TOOLS
For Missionaries
HARVESTING THE LORD'S WAY

By
Grant Von Harrison

Publishers Book Sales
1768 South Redwood Road
Salt Lake City, Utah 84104

Other books by Grant Von Harrison:

Trainer's Manual
Drawing on the Powers of Heaven
Converting Thousands
Every Missionary *Can* Baptize
Serve the Lord with Your Heart
Converting with the Book of Mormon

Contents

Foreword

The insights represented in this book were acquired by the author to a great extent while he was serving as a missionary. He has a deep sense of gratitude for these insights, and senses very keenly the profound influence they have had on his life. For this reason, all personal revenues realized from the sale of this book will be used to support missionary work.

The author requests that if the reader feels his life is significantly blessed as a result of this book he will make an additional donation to the Missionary Department of the Church of Jesus Christ of Latter-day Saints. This can be done by check or money order made payable to the L.D.S. Church and mailed to:

> Missionary Department
> Church Office Building
> 50 East North Temple
> Salt Lake City, Utah 84150

Introduction

During the first few months of my mission I was of the opinion that whether or not missionaries baptized people was determined primarily by chance. As I began to study the scriptures and the teachings of modern-day prophets and became conversant with the various commandments and revelations dealing with missionary work, I came to the realization that whether or not missionaries baptized people was determined by their willingness to comply with certain laws and principles, not by chance.

Later in my mission I had the opportunity to teach these laws and principles to other missionaries who had had little or no success thus far in their missions. In every case where the missionaries were willing to comply with the laws and use the principles they were much more successful in their missionary labors.

The Lord has promised missionaries that if they will approach their labors in the way he has prescribed they will be successful in bringing people into the Church.

In 1832 some missionaries who had encountered difficulty in bringing people to an understanding of their message desired to learn more about their duties. The following is a portion of a revelation that was received by the Prophet Joseph Smith in response to their desire:

> Hearken, O ye who have given your names to go forth to proclaim my gospel, and to prune my vineyard.
>
> Behold, I say unto you that it is my will that you should go forth and not

tarry, neither be idle but labor with your might—

Lifting up your voices as with the sound of a trump, *proclaiming the truth according to the revelations and commandments which I have given you.*

And thus, if ye are faithful ye shall be laden with many sheaves, and crowned with honor, and glory, and immortality, and eternal life. (D&C 75:2-5; italics added.)

This book has been written for those who desire to respond to the Lord's charge to do missionary work according to the revelations and commandments he has given.

The book is organized into five sections, each of which is based on one of President Kimball's admonitions concerning missionary work. The first chapter in each section serves as an introduction and the last chapter as a summary to the section. Section 1 deals with President Kimball's charge that missionaries learn to function properly, and gives them principles and procedures that will help them do so. Section 2 is concerned with President Kimball's plea that missionaries become more effective in bringing people into the Church, and provides principles and procedures that will help them become more productive. Section 3 introduces principles and procedures that will help missionaries meet President Kimball's charge to be more effective in getting people to listen to their message. Section 4 sets forth principles and procedures that will help missionaries be more successful in getting people to believe their message. The final Section (5) provides guidelines to assist missionaries in their responsibility to perfect their performance.

Chapter 1

Introduction to Section 1

President Spencer W. Kimball has said, "We've never had so many missionaries! Our great challenge now is *to cause them to function properly.*" (Italics added.) You have the Lord's promise that once you are functioning properly, you will be endowed with the Spirit and your talents and abilities will be greatly magnified. In contrast, if you fail in your efforts to function properly, the Lord has warned:

> ...and if ye receive not the Spirit ye shall not teach. (D&C 42:14.)

> Verily I say unto you, he that is ordained of me and sent forth to preach the word of truth by the Comforter, in the Spirit of truth, doth he preach it by the Spirit of truth or some other way?

> And if it be by some other way it is not of God. (D&C 50:17-18.)

> And this [people taught more perfectly] cannot be brought to pass until mine elders are endowed with power from on high.

> For behold, I have prepared a great endowment and blessing to be poured out upon them, inasmuch as they are faithful and continue in humility before me. (D&C 105:11-12.)

No amount of knowledge or skill can compensate for the absence of the Spirit, for only by the power of the Spirit can you magnify your calling. A missionary who has the Spirit can succeed in spite of weaknesses such as poor grammar or limited knowledge of a foreign language, because in a literal sense the Spirit compensates for human weaknesses. With the Spirit as your guide, your limitations, background, and physical characteristics

1

become insignificant. President Ezra Taft Benson has said, "The spirit is
the most important matter in this glorious work." (Mission Presidents
Seminar, June 21, 1975. See also D&C 50:13-14.)

The Lord has said that the gospel would be proclaimed to the world by
"the weak and the simple" and the "unlearned," who would preach "by the
power of my Spirit." (D&C 1:23; 35:13.) The Lord has promised that if you
are faithful you will be magnified in your calling. Therefore, if you are
faithful, the Lord will enhance your abilities so that you will be equal to the
task to which he has called you. (D&C 35:14.) "He that is weak among you
hereafter shall be made strong." (D&C 50:16.) He has promised you that if
you magnify your calling, your weaknesses will become strengths. (Ether
12:27.)

> Whether they [the missionaries] know much to begin with or not, the
> Lord will put his spirit into their hearts, and he will crown them with
> intelligence and power to save the souls of men. (Joseph F. Smith, *Gospel
> Doctrine,* p. 356.)

Unless you are willing to function (act in a required manner)
according to the standards the Lord has specified for those who are called
to the ministry, the results of your efforts as a missionary will be extremely
limited. As a missionary, it is essential that you understand that receiving
the Spirit is dependent on your compliance with specific laws. The
scriptures are explicit in explaining that you must be obedient to specific
laws in order to receive blessings from God.

> There is a law, irrevocably decreed in heaven before the foundations of
> this world, upon which all blessings are predicated—
>
> And when we obtain any blessing from God, it is by obedience to that law
> upon which it is predicated. (D&C 130:20-21.)

> We cannot preach the gospel of Christ without this spirit of humility,
> meekness, faith in God and reliance upon his promises and word to us. You
> may learn all the wisdom of men, but that will not qualify you to do these
> things like the humble, guiding influence of the Spirit of God will. (Joseph F.
> Smith, *Gospel Doctrine,* p. 356.)

> We should devote ourselves to the duties of that ministry, and we ought to
> strive with the utmost of our ability to qualify ourselves to perform that
> specific labor, and the way to do it is to live so that the spirit of God will have
> communication and be present with us to direct us in every moment and hour
> of our ministry, night and day. (Joseph F. Smith, *Gospel Doctrine,* p. 356.)

The following are the basic laws that govern the receipt of the Spirit
in missionary work: (1) personal worthiness, (2) righteous motives, (3)
fasting and prayer, (4) obedience, (5) total dedication, (6) scripture
reading, and (7) unity. Once you are complying with each of these basic

laws, you will be functioning properly, and you will receive a full endowment of the Spirit. When you receive a full endowment of the Spirit, you will teach with power and authority, and you will be magnified in your calling as a missionary. With the Spirit you will realize your full potential as an emissary for Jesus Christ. You should not be content with anything less.

At the present time one of the greatest deterrents to the success of many missionaries is the fact that they do not function properly. Some missionaries are very naive regarding how they are expected to function. Consequently, they do not qualify for the support of the Spirit in their labors.

> Many of our devoted missionaries are valiantly striving to do their best and to make their best better, day by day. Great is and greater yet shall be their reward. Others are lacking in energy and effort; their work is done, if at all, in a half-spirited way, and their thoughts are ever running ahead to the time of their release and return.

> To those of the first class the days are all too short and the months too few for the exalted labors in which they find such genuine satisfaction and happiness. To the others the days drag and the weeks are burdensome.

> The individual elder is left largely to the guidance of the spirit of his calling with which he should be imbued. If he fails to cultivate that spirit, which is the spirit of energy and application, he will soon become torpid, indolent, and unhappy....

> There is little excuse for the idle man in any walk of life; work is abundant for everyone who will labor; but least of all is there excuse or palliation in the case of a listless or idle missionary pretending to be busy in the service of the Lord. (Joseph F. Smith, *Gospel Doctrine*, pp. 363-364.)

As a missionary you will be held personally accountable before the Lord for your conduct during your mission. Jacob and Joseph in the Book of Mormon sensed this responsibility keenly and consequently approached their calling with all diligence.

> And we did magnify our office unto the Lord, taking upon us the responsibility, answering the sins of the people upon our own heads if we did not teach them the word of God with all diligence; wherefore, by laboring with our might their blood might not come upon our garments; otherwise their blood would come upon our garments, and we would not be found spotless at the last day. (Jacob 1:19.)

Speaking on this subject, the Prophet Joseph Smith said:

> If you do your duty [function properly], it will be just as well with you as though all men embraced the gospel. (History of the Church, 1:465-69.)

Your challenge in learning to function properly as a missionary is to become conversant with the laws and principles that govern the Spirit. It is difficult, if not impossible, to be obedient to given laws or principles unless you know what those laws are and have a clear understanding of what you must do to comply with them.

The chapters in this section have been written to assist you in knowing exactly how to comply with the laws that govern the Spirit. Reading these chapters will provide you with an understanding of these laws. If you will prayerfully and consistently reread the chapters in this section and the assigned scriptures throughout your mission, you will have a clear understanding of what it means to function properly as a missionary. You have the assurance that if you function properly, you will have success in your labors.

In contrast, if you are not totally diligent in your labors, you will be held responsible for those who would have accepted the gospel, had you been teaching by the Spirit. President John Taylor made the following statement regarding this responsibility:

> If you do not magnify your callings, God will hold you responsible for those whom you might have saved had you done your duty. (Journal of Discourses, 20:23.)

As you conduct yourself according to the standard of excellence taught in the chapters in this section, you can be assured that you will "stand blameless before God at the last day." (D&C 4:2.)

Chapter 2

You Must Be Found Worthy

President N. Eldon Tanner has counseled that it is much better to postpone a mission for a period of time than to go unworthily. The things in a person's life that are amiss should be straightened out before he goes on a mission. "It is a time to rejoice when a young man who has made mistakes clears his life and can start anew, clean and worthy to be an ambassador for the Lord." ("The Blessings of Church Interviews," *The Ensign,* Nov. 1978, p. 41.)

To be found worthy means you qualify to receive certain blessings or rewards as a result of obedience to the laws and ordinances associated with the gospel of Jesus Christ. Eternal salvation is the ultimate reward for worthiness.

As a missionary you must be worthy to qualify for the Spirit. Being found worthy as a missionary is dependent on the following:

1. Complete repentance.
2. Living righteously.
3. Compliance with rules and regulations designated for those called to the ministry.

It is essential that you consistently assess your worthiness, since all have sinned to some degree. Thus, we read in John's writings:

If we say that we have no sin, we deceive ourselves, and the truth is not in us. (1 John 1:8.)

President Spencer W. Kimball has said, "There is never a day in any man's life when repentance is not essential to his well-being in eternal progress." Because each of us has sinned, it is essential that we look to the mercies of God and take advantage of the law of repentance. It is the law of repentance that makes it possible for us to be worthy of our calling in the ministry. Repentance is absolutely essential in order for you to function properly.

To gain forgiveness through repentance one must recognize his guilt, have a godly sorrow for his sins, have a contrite heart, and have a burning desire to be relieved of the burden of his wrongdoing to the point of confessing completely to the proper priesthood authority. He must forsake his evil ways, make restitution in as far as it is possible, forgive those who have transgressed against him, ask God's forgiveness through prayer and faith, and then follow all of God's commandments.

Once you have repented you will be able to function properly as a missionary as you live righteously and comply with the rules and regulations stipulated for missionaries.

If you fail to qualify yourself in terms of worthiness, your efforts as a missionary will be futile to a great extent. The Lord has stipulated that "the powers of heaven cannot be controlled nor handled only upon the principles of righteousness." (D&C 121:36.) After you qualify yourself you will receive the Spirit in your missionary labors by seeking it through a prayer of faith.

> And the Spirit shall be given unto you by the prayer of faith; and if ye receive not the Spirit ye shall not teach. (D&C 42:14.)

Your ability to offer such a prayer of faith is dependent upon your worthiness. Elder Bruce R. McConkie tells us that "faith is a gift of God bestowed as a reward of personal righteousness. It is always given when righteousness is present. And the greater the measure of obedience to God's law, the greater will be the endowment of faith." Consequently, you will never enjoy a full endowment of the Spirit unless you are found worthy.

As a missionary you will be interviewed by your bishop and stake president. When they recommend you for a mission, they certify that you are worthy. Generally this clearance process is adequate for most missionaries. However, sometimes this clearance process fails to clear up major sins. When this happens, a missionary does not qualify for the Spirit.

President Spencer W. Kimball made this statement regarding missionaries who enter the mission field with major sins unresolved:

> While most missionaries go into the field clean and worthy, there is an

occasional one who has carried unadjusted guilt into his mission and has had a continual fight to keep the spirit of the mission. Some have even failed in the fight, for the conflict in the soul is near annihilating. (*The Miracle of Forgiveness,* p. 335.)

This occurs when (1) the missionary being interviewed is naive about what sins must be confessed, (2) the missionary being interviewed deliberately misrepresents during the interview, (3) the interview proves to be inadequate in terms of dealing with serious sins in the life of the missionary being interviewed, or (4) the missionary repeats the sin following the interviews.

Naivete Regarding Certain Sins

Unfortunately, some prospective missionaries are quite naive regarding some major sins. For example, a stake president was interviewing a young man for a mission and asked, "Are you morally clean?" The young man replied, "Yes." The stake president felt impressed to pursue the question further and asked, "Have you ever had sexual intercourse?" The young man replied, "Yes." When the stake president asked him why he answered "yes" when he was asked if he was morally clean, the young man replied, "I didn't catch any diseases." Obviously, this young man was extremely naive regarding the concept of morality. When you are being interviewed, if you have questions regarding any conduct with respect to moral cleanliness, you should definitely discuss the matter with your bishop. In this regard you should realize that all major sins must of necessity be confessed to your bishop. The Lord has commanded that major sins be confessed to proper Church authorities.

These sins include adultery, fornication, other sexual transgressions (e.g., petting, homosexuality, masturbation), allegiance to or involvement with any apostate group, and other sins of comparable seriousness for which the offender may be disfellowshipped or excommunicated.

Adultery

The sin of adultery occurs when someone who is married has intercourse with someone of the opposite sex who is not his or her spouse. The other person involved may be either single or married. In any case, the act is adultery. The act of adultery is a very grievous sin, but the magnitude of the sin is even greater if either of the parties involved has previously taken out his or her endowments or been married in the temple.

Fornication

Even though the Bible generally uses the terms *adultery* and *fornication* interchangeably, as a general rule fornication has reference to premarital heterosexual intercourse between two people who are unmarried. Unfortunately, in our society many rationalize that intercourse between two unmarried people is an expression of love and they attempt to justify the intimate relations. President Spencer W. Kimball says, "This is one of the most false of all of Satan's lies. It is lust, not love, which brings men and women to fornication.... No person would injure one he truly loves, and sexual sin can only result in injury." (*The Miracle of Forgiveness,* p. 65.)

Petting

Petting is one of the most common sexual sins committed by young people. Speaking of petting and other related sins, President Kimball has said:

> They awaken lust and stir evil thoughts and sex desires. They are but parts of the whole family of related sins and indiscretions. Paul wrote, as to modern young people who deceive themselves that their necking and petting are but expressions of love: "Wherefore God also gave them up to uncleanness through the lusts of their own hearts, to dishonour their own bodies between themselves." (Romans 1:24.) How could the evils of petting be more completely described?

> Too often, young people dismiss their petting with a shrug of their shoulders as a *little* indiscretion, while admitting that fornication is a base transgression. Too many of them are shocked, or feign to be, when told that what they have done in the name of petting was in reality fornication. The dividing line is a thin, blurry one, and Paul probably referred to these sins ranging from petting to fornication when he said: "For it is a shame even to speak of those things which are done of them in secret." (Ephesians 5:12.) And the Lord perhaps was referring to this evil when in our own time he was reiterating the Ten Commandments: "... neither commit adultery, nor kill, nor do anything like unto it." (D&C 59:6.)

> Our young people should know that their partners in sin will not love or respect them if they have freedom in fondling their bodies. Such a practice destroys respect, not only for the other person but for self. It destroys the ultimate respect for virtue. And it ignores the oft-repeated prophetic warning that one should give his or her life rather than yield to loss of virtue.

> Too many have lost themselves completely in sin through this doorway of necking and petting. The devil knows how to destroy our young girls and boys. He may not be able to tempt a person to murder or to commit adultery immediately, but he knows that if he can get a boy and a girl to sit in the car late enough after the dance, or to park long enough in the dark at the end of the lane, the best boy and the best girl will finally succumb and fall. He knows that all have a limit to their resistance.

> Those who have received the Holy Ghost after baptism certainly know that all bodily contacts of this kind are pernicious and abominable. They recognize, too, that the God of yesterday, today, and tomorrow continues to

demand continence and to require that people come to the marriage altar as virgins, clean and free from sex experience.

Almost like twins, "petting"—and especially "heavy petting"—and fornication are alike. Also like twins, the one precedes the other, but most of the same characteristics are there. The same passions are aroused and, with but slight difference, similar body contacts are made. And from it are likely to come the same frustrations, sorrows, anguish, and remorse. (*The Miracle of Forgiveness*, pp. 65-67.)

Homosexuality

The sin of homosexuality occurs when there is sexual desire for those of the same sex or sexual relations of any sort between individuals of the same sex, whether men or women. A homosexual act is a very repugnant sin. Because of the seriousness of this sin, it carries as heavy a penalty for the unrepentant as adultery and fornication. The Church authorities have taken a definite stand that the sin of homosexuality is equal to or greater than that of fornication and adultery, and that the Church will as readily take action to disfellowship or excommunicate the unrepentant practicing homosexual as it will the unrepentant fornicator or adulterer.

Masturbation

Nearly all books on sex produced by the medical doctors, psychiatrists, teachers, and others assert that masturbation is not harmful. Consequently, young people are left with the impression that it is natural and acceptable. However, the sanction of the sin of masturbation by society does not make it right. President Spencer W. Kimball has this to say regarding the sin of masturbation:

Many would-be authorities declare that it is natural and acceptable, and frequently young men I interview cite these advocates to justify their practice of it. To this we must respond that the world's norms in many areas— drinking, smoking, and sex experiences generally, to mention only a few— depart increasingly from God's law. The Church has a different, higher norm.

Thus prophets anciently and today condemn masturbation. It induces feelings of guilt and shame. It is detrimental to spirituality. It indicates slavery to the flesh, not that mastery of it and the growth toward godhood which is the object of our mortal life. Our modern prophet has indicated that no young man (or woman) should be called on a mission who is not free from this practice. (*The Miracle of Forgiveness*, p. 77.)

Masturbation is a form of perversion; it is very definitely a sin and it does have an adverse effect, both spiritually and physically. Medical doctors have reported that it dulls the mind, even causing an adverse effect on memory. It can destroy a person's self-confidence. Masturbaton is based on lust. It very definitely is a form of sexual perversion. Unless a

missionary is free of this sin, he will not qualify for or become worthy of
the Spirit.

Other Sins

All deviations from normal and proper heterosexual relations are
grievous sins in the sight of God, and naivete does not excuse you from the
adverse consequence of such sins.

Deliberate Misrepresentation

Sometimes prospective missionaries who are aware of the seriousness
of their sins choose to misrepresent their worthiness to Church authorities
during an interview for a mission. Generally, misrepresentation occurs in
one of two ways: either a denial of the transgression or a partial portrayal
of the transgression. For example, a young man may have fornicated
several times prior to his mission, and yet in his interview indicate that he
has only fornicated once.

There are many reasons why some prospective missionaries choose to
be dishonest in their interviews. Obviously, confession is one of the
hardest of all of the obstacles for the repentant sinner to negotiate.
Oftentimes our shame restrains us from making known and acknow-
ledging our errors. Sometimes there is not an element of trust between the
prospective missionary and the person conducting the interview. In some
instances the person's sense of guilt is not sufficient to motivate him to
confess.

Other reasons missionaries have given for misrepresenting in their
interviews include: "I didn't feel it was anyone else's business"; "The
bishop has had confidence in me my whole life and I couldn't bring myself
to admit to him what I had done"; "Everyone expected me to go on a
mission, and I was afraid if I told the truth I wouldn't be allowed to go on a
mission"; "It had been several years previously and I felt I had repented";
"I really didn't think it would matter"; or "I know others who have done
the same things who still went on missions."

The unfortunate thing is that prospective missionaries in this frame
of mind do not understand that they will be denied the Spirit no matter
how hard they work, because the Spirit will not dwell in unclean
tabernacles.

> Know ye not that ye are the temple of God, and that the Spirit of God
> dwelleth in you?
>
> If any man defile the temple of God, him shall God destroy; for the temple
> of God is holy, which temple ye are. (1 Corinthians 3:16-17.)
>
> What? know ye not that your body is the temple of the Holy Ghost which
> is in you, which ye have of God, and ye are not your own? (1 Corinthians 6:19.)

Inadequate Interviews

In some instances missionaries fail to confess serious sins because of inadequate interviews. President Kimball illustrates this:

> Another young couple showed a similar unawareness of the gravity of sin, and especially of sexual sin. They came to me in June, having become formally engaged with a ring the previous December, and in the six months' interval their sexual sin had been repeated frequently. In June they went to their respective bishops seeking recommends to the temple. The girl's bishop, knowing that she had always been active, did not searchingly question her as to cleanliness, and a recommend was soon tucked away in her purse for use in the planned June marriage. The bishop of the other ward questioned the young man carefully and learned of the six months of transgression.
>
> In my office the couple frankly admitted their sin and shocked me when they said: "That isn't so very wrong, is it, when we were formally engaged and expected to marry soon?" They had no comprehension of the magnitude of the sin. They were ready to go into the holy temple for their marriage without a thought that they were defiling the Lord's house. How lacking was their training! How insincere was their approach! They were very disturbed when their marriage had to be postponed to allow time for repentance. They had rationalized the sin nearly out of existence. They pressed for a date, the first possible one they could set up and on which they could plan their temple marriage. They did not understand that forgiveness is not a thing of days or months or even years but is a matter of intensity of feeling and transformation of self. Again, this showed a distortion of attitude, a lack of conviction of the seriousness of their deep transgression. They had not confessed their serious sin. They had but admitted it when it had been dug out. (*The Miracle of Forgiveness*, pp. 155-156.)

Interviews may be inadequate for several reasons. As in the example above, one of the most common reasons is that the authority conducting the interview *assumes* the worthiness of the person being interviewed and consequently is not thorough enough in the interview. Another reason is that some authorities may ask questions that are too general because they find it difficult to confront someone with questions like, "Have you ever had sexual intercourse?" or "Do you masturbate?" Another reason may be lack of communication. For example, the authority may ask, "Are you morally clean?" and the person may say, "Yes," only because to him moral cleanliness may not mean no petting or no masturbation. Another reason may be that the Church leader giving the interview is not sufficiently in tune to discern the unworthiness of the member. President Kimball alludes to this when he says:

> In connection with men's thoughts I discussed in a previous chapter the discernment often given to God's servants. If they are in sweet attunement, Church leaders are entitled "... to have it given unto them to discern ... lest

there shall be any among you professing and yet be not of God." (D&C 46:27.) Not only the General Authorities but bishops and stake and mission presidents have often discerned situations and thereby been enabled to protect the Church and bring the sinner to repentance. (*The Miracle of Forgiveness*, p. 184.)

Regardless of the reason, inadequate interviews do not excuse missionaries from their sins, when they are entering the mission field. If there were sins that should have been confessed but were not because of an inadequate interview, a missionary will be denied the Spirit of the Lord to a great extent until his sins are confessed to the proper authority.

You should take the initiative to insure your interviews are adequate to establish your worthiness. Take full advantage of the interviews and discuss any matter that is weighing on your conscience. In this way you can be certain that any previous transgression has been resolved.

Need for Complete Confession

In order to insure that you are worthy when you enter the mission field, you should discuss any major sins openly with your bishop. If you have any questions regarding what acts constitute sins that need to be confessed, you should read chapters 5 and 6 in President Kimball's book *The Miracle of Forgiveness*. You cannot be forgiven for major sins unless they are confessed to the proper Church authorities.

Why is it necessary to confess to Church authorities? First, because the Lord has commanded it. Second, because the offender cannot live and participate in the kingdom of God and receive the blessings therefrom with a lie in his heart. Bishops, stake presidents, and other local Church officers do not forgive sins when confessions are made to them. They only forgive in the sense of determining a person's participation in the Church. In other words, they remit the penalty which the Church on earth can impose, but the actual and ultimate forgiveness of sins comes from the Lord in heaven. Complete forgiveness is dependent on a person turning his whole heart to the Lord after confessing his sins. "He that repents and does the commandments of the Lord shall be forgiven." (D&C 1:32.) As a missionary, you must understand that no amount of hard work, fasting, prayer, etc., will result in the forgiveness of serious sins unless they are properly confessed to Church authorities.

Ideally, a person's confession should be voluntary and not forced. It should be prompted by the offender's conscience. Generally, when a confession is made voluntarily, it is a sign of true repentance and usually indicates that the person does desire to abandon the evil practice. President Spencer W. Kimball has made the following statement regarding voluntary confession:

The voluntary confession is infinitely more acceptable in the sight of the Lord than is forced admission, lacking humility, wrung from an individual by questioning when guilt is evident. Such forced admission is not the evidence of a humble heart which calls forth the Lord's mercy. "For I, the Lord forgive sins, and am merciful unto those who confess their sins with humble hearts." (D&C 61:2.) (*The Miracle of Forgiveness*, p. 182.)

Once a sin has been openly discussed and confessed to appropriate Church authorities, generally it is unwise and quite unnecessary to confess the same sin over and over again. If a major transgression has been fully cleared by the proper authority, the person may usually clear himself in any future interviews by explaining that all serious sins have been taken care of, and give the name of the person to whom they were confessed. (*The Miracle of Forgiveness,* p. 187.) This applies, however, only if there has been no repetition of any serious transgression. Usually the matter may be considered settled. (Note: It is never appropriate to discuss previous sins except with appropriate Church authorities. Never discuss them with companions, investigators, members, etc.)

Major Moral Sins Cleared by a General Authority

When a person is being considered for a mission, unless the person has comitted major moral sins, it is the prerogative of his bishop and stake president to decide in their hearts with the help of their Heavenly Father whether the person in question is worthy to go on a mission. It is their responsibility to determine whether the person is sufficiently repentant after they have examined all of the facts in the case. If they have determined that a person is worthy to serve on a mission, they will proceed with the recommendation unless there has been a major moral transgression. If the person has committed a major moral transgression, his transgression has to be reviewed by a General Authority, who will make the final determination as to whether the person is to receive a mission call.

Major Sins Reviewed by Local Authorities

A person going on a mission should understand that if a missionary confesses major sins after he has arrived at the Missionary Training Center or in the mission field, it is necessary that he contact the local bishop and stake president regarding the matter. It is much better to resolve the sins that require confession to a Church authority before you leave home, since the problem is compounded when for various reasons these sins are confessed after a missionary leaves for his mission.

Consequences of Repeating the Sin after the Interview

Altogether too frequently young people desiring to be called to go on a mission have not had their lives completely in order prior to being called in for an interview by their bishop. When this is the case, the bishop conducting the interview must use his own discretion as to whether or not the person should be cleared for a mission. If the person is cleared, usually the bishop will condition the clearance upon the prospective missionary's promise to keep his life completely in order from that time forth.

For example, in the course of the interview, a person reveals to his bishop that he has had a problem with smoking in the past. After the two discuss this problem, the bishop or stake president asks the person if he will refrain from smoking from now on. If the prospective missionary has repented and promises to always keep the Word of Wisdom, he will likely be cleared for a mission.

In instances when a missionary has made certain promises or commitments to his bishop or stake president in an interview and then, between the time he is interviewed and enters the mission field, fails to keep that promise by taking one last drink or smoke, or petting or fornicating, he will be denied the Spirit.

The degree or number of sins one commits after promising to abstain from sin is not the important point. The important point is that an individual has made a promise to a representative of the Lord and has broken it. Breaking the promise may be a lot more serious than the other sin. Unless a missionary who has broken a promise takes steps to clear himself with the authorities involved in his interview and to rectify the problem, his spirituality will be impaired throughout his entire mission. It is important that missionaries be aware of the seriousness of making a promise to a representative of the Lord and the consequences if they fail to live up to the promise. Complete honesty is an absolute necessity in interviews that precede a mission and interviews thereafter conducted by mission presidents or general authorities. The Lord will not tolerate misrepresentation to one of his designated representatives.

Conduct Following Confession

Confessing serious sins does not result in forgiveness unless a person (1) experiences remorse for his sins and (2) forsakes his sins. If he truly repents of a sin, he cannot escape the remorse for the sin. This remorse may not be immediate, but invariably it will come. Indifference may delay remorse for sin, but if a person begins to seek the Spirit, his conscience will be pricked and remorse will follow. The longer a person procrastinates repentance, the more intense will be the ultimate remorse. The following account of Alma vividly describes the suffering following serious transgressions:

But I was racked with eternal torment, for my soul was harrowed up to the greatest degree and racked with all my sins.

Yea, I did remember all my sins and iniquities, for which I was tormented with the pains of hell; yea, I saw that I had rebelled against my God, and that I had not kept his holy commandments.

Yea, and I had murdered many of his children, or rather led them away unto destruction; yea, and in fine so great had been my iniquities, that the very thought of coming into the presence of my God did rack my soul with inexpressible horror.

Oh, thought I, that I could be banished and become extinct both soul and body, that I might not be brought to stand in the presence of my God, to be judged of my deeds.

And now, for three days and for three nights was I racked, even with the pains of a damned soul. (Alma 36:12-16.)

Once a person has truly repented of his sins, and has confessed them to the proper Church authorities, he will forsake these sins. This is the ultimate test of repentance. In the process of a person's effort to overcome a sin, one of two things will happen. If he successfully refrains from repeating the sin, he will be forgiven. If he fails to refrain from a serious sin he has confessed, the guilt and consequences of previous forgiven sins will return.

...unto that soul who sinneth shall the former sins return.... (D&C 82:7.)

Following your initial interviews with the bishop and stake president, you should make the following resolves: (1) not to repeat any serious sins confessed, (2) not to read books that will cause you to think about vulgar or base things, (3) not to go to movies that will cause you to think about vulgar or base things, (4) not to listen to jokes that are vulgar or suggestive, (5) not to profane or use vulgar language, (6) not to steal, (7) not to lie, (8) not to argue, (9) to keep the Sabbath holy, (10) to comply totally with the Word of Wisdom, including going to bed early, (11) to be responsible and dependable, (12) to express gratitude to those with whom you associate, (13) not to find fault with others, (14) to study the scriptures, (15) to exercise, (16) to fast, (17) to pray every night and morning.

In addition, you should make every effort to insure that you are not harboring any hard feelings towards anyone. You cannot be forgiven of your sins unless you are willing to forgive others.

For if ye forgive men their trespasses, your heavenly Father will also forgive you:

But if ye forgive not men their trespasses, neither will your Father forgive your trespasses. (Matthew 6:14-15.)

You cannot receive the Spirit of the Lord if you have a grudge towards anyone, or any sense of animosity towards other people. You are required to "forgive all men." (D&C 64:8.) The spirit that accompanies anger, strife, revenge, malice, etc., is completely imcompatible with the Spirit of the Lord. If necessary, go to the people with whom you have had a disagreement or misunderstanding and express your desire to have the whole matter forgotten. Above all else, express your willingness to forgive and forget, and admit to your failings in the matter. If you will do this in the proper spirit, most people will respond in a positive way.

Missionaries Are Special Targets of Satan

You should realize that as you approach the time when you will receive your mission call, the adversary will exert an extra effort to get you to transgress in order to deny you the opportunity of filling a mission. It is very likely that you will experience more temptation after you receive your mission call than at any other time in your life. You should especially be on guard to insure that you do not succumb to Satan's enticings during this critical period. If you do, you will seriously jeopardize your prospects of having a successful mission.

Even after you arrive in the mission field, you will still be confronted with temptation. As a missionary you should realize that the temptations you will face during this time may be greater than before. President Kimball explains why this is the case:

> Satan wants all men, but especially is he anxious for the leading men who have influence. Perhaps he might try much harder to claim men who are likely to be his greatest opposition, men in high places who could persuade many others not to become servants to Satan.

> It seems that missionaries are special targets. The young man is going to spend two years exclusively in the service of converting people from error to truth, of teaching men to leave the employ of Lucifer and serve the Lord, of bringing people out of the dark where they are most vulnerable into the light where there is a measure of protection and where new strengths can be developed. Satan takes a special interest in all such workers. (*The Miracle of Forgiveness*, p. 175.)

Satan's effort to tempt you will be very subtle and you should be continuously on guard. He will continually attempt to exploit your weaknesses and vulnerable spots. For some it may be sleeping in. For others it may be eating too much. For others it may be contention. For still others it may be evil thoughts. In order to avoid sin you must consistently make every effort to protect your vulnerable spots by refusing to even flirt with temptation. In this way you insure that the adversary has no dominion over you as a person. Many of the mission rules are made to help you avoid the initial steps toward sin. You will not be vulnerable to major transgression during your mission if you will consistently comply with mission rules.

Recognizing Your Worthiness

As you approach your mission, the adversary may tempt you to doubt your worthiness. It is extremely important that you realize your acceptance by the Lord. If you have been honest in your interviews with your bishop and stake president and have conscientiously repented where necessary, the Lord has established your personal worthiness. Your bishop and stake president have recommended you to the President of the Church, and he has called you to serve as an ambassador of the Lord. With this call from the Prophet you have the assurance that the Lord accepts you and will sustain you as a missionary if you remain steadfast and faithful.

Having Faith in Yourself

Once your worthiness has been determined through interviews with your priesthood leaders, do not dwell on your past failings and short-comings, but learn to think of things that will enhance your faith in God and in yourself: (1) You are literally a child of God. (2) Because you were valiant in the pre-existence, you have been foreordained to fill a mission. (3) You are entitled to the promptings of the Holy Ghost. (4) You received a special blessing when you were set apart for your mission.

> For I will forgive you of your sins with this commandment—that you remain steadfast in your minds in solemnity and the spirit of prayer, in bearing testimony to all the world of those things which are communicated unto you. (D&C 84:61.)
>
> ...forgive, and ye shall be forgiven. (Luke 6:37.)

Accepting Full Forgiveness from the Lord

Some of the great missionaries of the past were men who had to experience a change of heart before they could be filled with the Holy Spirit and do the Lord's work (e.g., Paul, Alma, Zeezrom, the sons of Mosiah.)

> Nevertheless, he that repents and does the commandments of the Lord shall be forgiven. (D&C 1:32.)

When you have done what is necessary to repent (including, if necessary, confession to your bishop, branch president, mission president, etc.), you should completely accept the Lord's forgiveness and realize that his forgiveness is absolute. If you are unable to accept full forgiveness you will find it difficult to look to your Father in Heaven for the help you need in order to succeed as a missionary. You will not feel close to your Father in Heaven—almost as though you had not repented. You need to have an

abiding faith in the process of forgiveness and complete assurance that the
Lord has found you worthy to represent him.

> Behold, he who has repented of his sins, the same is forgiven, and I, the
> Lord, remember them no more. (D&C 58:42.)

Just as the Lord is willing to forget your sins, so should you be willing
to forget them.

> The essence of the miracle of forgiveness is that it brings peace to the
> previously anxious, restless, frustrated, perhaps tormented soul. (*The Miracle
> of Forgiveness,* p. 363.)

> What relief! What comfort! What joy! Those laden with transgressions
> and sorrows and sin may be forgiven and cleansed and purified if they will
> return to their Lord, learn of him, and keep his commandments. And all of us
> needing to repent of day-to-day follies and weaknesses can likewise share in
> this miracle. (*The Miracle of Forgiveness,* p. 368.)

The Lord desires that you accept his forgiveness so that you can fully
develop your potential.

Throughout your mission you should ask yourself the following
questions to review your personal worthiness.

1. Have I been totally honest and forthright in all of the interviews I
   have had since my initial interviews with my bishop?
2. Have I lived up to the commitments I made to my bishop, stake
   president, and others with respect to refraining from sins such as
   masturbation, etc.?
3. Am I doing all that I can to qualify for the Spirit of the Lord?
4. Am I worthy to represent the Savior as a missionary?
5. Am I determined to live all the rules and regulations of missionary
   work?
6. Am I argumentative?
7. Am I honest?
8. Am I virtuous?
9. Do I comply totally with the Word of Wisdom?
10. Am I responsible and dependable?
11. Am I completely free from any hard feelings toward other people?
12. Am I exercising proper discipline in my life?
13. Do I allow my mind to think about vulgar or base things?
14. Have I prayerfully approached my Heavenly Father and asked him to

reveal to my mind anything I have done or am doing which will keep me from realizing my full potential as a missionary?

15. Do I understand the atoning sacrifice of the Savior and the influence it can have in my life?

16. Do I have an abiding faith in the process of forgiveness and complete assurance that the Lord has found me worthy to represent him?

17. Do I express proper gratitude for the opportunity of repentance afforded me as a result of the atoning sacrifice of the Savior?

18. Do I feel the companionship of the Holy Ghost?

19. Do I consistently pray for the strength necessary to resist the influence of the adversary?

20. Do I refrain from dwelling on past failings and weaknesses?

21. Do I make a consistent effort to think of things that will enhance my faith in God and myself?

Chapter 3

Your Motives Must
Be Pure

In order to qualify for the Spirit as an emissary of Christ you must approach your work with an eye single to the glory of God. Be careful not to base your motives on personal honor and recognition.

Pure motives are a prerequisite to being blessed with the Spirit.

All progress in spiritual things is conditioned upon the prior attainment of humility. Pride, conceit, haughtiness, and vain glory are of the world and stand as a bar to the receipt of spiritual gifts. (Bruce R. McConkie, *Mormon Doctrine*, p. 147.)

Cultivating a Love for the People

You qualify for the gifts and blessings of the Spirit by serving with an eye single to the glory of God and developing a love for your fellow missionaries and for the people among whom you work. You are admonished to "pray unto the Father with all the energy of heart, that ye may be filled with this love." (Moroni 7:48.)

If a missionary does or says things that are inappropriate (e.g., offensive or irritating to others) or is easily offended, he does not possess the gift of charity and his efforts to teach the gospel will not be effective. (See 1 Corinthians 13:1.)

The pure love of Christ (charity) (Moroni 7:45; 1 Corinthians 13) is a gift of the Spirit. God will bestow this love upon those "who are true followers of his son Jesus Christ." You should earnestly fast and pray to receive this gift of the Spirit.

As you strive to qualify for this special endowment, you will begin to sense when your conversation or actions are inappropriate. If you continue in your effort to cultivate the gift of charity, you will find that the Spirit will prick your conscience when you are inclined to say or do anything that would be out of character for a missionary. When you are truly endowed with the true love of Christ, you will not be inclined to "behave unseemly" (1 Corinthians 13:5), which means that your conversations, your humor, your actions, your manners, your posture, etc. will be proper, fitting, in good taste and appropriate. You will have a keen awareness of how other people are reacting to everything you say and do, and you will desire to make every effort not to say or do anything that would offend or irritate. You will be motivated to do and say things that truly serve the interests of others. Your interests, aims, and desires will be totally unselfish. When you are in this frame of mind you also will find that you will not be irritated or hurt by the offensive remarks of others.

When you have unconditional love for people, you will receive revelation in their behalf and you will qualify for the other gifts of the Spirit. (See 1 Corinthians 14:1–3.)

The Influence of Love on Your Attitude

Cultivating true charity will bring you genuine joy and satisfaction in doing all aspects of missionary work. Only the love of God and the love of the people will sustain you in some aspects of missionary work.

Perhaps the real test of your desire to serve the Lord will not come until you have been in the mission field a few weeks. Occasionally a missionary's enthusiasm during the first few weeks is based more on excitement than on proper motives. Consequently, he experiences a letdown after a few weeks unless he is successful in cultivating love and esteem for the people and his fellow missionaries. "And let every man esteem his brother as himself." (D&C 38:24.)

You are charged with declaring the message of the restored gospel "without any respect of persons." (Alma 16:14.) You must work and pray to develop an unconditional love for the people where you are called to labor, no matter what they are like or how they treat you. One of the greatest examples of this type of love was the desire of Alma and the sons of Mosiah to preach the gospel to the Lamanites who were "a wild and a hardened and a ferocious people." (Alma 17:14.)

How the Adversary Can Stifle You

If your motives in the work are not based on love, you will find yourself consistently dissatisfied with one thing or another; and if the adversary can succeed in getting you disgruntled about something (weather, companion, area of labor), you will lose the Spirit and will be stifled in the work.

Missionaries are particularly vulnerable to the enticings of the adversary in this regard. Therefore, you should resolve to be continually on your guard.

Indications of Proper Motives

In trying to maintain proper motives, remember that your relationship with God can be no better than your relationship with your fellow men (companion, investigators, etc.). (Read 1 John 4:20-21.)

When you succeed in cultivating charity (the pure love of Christ), you will find you will not be inclined to complain or criticize in your conversations with people or in your letters to your family or friends. You will be content with your companion, area of labor, and other aspects of your missionary labors.

One of the Most Important Callings

You should not aspire to be assigned to leadership positions.

Aspiring to office can destroy the spirit of a mission as well as destroy missionaries. (Ezra Taft Benson, Mission Presidents Seminar, June 21, 1975.)

It does not matter where you serve, but how. If you prove your dependability, God will increase your capabilities and your responsibilities.

According to President Ezra Taft Benson, one of the most important callings of a missionary is training new missionaries. In order to be effective in this responsibility, you must be capable of giving of yourself totally. The greatest tribute your mission president can pay you will be to have you repeatedly training new missionaries. You can be assured that if you are successful in training new missionaries you will be successful in other aspects of missionary work.

Specific Self-Evaluation

Frequently evaluate yourself by answering these questions:

1. Am I kind?
2. Am I courteous and considerate?
3. Do I truly love the people I have been called to teach?
4. Do I envy?
5. Do I get provoked or irritated easily?
6. Do I complain about things (weather, companions, culture)?
7. Do I criticize and find fault?
8. Am I happy?

9. Do I put the interests of others before my own?

10. Do I enjoy all aspects of missionary work?

11. Am I aspiring unrighteously to become a district leader, a zone leader, or an assistant to the president?

12. Am I disgruntled about anything?

13. Am I willing to serve without special recognition?

True Spirit of Love and Gratitude

Once your motives are pure your sense of love and gratitude for the Lord, your parents, etc., will increase. This whole process can be facilitated if you will consistently express your feelings of love and gratitude. These expressions of gratitude and love should be expressed in public and in writing as well as in your personal prayers. Throughout your mission you should consistently express your love and appreciation to and for the Lord, your parents, your mission president, his wife, your companion, the people you teach, and others who influence your life for good.

There are two things you can train yourself to do on a daily basis that will help you catch and maintain a true spirit of gratitude. First, train yourself to ponder and reflect on your many blessings, God's mercy, etc., but most importantly those things you have been able to accomplish with the Lord's help. This process can be facilitated by reading the scriptures, reading Church hymns such as "When Upon Life's Billows," "Before Thee Lord, I Bow My Head," "I Need Thee Every Hour." As you learn to meditate and reflect on your blessings you will draw closer to the Spirit of the Lord and your sense of gratitude and appreciation will increase. Most importantly, your love for people will increase.

Second, as companions you must work at recognizing the workings of the Spirit throughout each day.

> And in nothing doth man offend God, or against none is his wrath kindled, save those who *confess not his hand in all things,* and obey not his commandments. (D&C 59:21; italics added.)

You should train yourself to discern and recognize the hand of the Lord in your work and then openly discuss with your companion the workings of the Spirit. Consistently look for examples where you have been inspired, people have been touched, etc. Each time you see the hand of the Lord evidenced in any aspect of the work, discuss it with your companion and then make it a point to express specific gratitude to the Lord for ways he has helped you during the day.

You should attempt to do this throughout the day, but most importantly at the end of each day take a few minutes to reflect and to identify specific instances where the hand of the Lord was made manifest. In addition, attempt to critique yourselves to see where you did or said things that distracted from your sensitivity to the Spirit. Resolve to make it a policy to do this on a regular basis.

If you consistently meditate on your blessings and discuss the workings of the Spirit with your companion and then express your gratitude specifically, your sensitivity to the Spirit will increase and inspiration regarding your investigators will become especially keen.

> A person may profit by noticing the first intimation of the spirit of revelation; for instance, when you feel pure intelligence flowing into you, it may give you sudden strokes of ideas, so that by noticing it, you may find it fulfilled the same day or soon; (i.e.) those things that were presented unto your minds by the Spirit of God and understanding it, you may grow into the principle of revelation, until you become perfect in Christ Jesus. (*History of the Church of Jesus Christ of Latter-day Saints*, 3:381.)

Specific Self-Evaluation

Frequently evaluate yourself by answering these questions.

1. Do I consistently express my gratitude and love to and for the Lord?
2. Do I consistently express my gratitude and love to and for my parents?
3. Do I consistently express my gratitude and love to and for my mission president and his wife?
4. Do I consistently express my gratitude and love to and for my companion?
5. Do I consistently express my gratitude and love to and for the people I am teaching?
6. Do I consistently express my gratitude and love to and for other people who influence my life for good?
7. Do I consistently take a few minutes each day to ponder and reflect on my blessings?
8. Do I consistently strive to recognize the hand of the Lord in all things and discuss specific instances of the workings of the Spirit with my companion?
9. Do I make it a policy to express gratitude for specific help I have received from the Lord throughout the day?

Throughout your mission you should continually ask yourself the following questions to determine if your motives are pure.

1. Do I recognize my dependence upon the Lord?
2. Do I love my companion?

3. Am I a true follower of Jesus Christ?

4. Am I praying with all the energy of my heart that I will be filled with the pure love of Christ?

5. Do I experience a genuine joy and satisfaction in doing all aspects of missionary work?

6. Do I have an unconditional love for the people I've been called to labor with?

7. Do I give of myself totally?

Chapter 4

Practice Proper Fasting

From the scriptures we learn that fasting plays a key role in a person's effort to draw close to the Lord and qualify to receive the Spirit.

Fasting is a Commandment

It is interesting to note that during the Savior's ministry in mortality there were many significant changes made in how people should worship. Most significant was the replacing of the law of sacrifice by a higher law. However, the commandments associated with fasting did not change. The people were told to continue in "fasting and prayer." (4 Nephi 12.) The law of the fast has been reconfirmed in our day through a modern-day prophet: "Also, I give unto you a commandment that ye shall continue in prayer and fasting from this time forth." (D&C 88:76.)

Throughout the history of the world those who have qualified to receive the Spirit in their missionary labors have "given themselves to much prayer, and fasting." (Alma 17:3.) If you desire to be sustained by the Spirit in your missionary labors, you must comply with the law of the fast.

There is more to fasting than abstinence from food and drink. You will not realize the full benefits of fasting unless you do it properly. If you fast properly, it can be a means of increasing your spirituality and faith. This chapter has been written to teach you how to fast properly.

In order to fast properly, you must:

1. Have proper motives. To be acceptable, fasting must be done for the

right reasons. (Read 3 Nephi 13:16-18.)

2. Open the fast with prayer. Take time to tell the Lord in prayer why you are going to fast, to ask him to accept your fast, and to pray that you will have the spirit of fasting.

3. Strive to think and pray about the purpose of the fast.

4. Fast an appropriate length of time. Generally your fast will be from the evening meal one day to the evening meal the following day (24 hours). When this is the case, it is important to remember that you begin fasting immediately following the evening meal, not the next morning.

5. Close the fast with prayer. Before breaking a fast, take time to offer a prayer and express your gratitude for the law of the fast and other blessings, even if circumstances allow you only to pray silently.

If you fast properly, you will find it a joyful and uplifting experience. In contrast, if you merely go without food and drink and fail to comply with the other aspects of fasting, the only result you will get from fasting will be hunger and thirst.

Reasons for Fasting

Many specific reasons for fasting are found in the scriptures.

1. It is a commandment. (D&C 59:13-14; 88:76; Luke 5:33-35; 2 Corinthians 6:5; 11:27.)

2. It is a form of worshipping God. (Luke 2:37; Acts 9:9; Alma 45:1; 4 Nephi 12.)

3. It brings special blessings. (Mosiah 27: 22-23.)

4. It helps you gain a testimony. (Alma 5:46.)

5. It can help you gain revelation. (Alma 17:3; 3 Nephi 27:1.)

6. It can bring about the conversion of nonmembers to the truth. (Alma 6:6; 17:9.)

7. It will bring you guidance. (Acts 13:3; Omni 26.)

8. It is an expression of righteous mourning and sorrow. (Alma 28:2-6; 30:2; Helaman 9:10.)

9. It is a means of sanctifying oneself. (Helaman 3:35.)

10. It is a means of qualifying for the Lord's help in accomplishing righteous desires, as when we fast in behalf of someone who is ill.

By fasting we demonstrate to the Lord our willingness to make a personal sacrifice in order to qualify for his help. We show him that we are willing to go the extra mile.

You should look forward to the opportunity of fasting once each month on the regular Fast Sunday. Additional fasts need be held only as specific needs arise and never longer than 24 hours at a time. Common sense and inspiration must govern fasting. Obviously, fasting too often can endanger your health. Learn to exercise good judgment concerning when and how often to fast. Your mission president is available for counsel and guidance.

In 1977 the First Presidency of the Church issued the following instructions for missionaries regarding fasting:

> Missionaries should not engage in excessive or lengthy fasting. Generally, once a month is sufficient for fasting. Occasionally there may be special matters for which missionaries might want to fast. If so, they should not extend the fast beyond one day.

> Missionaries should not request friends, relatives, or members of their home ward or branches to participate with them in special fasts for investigators.

> Missionaries should be encouraged to gain the full blessings of the law of the fast by paying fast offerings on Fast Sunday to the Bishop or Branch President in the area where they are serving. (Letter from First Presidency to Mission Presidents, Mar. 15, 1977.)

Missionary work requires self-discipline. There is no parent to wake you up in the morning, no one to remind you what to do. To a great extent missionaries are required to govern themselves. Unfortunately, many young people who enter the mission field lack self-discipline. Fasting is a means of learning self-control. As you fast properly on a regular basis, you will develop strength of character, gain a greater sensitivity to the promptings of the Spirit, and obtain the blessings you fast for.

Throughout your mission review the following checklist:

1. Do I enjoy fasting?

2. Do I make use of the law of the fast often enough?

3. When I fast do I remember to open the fast with prayer?

4. Do I make it a point to fast for specific reasons?

5. Do I make it a point to focus on the purpose of my fast in my thoughts and prayers while I am fasting?

6. Unless my health prohibits me, do I abstain from food and drink for an appropriate length of time?

7. Do I make it a policy to open and close each fast with prayer and express my gratitude for the law of the fast?

8. Am I fasting for the right reasons?

9. Do I consistently read the scriptures included in this section that deal with fasting?

10. What can I do to make my fasts more effective?

11. Do I consistently remember to pay my fast offering to the local branch president or bishop?

Chapter 5

Practice Fervent Prayer

From the beginning of time men have been commanded to pray. Prayer is not something that we may choose to do if we feel so inclined. It is an eternal decree: "thou shalt repent and call upon God in the name of the Son forevermore." (Moses 5:8.) The Lord has warned that we will be held in remembrance before him if we are negligent in our personal prayers. (D&C 68:33.) Fervent prayer is absolutely essential in missionary work. A person prays when he directs his conversation either vocally or mentally to God.

How to Make Your Prayers Effective

The following guidelines given by President Ezra Taft Benson will help you make your prayers more meaningful.

1. *We should pray frequently.* We should be alone with our Heavenly Father at least two or three times each day: "... morning, mid-day, and evening," as the scripture indicates. (Alma 34:21.) In addition, we are told to pray always. (2 Nephi 32:9; D&C 88:126.) This means that our hearts should be full, drawn out in prayer unto our Heavenly Father continually. (Alma 34:27.)

2. *We should find an appropriate place where we can meditate and pray.* We are admonished that this should be "in your closets, and your secret places, and in your wilderness." (Alma 34:26.) That is, it should be free from distraction, in secret. (3 Nephi 13:5, 6.)

3. *We should prepare ourselves for prayer.* If we don't feel like praying, then we should pray until we do feel like praying. We should be humble. (D&C

112:10.) We should pray for forgiveness and mercy. (Alma 34:17, 18.) We must forgive anyone against whom we have bad feelings. (Mark 11:25.) Yet, the scriptures warn, our prayers will be vain if we "turn away the needy, and the naked, and visit not the sick and afflicted, and impart [not] of [our] substance...." (Alma 34:28.)

4. *Our prayers should be meaningful and pertinent.* We should not use the same phrases at each prayer. Each of us would become disturbed if a friend said the same few words to us each day, treated the conversation as a chore, and could hardly wait to finish in order to turn on the TV and forget us.

In all of our prayers it is well to use the sacred pronouns of the scriptures—*thee, thou, thy,* and *thine* when addressing Deity in prayer, instead of the more common pronouns *you, your,* and *yours.* In this arrangement we show greater respect to Deity.

For what should we pray? We should pray about our work, against the power of our enemies and the devil, for our welfare and the welfare of those around us. (Alma 34:20; 22:25; 27.) We should counsel with the Lord pertaining to all our decisions and activities. (Alma 37:36-37.) We should be grateful enough to give thanks for all we have. (D&C 59:21.) We should confess his hand in all things. Ingratitude is one of our great sins.

The Lord has declared in modern revelation: "And he who receiveth all things with thankfulness shall be made glorious; and the things of this earth shall be added unto him, even an hundred fold, yea, more." (D&C 78:19.)

We should ask for what we need, taking care that we not ask for things that would be to our detriment. (James 4:3.) We should ask for strength to overcome our problems. (Alma 31:31-33.) We should pray for the inspiration and well-being of the President of the Church, the General Authorities, our stake president, our bishop, our quorum president, our home teachers, our family members, and our civic leaders. Many other suggestions could be made, but with the help of the Holy Ghost, we will know about what we should pray. (Romans 8:26.)

5. *After making a request through prayer, we have a responsibility to assist in its being granted.* We should listen. Perhaps while we are on our knees, the Lord wants to counsel us. "Sincere praying implies that when we ask for any virtue or blessing, we should work for the blessing and cultivate the virtue." (David O. McKay.)

Developing a Meaningful Relationship with God through Prayer

As a missionary you should find tremendous consolation in the fact that God is mindful of you and is ready to respond if you will place your trust in him and do what is right. If you truly understand this relationship with God, you will never be fearful in your missionary labors. There is no place for fear in missionary work if you will place your trust in the Lord and will be earnest in seeking divine guidance on a regular basis through prayer. Even though you will experience hardships and many aspects of the work will be trying and difficult, through prayer you will have the continual assurance that you can prevail and be successful in your labors.

God will sustain you and will speak peace to your soul. The peace that comes through the serenity of the Spirit is one of life's greatest blessings. As you develop a meaningful relationship with your Father in Heaven through prayer, your performance as a missionary will improve. You will be able to see things more clearly. You will be motivated to overcome your weaknesses. You will be able to see the joy and the growth that come through trials and testing, and no matter how trying your circumstances may be as a missionary, you will know peace, contentment, and true happiness in your labors. With the companionship of the Spirit, trials, frustrations, and headaches become blessings.

When you are praying you should refrain from using the word "might" (i.e., "Bless us that we might be better missionaries"). You should assume an attitude of confidence when you request the Lord's help and use the world "will" (i.e., "Bless us that we will be better missionaries.")

You must account to the Lord for your daily performance. At the conclusion of each day prior to prayer with your companion, you should evaluate your performance as companions. Discuss your use of time, your effectiveness in finding people to teach, your progress in your companion goals for your area, and where you can improve in your teaching ability. If you determine that there are areas of weakness in your daily performance, you should discuss those weaknesses in your prayer with your companion, together with the resolves you have made to correct them.

Likewise, prior to your personal prayer, you should evaluate your personal performance and determine areas where you need the help of the Lord in order to be more effective in your labors. In your prayers you should discuss your failings and shortcomings and ask for forgiveness. Request your Heavenly Father's help and support. An integral part of your personal prayers should be expressions of love to your Father in Heaven and your heartfelt gratitude for your bounteous blessings.

Throughout your mission you should be resolved not only to pray on a regular basis, but to insure that you pray with all the energy of your heart with sincere intent. You will find that as you are functioning properly in other respects (e.g., proper motives, obedience, and dedication), you will derive great strength from your prayers.

Throughout your mission ask yourself the following questions:

1. Am I alone with my Heavenly Father at least two or three times each day?

2. Is my heart full and drawn out in prayer to my Heavenly Father continually?

3. Do I prepare myself to pray?

4. Do I pray for forgiveness and mercy?

5. Am I willing to forgive others?

6. Do I avoid using the same phrases when I pray?

7. Do I use the sacred pronouns of the scriptures when I address Deity in my prayers?

8. Do I express gratitude in my prayers?

9. Do I listen for counsel from the Lord after I pray?

10. Do I earnestly seek divine guidance on a regular basis through prayer?

11. Do I refrain from using the word might, and instead use the word *will*, when I pray?

12. Do I make an accounting to the Lord for my daily performance?

13. Do I pray with all the energy of my heart and with sincere intent?

Chapter 6

You Must Be Obedient

Bruce R. McConkie has stated that "obedience is the first law of heaven, the cornerstone upon which all righteousness and progression rest." (*Mormon Doctrine*, p. 539.) The Lord said through an ancient apostle:

> Obey them that have the rule over you, and submit yourselves: for they watch for your souls, as they that must give account, that they may do it with joy, and not with grief: for that is unprofitable for you. (Hebrews 13:17.)

You should be obedient to senior companions, missionary leaders, and your mission president, who lead you in righteousness.

Measuring Your Obedience

You must be obedient to those in authority to qualify for the Spirit. One of the best ways to measure your obedience is to evaluate the degree of your compliance with the mission rules established by your mission president, the missionary guidelines stipulated in the *Missionary Handbook*, and the principles of conduct discussed in this book. You should read the *Missionary Handbook* the first week of your mission and reread it continually throughout your mission. President Ezra Taft Benson has recommended that you read portions of the handbook with your companion on a regular basis. (Mission Presidents Seminar, June 21, 1975.)

Growth Resulting from Obedience

Your growth and development as a missionary is primarily dependent on your obedience. Obedience to mission rules and the commandments of God will increase your stature and your effectiveness. There is virtually no limit to the power and influence for good you will realize if you are consistently obedient throughout your mission. The Lord will be able to use you continually to bring key people into the Church. However, if you are not obedient (watch TV, go to movies, get up late), you will not be as effective and will easily become discouraged. Consequently, the Lord will not trust you with the responsibility of bringing key people into the Church. No matter how talented you may be in other respects, if you are not obedient your effectiveness as a missionary will be limited.

Disobedience and Its Consequences

All acts of disobedience are sins, and one act of disobedience will offset numerous acts of obedience. Consequently, one act of disobedience can cause you to lose the Spirit which you have worked weeks, or maybe months, to obtain. The price of disobedience is extremely high. Remember also that minor acts of disobedience (sleeping in, watching TV) can lead to major acts.

Your Responsibility for Your Companion

You are also responsible for your companion's compliance with mission rules. In other words, you are your brother's keeper and should make an honest effort to prevent your companion from committing an act that jeopardizes his standing in the mission or in the Church. Do not excuse yourself by saying that you did not feel it was your responsibility to try to stop him. One of your major responsiblities is to keep your companion from evil.

Help your companion correct any minor acts in the spirit of love, not with a condemning or holier-than-thou attitude. If your pleas and prodding in the spirit of love do not produce results, tell your companion that unless he discusses the problem with a mission leader, you will do so.

Companions occasionally enter into conspiracies to conceal their sins by falsifying reports to the mission president and lying during interviews. When this happens, missionaries are extremely vulnerable to the enticements of Satan, and consequently they may fall victim to serious sin.

As a missionary you have entered into specific covenants with the Lord, and he expects you to live up to these covenants. For this reason, the consequences of sin are great while you are serving as a missionary. If you are obediently living up to these covenants, the Lord will endow you with His Holy Spirit and you will find satisfaction in doing His work. But if you are slothful and disobedient, you will find the work to be drudgery.

Throughout your mission you should continually ask yourself the following questions to evaluate your obedience.

1. Do I make every effort to learn what is expected of me?
2. Am I obedient to those who preside over me?
3. Do I systematically study the *Missionary Handbook?*
4. Do I comply fully with the mission rules?
5. Do I comply fully with the guidelines stipulated in the *Missionary Handbook?*
6. Do I comply fully with the principles of conduct discussed in this book?
7. Am I worthy of the Lord's trust?
8. Even though I may not understand the reasons behind certain rules, am I obedient regardless?

Chapter 7

With Your Heart, Might, Mind and Strength

O ne of the first scriptures you will commit to memory is the fourth section of the *Doctrine and Covenants*. As much as any scripture, this section contains the key to qualifying for the Spirit of the Lord. When you sense the tremendous significance of the second verse and respond accordingly, you will begin to understand the degree of dedication that the Lord requires of those who are called to the ministry.

Give Dedicated Service

As a missionary the Lord expects you to serve Him with all your heart, might, mind and strength, 24 hours a day, seven days a week. This, probably more than anything else, is the most difficult thing for missionaries to accept. Generally, throughout a person's life, he has always taken time off from school or work to entertain himself. Consequently, some missionaries find it difficult to meet the Lord's expectations to devote all their energies to missionary work 24 hours a day, seven days a week. Other than necessities (shopping, washing, writing your parents, etc.), any other activities that take you away from the work will distract from your spirituality.

To comprehend this type of dedication, you must understand the meaning of the terms *heart, might, mind,* and *strength.* By *heart,* the Lord means our emotions and sentiments. *Might* refers to our spiritual faculties, including our willpower. *Mind* refers to our entire thought process (intellect, reasoning ability). *Strength* means our physical attributes, our every action. (See Hyrum M. Smith and Janne M. Sjodahl, *Doctrine and Covenants Commentary,* p. 350.) In the second verse of the fourth section of the *Doctrine and Covenants,* the Lord is saying he expects those called to the ministry to serve him with their entire being.

From the outset of your mission you should concern yourself with mastery of the flesh (getting up by 6:30 a.m., working the designated number of hours per day, going to bed at the appointed time). You will never be able to achieve higher levels of dedication until you learn to serve the Lord with all your strength.

Use Time Wisely

Strive to avoid wasting time: "...see that ye refrain from idleness." (Alma 38:12.) "Thou shalt not idle away thy time...." (D&C 60:13.) For example, if you waste thirty minutes twice a day, every day of your mission, you will have wasted seventy-three days or two and one-half months. Make every effort to avoid being idle: "...the idler shall be had in remembrance before the Lord." (D&C 68:30.) Learn to use spare moments throughout the day to review your scriptures, study the discussions, read proselyting pamphlets, or improve yourself in some other way. Make it a policy to carry three-by-five inch cards or a note pad with things you need to learn or review.

Avoid spending time doing menial things (i.e., picking up a suit from the cleaners) during prime contacting time. Unless you make a strong, consistent effort to use your time constructively, you will waste a substantial part of every day.

Avoid Socializing with Members

Your first priority should be proselyting (teaching and proselyting nonmembers). If you spend time with members unwisely, your spirituality will be impaired. Your time with members should be restricted exclusively to talking about proselyting-related activities. President Ezra Taft Benson has made the following statement regarding missionaries' association with members:

> Too many missionaries are neutralized, and occasionally lost (excommunicated), because of oversolicitous members, member sisters who "mother" the missionaries, and socializing occurring between missionaries and members. Because of the importance of members and missionaries working effectively together on the member missionary program it is vital that missionaries maintain the proper missionary image and have the reputation as great proselyting elders and not just "good guys". The greatest help members can be to a missionary is not to feed him, but to give names of their friends so he can teach them with the spirit in their homes and challenge them, with the wonderful members helping to fellowship. (Mission Presidents Seminar, June 21, 1975.)

If you become too familiar in your association with members, they will have only limited confidence in you and will not fully trust you to teach their friends.

Avoid Inappropriate Conversations

As a missionary you should learn to scrutinize your casual conversations. What you talk about is an indication of the degree to which you are dedicated to the Lord's work.

The scriptures teach us that we will be judged by what we talk about: "For our words will condemn us...." (Alma 12:14.) Our words reveal what is in our heart.

> ...for of the abundance of the heart his mouth speaketh. (Luke 6:45.)

> But I say unto you, that every idle word that men shall speak, they shall give account thereof in the day of judgment.

> For by thy words thou shalt be justified, and by thy words thou shalt be condemned. (Matthew 12:36-37.)

> Not that which goeth into the mouth defileth a man; but that which cometh out of the mouth, this defileth a man. (Matthew 15:11.)

You should make every effort to insure that your casual conversations are in harmony with the spirit of the work. You will not enjoy a full endowment of the Spirit if you engage in inappropriate conversations. Inappropriate conversations take many forms. For example, foolish talking and jesting (Ephesians 5:4) and light speech (D&C 88:121). Also sarcasm and needling should be avoided in conversations with other missionaries. The Prophet Joseph Smith said:

> How vain and trifling have been our spirits, our conferences, our councils, our meetings, our private as well as public conversations—too low, too mean, too vulgar, too condescending for the dignified characters of the called and chosen of God.... (*Teachings of the Prophet Joseph Smith*, p. 137.)

> If any man offend not in word, the same is a perfect man, and able also to bridle the whole body. (James 3:2.)

> Who is a wise man and endued with knowledge among you? let him shew out of a good conversation his works with meekness of wisdom. (James 3:13.)

You should not use slang, such as "flip," "gross," "jacked," and similar expressions. You are obligated to learn to use speech that is appropriate for an emissary of the Lord Jesus Christ. Generally, the possibility of detrimental conversations occurring increases when more than two missionaries get together on preparation days.

Discern What Are Appropriate Topics of Conversation

You must have the spirit of discernment to determine whether or not a topic of conversation will be detrimental to your spirituality. The effect of casual and incidental conversation on your spirituality is not neutral; it is either constructive or detrimental. (Read D&C 50:23.) Missionaries who learn to scrutinize their casual and incidental conversation qualify for a more abundant endowment of the Spirit. They realize that a few minutes of idle or inappropriate conversation can destroy the level of spirituality that requires several days of hard work to achieve.

One important key to avoiding inappropriate conversation is to focus on the people you are teaching and on other aspects of missionary work, rather than on those things that occupied your thoughts and conversations before you entered the mission field. Learn to be people-centered instead of self-centered or world-centered. The Lord expects you to set aside your personal interests (cars, girls, sports, inappropriate music) for two years and to maintain this standard every day, including your preparation day.

Avoid Inappropriate Conversations with the Opposite Sex

One of the most hazardous types of conversation is incidental conversation with young people of the opposite sex, including missionaries of the opposite sex. Frequently, this type of conversation is not constructive and is inappropriate because it is a form of idleness. Beyond a simple greeting, avoid conversations with young people of the opposite sex. Many missionaries lose the spirit of the work as a result of innocent fraternizing with the opposite sex. Missionaries should realize the negative consequences of idle conversation with members of the opposite sex and make every effort to refrain from it.

Because of the strong desire of young people to talk to persons of the opposite sex, you may find this to be a very difficult policy to comply with. You should seek spiritual confirmation of the validity of this counsel so that you will be strongly motivated to heed it. Remember, to test the truthfulness of a principle, you have to comply with it for a sustained period of time. (See John 7:17.)

Realize What Your Thoughts Indicate about You

Serving the Lord with all your mind requires the ultimate level of dedication, because your thoughts are the true indicator of your dedication: "For as he thinketh in his heart, so is he...." (Proverbs 23:7.)

> A man is literally what he thinks, his character being the complete sum of all his thoughts. (*The Miracle of Forgiveness,* p. 103.)

> The thought in your mind at this moment is contributing, however infinitesimally, almost imperceptibly to the shaping of your soul.... Even passing and idle thoughts leave their impression. (David O. McKay, quoted in *The Miracle of Forgiveness,* p. 105.)

I will know what you are if you tell me what you think about when you don't have to think. (David O. McKay, *True to the Faith*, p. 170.)

Control Your Thoughts

As a missionary you have the responsibility to exert every effort to control your thoughts. You need to realize you exercise your agency in what you think about as well as in your actions. The Lord expects you to discipline your mind to insure that your thoughts are productive and edifying.

Yea, and cry unto God for all thy support; yea, let all thy doings be unto the Lord, and withersoever thou goest let it be in the Lord; yea, let thy thoughts be directed unto the Lord; yea, let the affections of thy heart be placed upon the Lord forever.

Counsel with the Lord in all thy doings, and he will direct thee for good; yea, when thou liest down at night lie down unto the Lord, that he may watch over you in your sleep; and when thou risest in the morning let thy heart be full of thanks unto God; and if ye do these things, ye shall be lifted up at the last day. (Alma 37:36, 37.)

... let virtue garnish thy thoughts unceasingly.... (D&C 121:45.)

Look unto me in every thought.... (D&C 6:36.)

... if ye do not watch yourselves, and your thoughts,... ye must perish.... (Mosiah 4:30.)

For to be carnally [worldly] minded is death; but to be spiritually minded is life and peace.

Because the carnal mind is enmity [hatred] against God.... (Romans 8:6-7.)

To achieve this level of dedication, you must first become continually aware of your thoughts. Then you must learn to examine them to determine if they are appropriate.

You will be more able to control your thoughts if you will consistently remind yourself that God "... knowest thy thoughts and the intents of thy heart." (D&C 6:16.) You will achieve this level of dedication by striving consistently over a sustained period of time to obtain it. You will have to make an extremely strong effort initially to control your thoughts, but once you cultivate the Spirit, you will find that this level of dedication is much easier to maintain. When you apply yourself and make the effort, the Lord will help you control your thoughts and you will receive the Spirit as your teacher and guide.

Unless you are willing to respond to the Lord's charge to serve Him with all your mind, you will never experience the full endowment of the Spirit in your missionary labors.

As you learn to control your mind so that it is not distracted by events around you or other preoccupations (e.g., the weather, not receiving a letter from home), you will qualify for the full endowment of the Spirit.

A missionary who reaches this level of dedication will be able to teach with power and authority and will be an instrument in the hands of the Lord in bringing many converts into the Church (read Alma 17:3): "... he that is righteous is favored of God" (read Alma 17:35); "... he that is faithful shall be made strong.... (D&C 66:8). If you dedicate yourself you will not be juvenile, immature, and light minded; even more importantly, you will not be as vulnerable to the enticings of Satan. You have the promise that if you truly dedicate youself to the work, the Lord will provide you people to teach.

Your Responsibility to Your Companion

If you are assigned to labor with a missionary who does not have the Spirit and who is not dedicated, the Lord will not excuse you if you are also slothful. He expects you to strengthen your companion.

> And if any man among you be strong in the Spirit, let him take with him him that is weak, that he may be edified in all meekness, that he may become strong also. (D&C 84:106.)

Throughout your mission you should continually ask yourself the following questions to evaluate your level of dedication.

1. Am I serving the Lord with all my heart?

2. Am I serving the Lord with all my might?

3. Am I serving the Lord with all my mind?

4. Am I serving the Lord with all my strength?

5. Do I use my spare moments throughout the day to improve myself in some way?

6. Do I make constructive use of my time rather than merely putting in time?

7. Do I restrict my time with members to talking about proselyting and related activities?

8. Am I too familiar in my associations with members?

9. Are my casual conversations in harmony with the Spirit of the work?

10. Have I eliminated any use of slang expressions?

11. Do I focus my thoughts and conversation on the people we are teaching and other aspects of missionary work, rather than things which occupied my thoughts and conversation before I entered the mission field?

12. Do I make every effort to refrain from idle conversations with members of the opposite sex?

13. Do I continually examine my thoughts to determine if they are appropriate?

14. Do I do all I can to assist my companion in maintaining the level of dedication expected of missionaries?

15. Am I putting forth a consistent effort each day to maintain the level of dedication necessary for me to receive a full endowment of the Spirit?

16. Do I fulfill my responsibilities as a missionary with a glad heart and a cheerful countenance?

Chapter 8

Feast upon
the Words of Christ

In the early history of the Church the brother of Joseph Smith made his desires to do missionary work known to the prophet. Section 11 of the *Doctrine and Covenants* is the revelation the prophet received in response to Hyrum's request.

In this revelation a very basic truth is revealed. The Lord made it clear that you should not attempt to do missionary work until you have a good understanding of Church doctrine. The Lord explained that you cannot have the power to convince people that the Church is true until you "obtain my word" (a clear understanding of the doctrines of the Church).

Why Study

The Lord promises that specific blessings will follow once you gain a knowledge of the doctrines of the Church: "... then shall your tongue be loosed; then, if you desire, you shall have my Spirit and my word, yea, the power of God unto the convincing of men."

As you approach a mission, it is absolutely essential that you are obedient to the Lord's commandment to study his word so you can qualify for the endowment of the Holy Spirit.

A knowledge of Church doctrine is *not* obtained by attending Church, seminary, institute, or other Church classes. You will never acquire a knowledge of the doctrines of the Church unless you systematically study the gospel on your own.

The fact that many members of the Church do not study the gospel independently is a major concern of the Church leaders. President Kimball made the following remarks:

> ... we are saddened to learn as we travel about the stakes and missions of the Church that there are still many of the saints who are not reading and pondering the scriptures regularly and have little knowledge of the Lord's instructions to the children of men. Many have been baptized and received a testimony, and have 'gotten into this straight and narrow path,' yet have failed to take the further required step—to 'press forward, *feasting upon the word of Christ*, and endure to the end.' (2 Nephi 31:19, 20. Italics added.) One cannot become a 'doer' of the word without first becoming a 'hearer'. And to become a 'hearer' is not simply to stand idly by and wait for chance bits of information, it is to seek out and study and pray and comprehend. Therefore, the Lord said, 'Whoso receiveth not my voice is not acquainted with my voice, and is not of me.' (D&C 84:52.)
>
> ... Lest the foregoing be lightly passed over, let me pause here to point out a common error in the mind of man—that is, the tendency, when someone speaks of faithfulness or success in one thing or another, to think 'me,' and when someone mentions failure or neglect, to think 'them.' But I ask us all to honestly evaluate our performance in scripture study. It is a common thing to have a few passages of scripture at our disposal, floating in our minds, as it were, and thus to have the illusion that we know a great deal about the gospel. In this sense, having a little knowledge can be a problem indeed. *I am convinced that each of us, at some time in our lives, must discover the scriptures for ourselves*—and not just discover them once, but rediscover them again and again.
>
> ... I feel strongly that we must all of us return to the scriptures just as King Mosiah did and let them work mightily within us, impelling us to an unwavering determination to serve the Lord.
>
> ... The Lord is not trifling with us when he gives us these things, for 'unto whomsoever much is given, of him shall much be required.' (Luke 12:48.) Access to these things means responsibility for them. We must study the scriptures according to the Lord's commandment. (See 3 Nephi 23:1-5); and we must let them govern our lives....
>
> ... The Lord's teachings have always been to those who have 'eyes to see' and 'ears to hear.' The voice is clear and unmistakable, and against those who neglect so great an opportunity the witness is sure.
>
> So I ask all to begin now to study the scriptures in earnest, if you have not already done so. (Spencer W. Kimball, "How Rare a Possession—the Scriptures!," *The Ensign*, Sept. 1976; italics added.)

What to Study

Before you enter the mission field you should read the following: *The Book of Mormon, A Marvelous Work and a Wonder, The Articles of Faith, The New Testament, Jesus the Christ*, and the *Doctrine and Covenants*.

In addition, once you are in the field, you should study the scriptures daily. Reading the scriptures each morning before you begin your proselyting efforts will make you more receptive to the Spirit which is required to convince men of the truthfulness of your message.

Daily scripture study is one of the most difficult aspects of missionary work. Other demands in the morning will encroach on the time that should be devoted to scripture study unless you remind yourself every morning that seeking the word through systematic study as the Lord admonished will entitle you to the Spirit of the Lord. This is just as true on the last day of your mission as it is on the first day. Generally you will be expected to devote portions of your study time to various activities. However, no matter what demands are made of you to study other things, if you want to qualify for the Spirit you must make it a practice to read the scriptures every day.

Becoming lax in your scripture study any time during your mission will impair your effectiveness. Indeed, the need for daily scriptural study will continue throughout your lifetime.

How to Study

Since we are admonished to "feast upon the words of Christ" (2 Nephi 32:3), you need to develop a genuine love for the scriptures, not merely read them out of duty. Your intent in studying the scriptures should be to draw closer to your Father in Heaven and to be better grounded in the first principles of the gospel. As you study the scriptures you should note and mark scriptures that will assist you in your efforts to be a good missionary and that deal with the doctrines covered in the discussions.

Examples:

... having great desires to know of the mysteries of God, wherefore, I did cry unto the Lord; and behold he did visit me, and did soften my heart that I did believe all the words which had been spoken by my father; wherefore, I did not rebel against him like unto my brothers. (1 Nephi 2:16.)

Adam fell that men might be; and men are that they might have joy. (1 Nephi 2:25.)

It is essential that you train yourself to study and ponder as you read the scriptures. As you read a chapter, identify at least one concept or idea that you consider to be the most important for you. Write the verse(s) down and then make it a point to think about the concepts or ideas during your spare moments during the day. The process of selecting, writing and reflecting will help you to learn to ponder as you read the scriptures. As you study the scriptures, you should maintain a log of your activities.

Example:

Date: September 10, 1978
Chapters read: Alma 17, 18
Time spent: 15 minutes
Verses selected: 17:2-3 and 18:16

... they had searched the scriptures diligently, that they might know the word of God....

they had given themselves to much prayer and fasting.... (Alma 17:2-3.)

... Ammon, being filled with the spirit of God, therefore he perceived the thoughts of the king.... (Alma 18:16.)

Make it a policy to discuss the scriptures you select in each chapter with your companion on a daily basis. This will help you train your mind to focus on things related to missionary work instead of home, girls, and other distractions.

More than any other books, the *Book of Mormon* and the *Doctrine and Covenants* should be the focus of your reading. The collection of scriptures dealing with missionary work at the end of this chapter should be read and reread frequently throughout your mission.

Remember that compliance with this requirement of scripture study as it relates to the Spirit is based on continually feasting upon the word of the Lord by reading the scriptures each day. If you consistently comply with this requirement, your spirituality and effectiveness will increase throughout your mission.

When to Study

Ideally you should enter the mission field well-grounded in the doctrines of the Church and well-acquainted with scriptures that deal with the doctrines covered in the discussions and scriptures that explain how the Lord expects you to perform your duties as a missionary. However, if you arrive in the mission field without this background, you still should not study in your apartment during proselyting hours. You will find that if you do, it will become counter-productive. There is a time and a place appointed for each aspect of missionary work: prayer, study, contacting, teaching. It is very important that you do each of these at its appointed time.

Throughout your mission you should consistently ask yourself the following questions:

1. Do I read the scriptures each day?

2. Do I remind myself every morning that seeking the word of God through systematic study will entitle me to the Spirit of the Lord?

3. Do I study because of a genuine love for the scriptures rather than out of duty?

4. Do I study only the books outlined in the missionary handbook?

Selected References

1 Nephi 8; 2 Nephi 25-26; Jacob 1, 7; Enos 1; Mosiah 1-2, 4, 6, 18, 23, 25, 27, 28; Alma 1, 4-5, 8-9, 13-24, 26, 29-32, 34, 37-39, 42-46, 48-49, 62; Helaman 3-7, 11, 13, 15-16; 3 Nephi 1-2, 6-7, 15, 19, 23, 26, 28; Mormon 1, 9; Moroni 3, 6-8, 10.

D&C 4; 5:6-16; 6; 9:7-9; 11-12; 15; 18; 19:28-31, 37-41; 33; 35:6-9; 42:6-17; 43:5-35; 50:13-18; 79; 84:60-95, 100; 121; 122; 135.

Chapter 9

"If Ye Are Not One, Ye Are Not Mine"

No matter what your efforts are in terms of hard work, long hours, and prayer, if you fail to maintain a harmonious relationship with your companion and those who preside over you, you will not enjoy the support of the Spirit in your labors. The Lord has declared, "If ye are not one ye are not mine." (D&C 38:27.) Merely tolerating your companion and your mission leaders is not good enough. The Lord expects you to develop a relationship that is completely harmonious.

> And he commanded them that there should be no contention one with another, but that they should look forward with one eye, having one faith and one baptism, having their hearts knit together in unity and in love one towards another. (Mosiah 18:21.)

Eliminate Disagreements

The key to this type of relationship is to eliminate disagreements. You will not achieve this type of relationship unless you are willing to work at it consistently.

Because people are different in disposition, eating habits, and likes and dislikes, invariably disagreements will occur unless companions are willing to bend and give in order to maintain harmony. Your ability to work harmoniously with your companion and others will test your maturity in the gospel as much as anything else. You have the responsibility to be kind, considerate, thoughtful, understanding, patient, etc. with your companion and with those who preside over you.

Most disagreements involve very trivial things. You will avoid disagreements with others as you do the following:

1. If they make a statement that is inaccurate or that you do not agree with, do *not* say anything unless the consequence is critical.

   Example:

   In a conversation, if your companion gives you an incorrect reference for a scripture, you should not correct him.

2. If they disagree with your choice in a decision, go along with them unless the consequence is critical.

   Examples:

   Which brand of milk you buy.

   Who should speak first if both of you are in a sacrament meeting.

3. If they disagree with something you say, let the point drop unless the consequence is critical.

   Example:

   You say you like a particular style of house, and your companion disagrees with you.

Avoid Contention

You cannot have a harmonious relationship with someone if there is any element of a struggle, quarrel, or misunderstanding between the two of you. Contention never was and never will be constructive. Any disagreement between you and anyone else that results in contention will canker both of your spirits, and will deprive both of you of spiritual growth. In your relationships with other people you should avoid any arguing, careless words spoken in anger, disgust, or intolerance. All contention originates from the devil.

For verily, verily I say unto you, he that hath the spirit of contention is not of me, but is of the devil, who is the father of contention, and he stirreth up the hearts of men to contend with anger, one with another. (3 Nephi 11:29.)

If the adversary can get you to succumb to a contentious frame of mind, he can gain power over you. In contrast, if you maintain a harmonious relationship with others and comply with mission rules, the adversary will have no power over you. You must learn to express your views to people without resorting to any sentiment that results in the spirit of contention. Elder Ashton offers the following suggestions for avoiding contention.

1. Pray to have the love of God in your heart. Sometimes this is a struggle, but the Spirit of the Lord can soften hard feelings and mellow a callous spirit.

2. Learn to control your tongue. There is an old maxim and an excellent one: "Think twice before you speak and three times before you act."
3. Don't allow emotions to take over; rather, reason together.
4. Refuse to get embroiled in the same old patterns of argument and confrontation.
5. Practice speaking in a soft, calm voice. The peaceful life can best be attained not by those who speak with a voice of "great tumultuous noise" but by those who follow the Savior's example and speak with "a still voice of perfect mildness." (Helaman 5:30.)

Never Compromise Righteousness

You should never compromise righteousness under the guise of maintaining harmony. Some missionaries may rationalize their failure to fulfill certain responsibilities because they don't want to create disharmony with their companions. If you are ever in a situation where your companion or anyone else asks you to do something which conflicts with mission rules or the commandments of the Lord, you should decline. The Lord does not expect you to follow your companion or others in unrighteousness. As you develop and express love for your companion and openly discuss your desire to serve your Heavenly Father with all your heart, might, mind, and strength, you will find that you can disagree when the outcome is critical without creating contention.

Discipline Yourself

You must formulate the will and the discipline in your relationship with others to avoid contention. Train yourself to say things that are complimentary and supportive of your companion and others with whom you associate.

> We must eliminate the individual tendency to selfishness that snares the soul, shrinks the heart, and darkens the mind. (President Spencer W. Kimball, "Becoming the Pure in Heart," *Ensign*, p. 81)

> If the spirit of the Lord is to magnify our labors, then the spirit of oneness and cooperation must be the prevailing spirit in all we do. Moreover, when we do so we are told by the Prophet Joseph Smith "the greatest temporal and spiritual blessings which always come from faithfulness and consecrated effort never attend individual exertion or enterprise." (President Spencer W. Kimball, "Becoming the Pure in Heart," *Ensign*, p. 81.)

The bond of love between you and your companions and mission leaders will be enhanced as you consistently follow the guidelines in this chapter.

Throughout your mission ask yourself the following questions:

1. Am I willing to bend and give in order to maintain harmony?

2. Am I able to express my views to everyone without resorting to any sentiment that results in the spirit of contention?

3. Do I pray to have the love of God in my heart?

4. Have I learned to control my tongue?

5. Am I able to reason together with others rather than allowing my emotions to take over?

6. Do I practice speaking in a soft, calm voice?

7. Do I express my love for my companion openly and discuss my desire to serve my Heavenly Father with all my heart, might, mind and strength?

8. Do I say things that are complimentary and supportive of my companion and others with whom I associate?

Chapter 10

Summary of Section 1

Righteousness is an absolute prerequisite in missionary work, and the Lord's expectations of missionaries are very demanding. More than anyone else on the face of the earth, President Spencer W. Kimball understands these expectations. Speaking to new mission presidents in 1976, he told them that they should not take time off to tour, see the sights, or entertain friends. He made it clear that when someone is called to the ministry, it is for twenty-four hours a day, seven days per week.

The Lord expects missionaries to set aside their personal interests for two years. Many missionaries find it difficult to do so and resist this charge throughout their missions. As long as a missionary is preoccupied with personal interests (i.e., home, sports, cars) he will not cultivate a genuine love of the people he is called to teach. When a missionary is in this frame of mind, he will be inclined to do things that are out of character for a missionary (i.e., horse play, practical jokes, being boisterous, loud laughter). Any conduct that distracts from a missionary's dignity is out of character. So often, comments and actions that missionaries feel are harmless prove to be totally inappropriate.

You will find it easy to determine what you should or should not do if you earnestly pray for the power of discernment. Once you have the power of discernment, you will know when your speech or conduct is offensive to the Lord. If you want to function properly you must accept the fact that the Lord expects you to conduct yourself in a dignified way at all times, and your preparation day is no exception. The Lord expects you to be as conscientious in the use of your time and controlling your conversation and thoughts on your preparation day as on any other day.

If you hope to function properly as a missionary and qualify for the Spirit, you must be willing to accept the fact that a mission is a period of time in your life when you're expected to sacrifice your own interests and devote all of your energies to serving the Lord. Unless you're willing to function properly as a missionary, the principles and procedures discussed in this book will be of limited value to you, because receiving the Spirit is prerequisite to every other aspect of missionary work discussed in this book.

Chapter 11

Introduction to Section 2

We must convert more people ... ; how can we be satisfied with 100,000 converts out of four billion who need the gospel?" President Spencer W. Kimball made these statements when he spoke to the General Authorities and Regional Representatives in conjunction with a general conference of the Church in 1974. The theme of his talk was that missionaries must become much more productive in terms of convert baptisms.

Since that time the number of convert baptisms has increased significantly; and yet the prophet expressed the same concern when he spoke to the Church leaders in 1978. "How can we be satisfied with 200,000 converts in a year out of four billion people in the world who need the gospel? ... We have hardly scratched the surface."

President Kimball is confident that missionaries can become much more effective in their efforts to bring people into the Church. He has said:

> From now on brethren, we expect that every year there will be *a great increase in convert baptisms*.
>
> We must change our sights and raise our goals.
>
> Do you believe the doors of Russia can be pushed wide open? Do you think the gates of China, Egypt, India, Burma, the Arab countries can be swung wide so that we may enter and teach the gospel to them? Is it possible? As with your faith, so shall it be....
>
> "For with God nothing shall be impossible" (Luke 1:37), and I think that

is the way we must go into this, knowing that the Lord is able to do whatever is necessary to bring the gospel to the people of this world. (Regional Representatives'Seminar, Oct. 2, 1975.)

President Kimball has consistently said that he has every confidence that the work will go faster, will, in fact, be hastened considerably. He has said:

As we double the number of missionaries, we can easily multiply the number of conversions, *and there are many other ways the Lord can find to increase the success of the missionary work. (Ensign,* May, 1978, p. 108; italics added.)

We can increase our production and that's what we're talking about, and we want it to be real production, of course. We're not talking about baptisms—we're talking about conversions....

And we must increase our real conversions, not just the baptisms, but the real conversions. We must do a better work in convincing them of the truths of the gospel enough to change their lives. (Regional Representatives Seminar, Oct. 2, 1975.)

President Kimball has complete faith in the declarations of the Savior and ancient prophets that the gospel of Jesus Christ will be carried to all of the inhabitants of the earth. The following are statements he made in a talk in 1974:

And as he [the Savior] commanded them [his disciples] to go forth, do you think he wondered if it could be done? He reassured us. He had the power. He said, "All power is given me in heaven and in earth ... and I am with you always."

And again, as Mark records the events after the resurrection,' he upbraided those who had some doubts about his resurrection; then commanded them:

"Go ye into all the world, and preach the gospel to every creature." (Mark 16:15.)

...Surely there is significance in these words! Certainly his sheep were not limited to the thousands about him and with whom he'rubbed shoulders each day. A universal family! A universal command!

My brethren, I wonder if we are doing all that we can. Are we complacent in our approach to teaching all the world? We have been proselyting now for 144 years. Are we prepared to lengthen our stride? To enlarge our vision? Remember, our ally is our God. He is our commander. He made the plans. He gave the commandments. Remember what we have quoted thousands of times...

"And it came to pass that I, Nephi, said unto my father: I will go and do the things which the Lord hath commanded, for I know that the Lord giveth no commandments unto the children of men, save he shall prepare a way for them that they may accomplish the thing which he commandeth them." (1 Nephi 3:7.)

"Wherefore, whithersoever they shall send you, go ye, and I will be with you; and in whatsoever place ye shall proclaim my name an effectual door shall be opened unto you, that they may receive my word." (D&C 112:19.) (Seminar for Regional Representatives of the Twelve, Oct. 1974.)

The chapters in this section are designed to help you catch the vision of your potential to bring people into the Church if you function properly as a missionary and truly desire to see people join the Church.

Chapter 12

Catch the Vision
of Your Potential

Even though we have been sending missionaries out since the gospel was restored and the number of missionaries is greater today than ever before in the history of the Church, according to President Kimball we "have hardly skimmed the surface" as far as the charge to carry the gospel to the ends of the earth is concerned. "Our objective is to bring the gospel to all the world." To quote the prophet further, "Some few missionaries move toward their work as though they had all time and eternity to convert a few people in their part of the world. The word is URGENCY—it is *now*."*

In 1974 there were 75,000 convert baptisms. In 1975 there were 90,000. This increase in convert baptisms was primarily the result of more missionaries in the field, not increased effectiveness. The average number of baptisms per missionary in 1974 was 4.3, and in 1975 it was 4.9. Over the years we have failed to consistently become more effective in bringing people into the Church.

Regarding this situation, the prophet has said, "... we can hardly be content with this record. *We must find ways to inspire and teach better ways of doing missionary work.*" (President Spencer W. Kimball, Regional Representatives Seminar, Apr. 5, 1976; italics added.)

---

*The quotations from President Spencer W. Kimball in this chapter were taken from his remarks during a Regional Representatives Seminar, Apr. 5, 1976.

President Kimball asked the question, "Could we develop missionaries who could increase eight or twenty times the present production of converts?" Unless this challenge is met, the missionary effort of the Church is going to fall short of the Lord's expectation. Even if we increased the missionary force to 100,000, at 4.9 baptisms per year, that would only be a half million people joining the Church a year. At that rate it would take 10,000 years to proselyte the world. In response to this rate of growth the prophet has said, "That may be all right for you, but it's a little long for me."

If we are going to meet President Kimball's challenge, missionaries must become more productive. In missions where missionaries are productive, the average convert baptism for each missionary per year is between 20 and 30. If all missions were this effective, there would be more than one million people a year joining the Church.

President Kimball has faith in the promise made by the Prophet Alma:

> Yea, he that repenteth and exerciseth faith, and bringeth forth good works, and prayeth continually without ceasing ... it shall be given unto such to bring thousands of souls to repentance. ... (Alma 26:22.)

President Kimball has prayed:

> Oh, our beloved Father in Heaven, bring about the day when we may be able to bring in large numbers as Ammon and his brother did, thousands of conversions, not dozens, not tens or fives or ones, thousands of conversions. The Lord has promised it; he fulfills his promises. Our Father, may we move forward with Jesus Christ as our advocate to establish the Church among the inhabitants of the earth. May Jacob flourish in the wilderness and blossom as the rose upon the mountains. May we merit the promise that the Lord will do things that we can hardly believe. May we *improve the efficiency of our missionaries, each bringing thousands of converts into the Church.* Please, Father, open the doors of the nations. I pray this in the name of Jesus Christ. Amen. (Spencer W. Kimball, Regional Representatives Seminar, Apr. 5, 1976; italics added.)

Elder Bruce R. McConkie made the following statement regarding the growth of the Church:

> I think this statement summarizes what ought to be: If you will ponder it in your mind, you will come up, in my judgment, with the conclusion that we could bring immeasurably more people into the Church than we are now doing. We could fellowship more than we are fellowshipping. In practice this could be five or ten or twenty times as many as we are now baptizing. Perhaps in due course it should be 24 times or 100 times as many as at present. (Bruce R. McConkie, Mission President Seminar, June 21, 1975.)

This prophecy has been fulfilled in some sectors of the world. For example, in 1978 less than 20 people were joining the Church a month in the Tokyo South Mission. Today, nearly 1,000 people are joining the Church a month in the same mission.

As you catch the vision of your potential as a missionary, your motivation to do everything in your power to be a good missionary will be greatly enhanced because you will realize the Lord desires to use you to bring many good people into the Church.

When missionaries catch the vision of what they can accomplish if they will function properly, we will begin to see millions join the Church each year.

Throughout your mission you should consistently ask yourself the following questions:

1. Do I move toward my work as a missionary with the attitude of urgency expressed by President Kimball?

2. Am I consistently becoming more effective in bringing people into the Church?

3. In my prayers, do I ask my Heavenly Father to bless me with the same vision and perspective that President Kimball has regarding missionary work?

4. Am I doing all that I can to become proficient in using the various proselyting principles discussed in this book?

5. Do I read this book frequently?

6. Are my insights into and understanding of the principles contained in this book increasing?

7. Do I always pray and seek spiritual inspiration each time I read one of the chapters in this section?

Chapter 13

Use Faith as a Principle of Power

Faith is the moving cause of all action." (Joseph Smith, *Lectures on Faith.*) Your faith and conviction that the gospel of Jesus Christ has been restored to the earth is the reason you are willing to go on a mission. Your faith in God gives you the desire to live righteously. Your faith in the atoning sacrifice of Jesus Christ gives you the incentive to repent of your sins. It is faith that gives you the resolve and determination to do things like get up consistently at six o'clock, memorize so many scriptures a week, and read so many minutes a day in the scriptures. It is your faith in the results of your actions that motivate you to do things. For example, you get up a half-hour early and devote the extra time to your discussions because you are confident your ability to present the discussions will improve.

If you can see clearly in your mind's eye how you can realize a certain desire if you apply yourself, faith as a principle of motivation is all that you will need to achieve your desire.

Faith and Desires

However, as a missionary there will be many things you will desire to achieve (e.g., baptize a certain number of people per month, get someone to quit smoking), but you will not be able to see clearly in your mind's eye how they will be achieved even if you apply yourself. This type of desire not only requires you to be motivated to action by faith but also to use faith as a principle of power. These are desires you cannot achieve without

61

drawing on the powers of heaven. Your ability to use faith as a principle of power will have more influence on your mission than anything else.

Joseph Smith summarized the role of faith in our lives in the following statement:

> Faith is not only a principle of action, *but of power also.*

In order to realize your full potential as a missionary, you must learn to use faith as a principle of power as well as a principle to motivate. When you learn to use faith as a principle of power, you will be able to draw on the powers of heaven. No amount of knowledge or skill can compensate for the absence of the powers of heaven in your missionary labors. With these powers to assist you, you will be successful in your missionary labors in spite of weaknesses. In a very literal sense, the powers of heaven compensate for human weaknesses. With the powers of heaven to assist you, your limitations, such as aptitude and physical characteristics, will become insignificant. The Lord has promised that if you come to him in humility your weaknesses will become strengths.

> And if men come unto me I will show unto them their weakness. I give unto men weakness that they may be humble; and my grace is sufficient for all men that humble themselves before me; *for if they humble themselves before me, and have faith in me, then will I make weak things become strong unto them.* (Ether 12:27; italics added.)

The realization of this promise is made possible through faith as a principle of power. In our relationship with Deity, the powers of heaven include any influence or power (inspiration, gift of the spirit, power of the priesthood, etc.) which is governed by God and operates in our behalf. A study of the scriptures reveals that the ways in which the powers of heaven can assist missionaries are virtually unlimited. These powers are indeed very real and can dramatically influence your effectiveness as a missionary. As you learn to draw on the powers of heaven, your talents and abilities will be greatly magnified. Your ultimate effectiveness as a missionary will be determined by your ability to draw on the powers of heaven, not your natural ability. This chapter will teach you how to exercise the faith required to release the powers of heaven.

The Nature and Function of Faith

The following example illustrates the role of faith in motivating a person to action.

> If a man desires to lose 10 lbs., he must take the following steps:
> 1. Have faith in the laws that determine weight loss.
> 2. Make a resolve to exercise daily and eat less.
> 3. Maintain a constant effort, motivated by faith.

If you use faith only as a principle to motivate you to act, you will limit your performance as a missionary. Consider the task of memorizing the discussions. If you rely on the faith that motivates you to action exclusively, the time it takes you to memorize the discussions will be determined by your ability. However, if you exercise the faith necessary to call down the powers of heaven to assist you, your ability to memorize will be facilitated through the Spirit and you will be able to memorize the discussions in much less time.

The same holds true in learning a foreign language. If a missionary relies on faith as a principle of motivation, his rate of learning will be determined by his ability and how much time he devotes to studying the language. In contrast, if a missionary draws on the powers of heaven to assist him in learning the language, his ability to learn the language will be greatly facilitated.

The diagram below depicts the powers of heaven released through faith when someone is motivated to repent.

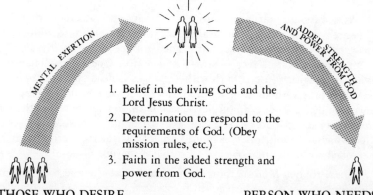

MENTAL EXERTION

ADDED STRENGTH AND POWER FROM GOD

1. Belief in the living God and the Lord Jesus Christ.
2. Determination to respond to the requirements of God. (Obey mission rules, etc.)
3. Faith in the added strength and power from God.

THOSE WHO DESIRE
TO SEE SOMEONE REPENT

PERSON WHO NEEDS
TO REPENT

Your Faith Governs the Powers of Heaven

Once you develop a basic faith in the overall plan of salvation, repent, acquire a testimony of the restored gospel, live in harmony with the gospel and comply with the rules and regulations specified for missionaries, you are in a position to exercise the type of faith that unlocks the powers of heaven. With this power you will be able to accomplish righteous desires that require the Lord's help, such as healing someone through the power of the priesthood, speaking with the power of the Holy Ghost when you teach, or baptizing a certain number of people in a given month.

Unless you learn to exercise the faith required to release the powers of heaven, *you deny the Lord the opportunity to help you in your missionary labors.* The scriptures teach us that the powers of heaven are governed by the faith of mortal men.

> And neither at any time hath any wrought miracles *until after their faith.* (Ether 12:18; italics added.)

> The Lord is able to do all things according to his will, for the children of men, *if it so be that they exercise faith in him.* (I Nephi 7:12; italics added.)

> Deny not the power of God; for he worketh by power, *according to the faith of the children of men.* (Moroni 10:7; italics added.)

> For behold, I am God; and I am a God of miracles . . . and *I work not among the children of men save it be according to their faith.* (2 Nephi 27:23; italics added.)

> And Christ hath said: If ye will have faith in me ye shall have power to do whatsoever thing is expedient in me. (Moroni 7:33.)

> Remember that *without faith you can do nothing.* (D&C 8:10; italics added.)

As a missionary it is very important that you understand that the influence of the powers of heaven in your proselyting activities is governed or controlled by your faith. The Prophet Joseph Smith said, "If the present generation receive any assistance from God, they will have to obtain it by faith." Just as faith without works is dead (James 2:14-16), likewise works without faith are dead, since they are not sustained by the powers of heaven. For example, if you lack faith, you can spend long hours proselyting and still not be successful. No matter how hard you work, your effectiveness as a missionary is limited unless you learn to exercise faith in the added strength and power of God that is at your disposal.

The Prophet Moroni thoroughly understood the role of faith in releasing the powers of heaven. In response to a revelation he received regarding his ability to overcome his weaknesses, he made the following statement when he expressed his gratitude to the Lord.

> . . . I know that thou workest unto the children of men according to their faith;

> . . . thou workest after men have faith.

> . . . after they had faith, . . . thou didst show thyself unto them in great power. (Ether 12:29-31.)

Of those missionaries who are motivated to work hard, there are significant numbers who in turn deny themselves the full blessings that come through dedicated service because they fail to exercise sufficient faith to allow the Lord to bless them for their obedience and dedication. Obedience and dedication alone will not release the powers of heaven. There are many blessings the Lord would like to extend to individual missionaries if they would merely exercise the faith that would allow him to extend the blessings. In other words, in some instances obedience and dedication on the part of missionaries exceeds their faith. If their faith were greater, they would realize many blessings which the Lord wishes them to have and for which they have qualified as a result of their obedience and dedication.

Faith has a very important role in the receiving of inspiration. For example, a missionary may be faced with a difficult decision. Faith can motivate the missionary to pray and seek guidance from his Father in Heaven. However, unless the missionary exercises the faith required to call down the powers of heaven, the Lord cannot inspire him regarding his problem. In other words, the missionary's faith governs his ability to receive inspiration. All of the powers of heaven (witness of the Spirit, inspiration, gifts of the Spirit, etc.) are governed by your faith. In the course of your mission you will repeatedly call upon the Lord to bless and assist you in various ways. You must make certain that you exercise the necessary faith to allow the Lord the opportunity to grant your requests.

Throughout your mission you should analyze the role of faith in all your endeavors. By doing so, you will become much more aware of faith as a principle of power.

Faith—the Key to Excellence

In the course of your mission, there will be many things required of you that you cannot accomplish to a degree of excellence without the Lord's help. There will be many things you will do every day as a missionary that you could do much better if you knew how to call down the powers of heaven to help you. In order to realize your full potential, you must learn to exercise abiding faith that the Lord will help you achieve goals and expectations that you cannot achieve without the Lord's help. Exercising such faith involves a very specific process which has to be both learned and mastered.

The Principles that Govern Faith

Once you are functioning properly in terms of being worthy, having proper motives, being obedient, making constructive use of your time, avoiding inappropriate conversation, and directing all of your thoughts to the work, you will be able to exercise the faith required to call upon the powers of heaven.

... the powers of heaven cannot be controlled nor handled only upon the principles of righteousness. (D&C 121:36.)

I, the Lord, am bound when ye do what I say; but when ye do not what I say, ye have no promise. (D&C 82:10.)

Faith is a gift of God bestowed as a reward for personal righteousness. It is always given when righteousness is present, and the greater the measure of obedience to God's laws the greater will be the endowment of faith. (Bruce R. McConkie, *Mormon Doctrine*, p. 264.)

Consequently, unless you are willing to completely dedicate yourself to the work you will be very limited in your ability to draw on the powers of heaven.

In order to be effective in using faith as a principle of power, you must understand the process thoroughly and then learn to use the process in your missionary labors. The following steps will help you understand the process required for calling upon the powers of heaven to assist you in your missionary labors.

1. Select Righteous Desires

Once you are functioning properly, the first step in drawing on the powers that come through faith is to select a righteous desire that will require you to draw on the powers of heaven in order to achieve it. It is impossible to exercise faith in the powers of heaven at your disposal without having a very specific end in mind. The most serious failing on the part of many missionaries with respect to faith is their failure to make specific decisions regarding things they want the Lord to assist them with. For example, unless you systematically make the decision that you want to see someone join the Church each month you are in the mission field, the chance that you will see someone join the Church each month of your mission is quite remote.

In your dealings with the Lord, the need to ask for specific blessings is an absolute requirement. Dedication alone is not sufficient. You must request blessings.

> Therefore, if you will ask of me you shall receive; if you will knock it shall be opened unto you. (D&C 11:5.)

This same promise is reiterated at least 100 times throughout the scriptures. However, you cannot take advantage of this promise unless you are willing to ask the Lord in faith to help you achieve your desires.

> I can promise you that the spirit is a whole lot more anxious to help you than you are to be helped. (S. Dilworth Young, Talk given in the Missionary Home, June, 1975.)

If we realized blessings as a direct result of dedication, we would lose sight of the hand of the Lord in the blessings we receive. It is for this reason the Lord has stipulated we must ask in order to receive blessings.

It is your responsibility to make certain your desires are righteous and properly focused. The Lord has said:

Remember that without faith you can do nothing; therefore ask in faith. Trifle not with these things; *do not ask for that which you ought not.* (D&C 8:10; italics added.)

Whatsoever ye ask the Father in my name it shall be given unto you, *that is expedient for you; And if ye ask anything that is not expedient for you, it shall turn unto your condemnation.* (D&C 88:64-65; italics added.)

And now, if God, who has created you, on whom you are dependent for your lives and for all that ye have and are, *doth grant unto you whatsoever ye ask that is right, in faith, believing that ye shall receive,* O then, how ye ought to impart the substance that ye have one to another. (Mosiah 4:21; italics added.)

And now, because thou hast done this with such unwearyingness, behold, I will bless thee forever; and I will make thee mighty in word and in deed, in faith and in works; yea, even that all things shall be done unto thee according to thy word, *for thou shalt not ask that which is contrary to my will.* (Helaman 10:5; italics added.)

...ye must not perform any thing unto the Lord save in the first place ye shall pray unto the Father in the name of Christ, that he will consecrate thy performance unto thee, that thy performance may be for the welfare of thy soul. (2 Nephi 32:9. See also D&C 46:31.)

If your motives are pure, you will be inspired to pray for the right things. (See 3 Nephi 19:24; D&C 50:29,30; D&C 46:30.)

Even if you are consistently prayerful in the process of selecting righteous desires, there will be times when you will begin to exercise faith in a desire that is not approved by your Father in Heaven. When this is the case you will experience a stupor of thought and will find it virtually impossible to focus your mind on your desires. When this happens you should cease your effort to petition the Lord's help and prayerfully determine why the desire is not appropriate.

In your effort to exercise faith, it is your responsibility to insure that you do not confuse either your lack of personal worthiness, desire, personal discipline, or opposition from the adversary with the stupor of thought just described. If you are sensitive to the Spirit, you will be able to distinguish very clearly between opposition from the adversary and the stupor of thought that occurs when a desire, for one reason or another, is inappropriate.

With this understanding you should be able to consistently have the assurance that your desires are righteous. You should keep this caution in mind, because through persistence it is possible to realize desires that in the wisdom of the Lord are not in your best interest. The Lord honors our agency in the desires we seek.

As you prayerfully select righteous desires it is important that you realize that a desire is more than a mere wish. It is a motivating conviction that moves one to action. We are ambitious or lazy, interesting or dull, faithful or disobedient, loyal or undependable, successful or unsuccessful according to our desires. Learn to concentrate on your desire every day—when you are praying, walking, or traveling, or at night before you retire. Otherwise the things for which you are striving will not actually be desires. Remember, desires are not just passing thoughts, but those things we seek earnestly.

The Lord has promised he will grant unto men according to their desires.

> ...I know that he granteth unto men according to their desire.... (Alma 29:4.)

> ...if you desire, you shall have my Spirit and my word, yea, the power of God unto the convincing of men. (D&C 11:21.)

In the process of selecting a righteous desire that you want to achieve you should (a) specify your desire in writing, and (b) specify when the desire will be attained. As you do this you are, in effect, setting a goal.

Goal setting is very critical to effective missionary work. President Spencer W. Kimball has stressed the importance of goal setting in missionary work:

> We do believe in setting goals. We live by goals. In athletics, we always have a goal. When we go to school, we have the goal of graduation and degrees. Our total existence is goal-oriented.
>
> ...we must have goals to make progress, encouraged by keeping records. I believe it is proper for a missionary to set his own goals, as the swimmer or the jumper or the runner does.
>
> ...Goals are good. Laboring with a distant aim sets the mind in a higher key and puts us at our best.
>
> ...Goals should always be made to a point that will make us reach and strain. (Regional Representatives Seminar, Apr. 3, 1975.)

Some goals can be accomplished by means of the resolve and determination that come through faith. Others will require faith as a principle of power to be achieved.

Each time you set a goal that will require assistance from the various powers of heaven in order to be achieved it is essential that you remind yourself of your responsibility to function properly and to exercise the faith necessary to release the powers of heaven.

Many of your righteous desires that will require assistance from the Lord to be achieved will grow out of expectations. For example, while you are at the Missionary Training Center there will be certain expectations associated with the experience that you cannot accomplish without the Lord's help. When you arrive in the mission field your mission president will also establish certain expectations you will not be able to meet without the Lord's help. These expectations, coupled with the expectations that are introduced in this book that involve the Spirit, should be the primary focus of many of your desires. However, it is important that you set other goals for yourself that will require you to draw on the powers of heaven in order to achieve them.

> For behold, it is not meet that I should command in all things; for he that is compelled in all things, the same is a slothful and not a wise servant; wherefore he receiveth no reward.
>
> Verily I say, men should be anxiously engaged in a good cause, and do many things of their own free will, and bring to pass much righteousness;
>
> For the power is in them wherein they are agents unto themselves. And inasmuch as men do good they shall in nowise lose their reward.
>
> But he that doeth not anything until he is commanded, and receiveth a commandment with doubtful heart, and keepeth it with slothfulness, the same is damned. (D&C 58:26-29.)

As a general rule, it is much better to focus on a few pertinent desires at one time rather than attempting to focus on many desires simultaneously. You should use wisdom in determining how many desires you attempt to focus on at the same time according to your particular temperament, ability, etc.

Goals (desires), of course, need to be realistic, something that you are not currently achieving and something that will require the Lord's help. Otherwise you will not be required to use faith as a principle of power.

Even though you will not be able to see clearly in your mind's eye how you will achieve some desires, you must maintain the faith that if your desire is righteous and you make a determined effort, the Lord will prepare a way for your desire to be accomplished.

> And it came to pass that I, Nephi, said unto my father: I will go and do the things which the Lord hath commanded, for I know the Lord giveth no commandments unto the children of men, save he shall prepare a way for them that they may accomplish the thing which he commandeth them. (I Nephi 3:7.)

Throughout your mission you should follow President Kimball's admonition to set goals for yourself, especially goals that will require you to draw on the powers of heaven. You are entitled to draw on the powers of heaven in realizing righteous desires related to your health, your ability to get along with your companion, effectiveness in giving the discussions, baptizing people, etc. You need to remember that the power of faith has "power, dominion, and authority over all things." You should learn to approach everything you desire to achieve with faith as a principle of power in mind. The Lord is willing and anxious to assist you in achieving your righteous desires if you will let him. Through faith, the powers of heaven can assist you in realizing any righteous desire, be it emotional, intellectual, or spiritual in nature.

2. Plead Your Case before the Lord

Once you have selected a righteous desire, your next step is to plead your case before the Lord. Go to the Lord in earnest prayer. Explain your rationale in selecting your particular desire, and, most important, explain in great detail why you want the particular desire to be realized. Throughout history we see that the Lord is responsive to the request of mortal men if they go to Him in faith and can present a strong case for the blessing they are seeking. In a very literal sense, you need to learn to reason with the Lord. A good example of this process is found in Helaman 11:9-16:

> And it came to pass that the judges did say unto Nephi, according to the words which had been desired. And it came to pass that when Nephi saw that the people had repented and did humble themselves in sackcloth, he cried again unto the Lord, saying:
>
> O Lord, behold this people repenteth; and they have swept away the band of Gadianton from amongst them insomuch that they have become extinct, and they have concealed their secret plans in the earth.
>
> Now, O Lord, because of this their humility wilt thou turn away thine anger, and let thine anger be appeased in the destruction of those wicked men whom thou hast already destroyed.
>
> O Lord, wilt thou turn away thine anger, yea, thy fierce anger, and cause that this famine may cease in this land.
>
> O Lord, wilt thou hearken unto me, and cause that it may be done according to my words, and send forth rain upon the face of the earth, that she may bring forth her fruit, and her grain in the season of grain.
>
> O Lord, thou didst hearken unto my words when I said, Let there be a famine, that the pestilence of the sword might cease; and I know that thou wilt, even at this time, hearken unto my words, for thou saidst that: If this people repent I will spare them.
>
> Yea, O Lord, and thou seest that they have repented, because of the famine and the pestilence and destruction which has come unto them.
>
> And now, O Lord, wilt thou turn away thine anger, and try again if they will serve thee? And if so, O Lord, thou canst bless them according to thy words which thou hast said. (Helaman 11:9-16.)

As you study the life of Joseph Smith, you will find that he never did receive new doctrine or revelation until he exerted himself and went to the

Lord and requested clarification on a point. (Read the preface to Sections 76 and 132 of the Doctrine and Covenants.) Make every effort to exercise faith in the prophet Alma's promise:

> Counsel with the Lord in all thy doings, and he will direct thee for good....(Alma 37:37.)

In your relationship with your Father in Heaven, you must *ask* in order to receive. Missionaries have a tendency to be too general in their petitions to God (e.g., please bless, please help.) You should resolve to be more specific in your requests, expressing much more specifically the desires for which you are striving. Being more specific in prayers on a regular basis enhances the chance that your prayers will become earnest and sustained by faith. Unfortunately, most people do not petition the Lord unless they are faced with a crisis. You will find that your relationship with your Father in Heaven will be greatly enhanced if you are consistently seeking His help in achieving righteous desires you have selected instead of desires that grow out of a crisis. Obviously, if you are seeking and experiencing the Lord's help on a daily basis, when you are faced with a crisis your ability to exercise faith sufficient to call down the powers of heaven will be much greater. It is man's tendency to forget his dependence upon God when he is not faced with hardships.

> And because of this their great wickedness, and their boastings in their own strength, they were left in their own strength; therefore they did not prosper, but were afflicted and smitten, and driven before the Lamanites, until they had lost possession of almost all their lands. (Helaman 4:13.)
>
> And thus we can behold how false, and also the unsteadiness of the hearts of the children of men; yea, we can see that the Lord in his great infinite goodness doth bless and prosper those who put their trust in him. (Helaman 12:1.)
>
> They were slow to hearken unto the voice of the Lord their God; therefore, the Lord their God is slow to hearken unto their prayers, to answer them in the day of their trouble. In the day of their peace they esteemed lightly my counsel; but, in the day of their trouble, of necessity they feel after me. (D&C 101:7-8.)

The elect of God are those who do not lose sight of their dependence on God, even when they are not faced with adversity. You should make every effort to make your daily prayers earnest, even when you are not faced with pressing problems. Your prayers will be mighty prayers if they are persuasive, because a mighty prayer is one that is heard and answered. If your prayers are not being answered, it may be due to your failure to pray with the power of faith or sufficiently plead your case to God.

Very critical in your effort to petition help from the Lord is your willingness to resolve that you will do everything in your power to achieve

the righteous desire. Only when you're doing all you can to bring about
your desire will you qualify for the added strength and power from God.
You should never expect the Lord to do what you can do on your own. Only
when you're doing all you can to bring about your desire will you receive
the necessary assistance from your Heavenly Father. When you plead your
case before the Lord, you should make it a point to tell the Lord very
specifically what things you will do in your effort to bring about your
righteous desires. You will find that when you promise the Lord that you
will do certain things (e.g., make specific sacrifices, keep mission rules, be
willing to go the extra mile, etc.), your personal resolve and determination
will be enhanced. If your motives are righteous, you will find the Lord will
be very responsive to your requests when you express a resolve to live
more righteously, etc.

When you make commitments to the Lord, you are in effect entering
into a covenant with him. Such a covenant should never be construed as
bartering with God. You barter with man. You covenant with God. You
should make a clear distinction between the two when you petition your
Father in Heaven regarding your righteous desires.

In your effort to solicit the Lord's help in realizing your righteous
desire, you cannot rely on vocal prayers alone. You must learn to offer
frequent silent prayers.

> And again, I command thee that thou shalt pray vocally as well as in thy
> heart.... (D&C 19:28.)

When you encounter a situation that causes you to doubt your ability to
achieve your desire, request the Lord's help in maintaining an attitude of
faith.

When you are seeking the powers of heaven to assist you in realizing a
righteous desire, you should plead your case to your Heavenly Father daily
until your desire is realized.

3. Exert Yourself Mentally

Exercising the faith required to release the powers of heaven involves
continual mental exertion. This basic truth was revealed to Joseph Smith:

> When a man works by faith he works by mental exertion instead of by
> physical force. (*Lectures on Faith*, 7:3.)

The thought process itself is the key to exercising faith—we
accomplish what we think about. In other words, what you think about
today, tomorrow, or next month will mold your attitude and determine
what you will accomplish during your life. Your life is influenced more by
your own thoughts and desires than anything else.

> How could a person possibly become what he is *not* thinking? Nor is any

thought, when persistently entertained, too small to have its effect. The "divinity that shapes our ends" is indeed in ourselves. (Spencer W. Kimball, *The Miracle of Forgiveness*, pp. 104, 105.)

Thoughts are indicative of our desires. The Lord has said we achieve according to our desires. (Read Alma 29:4, 5.) It is essential that you learn to control your thoughts and focus them on righteous desires. The Savior said to a centurion:

> ...as thou hast believed, so be it done unto thee.... (Matthew 8:13.)

Once you have prayerfully selected a goal (righteous desire) you want the Lord to assist you with, in order to exercise faith, you must become preoccupied with your desire. Faith can be gauged, to a great extent, by the amount of time spent thinking about the goal.

The mind is like a field; you will harvest whatever you plant in it if it is nourished. You should learn to follow the Lord's admonition:

> Look unto me in every thought; doubt not, fear not. (D&C 6:36.)
>
> ... where doubt and uncertainty are there faith is not, nor can it be. For doubt and faith do not exist in the same person at the same time; so that persons whose minds are under doubts and fears cannot have unshaken confidence; and where unshaken confidence is not there faith is weak. (Joseph Smith, *Lectures on Faith*, pp. 59-60.)

Research has demonstrated that most people use their minds in a constructive way only about ten percent of the time. Similarly, the amount of faith they exercise is extremely limited. Thinking negatively does not require any effort; exercising faith, however, requires an exerted effort over a sustained period of time.

By the process of faith thoughts produce an effect as literal as physical exertion. Your thoughts, more than anything else, will be the determining factor in how much success you have during your mission.

Some people are prone to blame their circumstances for their failure to realize their righteous desires. As you understand faith as a principle of power, you will realize that you can change your circumstances by changing your attitude and by exercising faith:

> Let a man radically alter his thoughts, and he will be astonished at the rapid transformation it will effect in the material conditions of his life. Men imagine that thought can be kept secret, but it cannot, it rapidly crystallizes into habit and habit solidifies into circumstance." (James Allen, *As a Man Thinketh*, pp. 26-27.)

You exercise your agency in what you think about as literally as you do in your actions. Man alone, of all creatures on earth, can change his thought pattern and become the architect of his destiny. When a person is groping in life, we say: "He has not found himself." This statement is not accurate. Self is created—not found.

> Each one of us is the architect of his own fate; and he is unfortunate indeed who will try to build himself without the inspiration of God, without realizing that he grows from within, not from without. (David O. McKay, "True End of Life," *Instructor*, Jan. 1964, p. 1.)

You cannot blame your circumstance (slothfulness of companion, negative attitude of the people) for your failure to baptize souls into the Kingdom of God. As you understand the process of faith, you will realize you will consistently baptize people if you have the faith. Speaking of this subject, President Ezra Taft Benson has said, "The Lord calls nobody to fail, but to succeed; and they (the missionaries) should understand this fully." (Mission Presidents Seminar, June 21, 1975.) Also, Elder Bruce R. McConkie has said, "Now, very frankly, whether we gain many converts or few depends in large measure upon *our frame of mind*." (Mission Presidents Seminar, June 21, 1975; italics added.) In the work of the Lord, mental attitude is much more important than mental ability. You must realize that your success in baptizing people will be in direct proportion to your faith and effort, not your ability or circumstances.

Although you cannot violate someone's free agency by exercising faith, in many instances your faith will be the determining factor as to whether or not people join the Church. Your faith can cause doors to be opened and elicit stronger witnesses of the Spirit, so that people will know your message is true.

The missionary labors of Nephi and Lehi provide an example of the potential of faith in changing circumstances.

> Behold, it was the faith of Nephi and Lehi that wrought the change upon the Lamanites, that they were baptized with fire and with the Holy Ghost. (Ether 12:14.)

The missionary labors of Ammon and his brethren are another example of the potential of faith to change circumstances.

> Behold, it was the faith of Ammon and his brethren which wrought so great a miracle among the Lamanites. (Ether 12:15.)

You will be successful in exerting yourself mentally when you learn to control your mind.

You will be successful in controlling your mind as you do the following: (a) train yourself to be conscious of your thoughts, (b) learn to scrutinize your thoughts to determine whether they add to or detract from your faith, and (c) if a thought detracts from your faith, replace it with a thought that is based on faith (e.g., remind yourself of the Lord's goodness and willingness to bless you, remind yourself of the numerous promises in the scriptures that if we ask in faith the Lord will bless us). If you learn to put forth the necessary mental exertion you will be successful in cultivating the faith required to qualify for the power and force for righteousness that comes through faith.

To exercise mental exertion effectively you must have power and dominion over your mind. You cannot allow your mind to be easily distracted—to focus on something that is extraneous to the purpose or object of your desired blessing. For instance, when you call upon the Lord for his blessings, do you find thoughts popping into your mind regarding things you need to do or other mundane preoccupations? The next time you pray or meditate, see if you have power and control over your mind sufficiently that you can keep it from wandering when you are attempting to communicate with the Lord. Consider how offensive it is to you when someone fails to give you his undivided attention during a conversation. For example, if you are in a man's office talking to him and he is reading or writing while you are attempting to talk to him, you generally will take offense at his lack of courtesy. In the same way our behavior is offensive to the Lord when we are attempting to communicate with him and allow our mind to be distracted. Until you learn to discipline your mind and have complete control over it, you will be limited in your capacity to exercise faith. The full power of the mind is only realized when it is specifically focused and directed to a specific end.

> And if your eye [mind's eye] be single to my glory, your whole bodies shall be filled with light.... (D&C 88:67.)

If you allow your mind to randomly dwell on various matters, you will be limited in your ability to draw on the power of faith and your mind will not be a source of power for you.

You will discover as you attempt to control and focus your mind that the devil will bring things to your view to divert you. When you can control your mind and not allow it to be distracted, your eye will be single, and you will be able to unlock the powers of heaven by your faith.

> The greatest mystery a man ever learned is to know how to control the human mind and bring every faculty and power of the same in subjection to Jesus Christ; this is the greatest mystery we have to learn while in these tabernacles of clay. (Brigham Young, *Journal of Discourses,* 1:46.)

You need to consistently remind yourself that your mind, in a very literal sense, is a source of power, if you learn to control it.

> It (the mind) is the agent of the Almighty clothed with mortal tabernacles, and we must learn to discipline it, bring it to bear on one point, and not allow the devil to interfere and confuse it, nor divert it from the great

object we have in view.

If we could control our minds, we could control our children, our families, and the kingdom of God, and see that everything went right, and with much more ease than we can now. (Orson Hyde, *Journal of Discourses*, 7:153.)

You need to be able to control your mind so it is not distracted by those events or other preoccupations around you, and make it focus with all its force on a particular problem you are trying to solve or blessing you are seeking.

If a person trains his mind to walk in the spirit, and brings his whole mind to bear upon its operations, and upon the principles of faith which are calculated to put him in possession of the power of God..., how much greater will be his faculties for obtaining knowledge. (Orson Pratt, *Journal of Discourses*, 7:155,156.)

One of the best ways to exert yourself mentally is to frequently create a mental picture of the thing you are striving for. In a very literal sense, desired ends must be created spiritually in the mind before they can be realized. Through the process of faith, you can see clearly in your mind what you can accomplish with the Lord's help. Being allowed to see clearly what we can accomplish with the Lord's help is a form of vision. Seeing things in your mind's eye is an example of seeing with an "eye of faith." (Alma 5:15; 32:40; Ether 12:19.)

You also can exert yourself mentally by rehearsing things in your mind. The mind is capable of rehearsing anything you are trying to accomplish (e.g., giving a discussion, giving a talk, making a first contact.)

Your ability to exert yourself mentally will be facilitated if you will learn to devote certain periods of time each day to meditation. These should be periods of time devoted exclusively to prayer, when you reason with the Lord, or to mental exertion regarding your desired goal. If you are so inclined, you can find numerous opportunities during the day to devote to mental exertion.

Throughout the day there are numerous segments of time when you are not required to think about anything in particular. Obviously when you are praying you are in a position to focus your mind exclusively on your dealings and relationship with the Lord. However, to exercise greater faith you need to learn to focus your mind on your righteous desires during those segments of time when you are not required to deal with anything in particular. This can be while you prepare to leave in the morning, while you prepare your meals, while you are eating, after you retire at night, etc. Most people have formed very poor mental habits; consequently, they make no effort to control or direct their thinking during these segments of the day.

Silent prayer will help you control your thoughts and maintain an attitude of faith over a sustained period of time.

When you face a situation that causes you to begin to doubt your ability to achieve your desire, learn to offer a mental prayer and request the Lord's help. Then exercise faith that he will help you so that you will not deny him the opportunity. Remember that the help you receive from the Lord is contingent on your faith.

Your Efforts Must Be Sustained

You will begin to feel the power of faith in your work when you have been successful in maintaining the necessary mental discipline and total dedication to the work for *several consecutive weeks.* Thinking positively for a sustained period of time may be very difficult because you most likely will have to form new habits and new habits are not easily formed. If you allow your mind to dwell on supposed obstacles to achieving your desire, your desires to achieve your goals will not be sufficiently strong to motivate persistence. During the day, repeatedly think about the following statements: "Ask, and it shall be given unto you; seek, and ye shall find; knock, and it shall be opened unto you." (Matthew 7:7.)

"...Doubt not but be believing...." (Mormon 9:27.)

You can only test the principle of faith by working at it consistently over a sustained period of time. Resolve to test this principle by putting forth the required effort for several consecutive weeks even though it may be difficult at first.

As you acquire this ability, doubts and fears will be eliminated from your thought process. Once you learn to control and direct your thoughts over a sustained period of time, you will begin to see the powers of heaven evidenced in your labors. As you begin to receive heavenly endowments, your abilities and capacities will be increased tenfold.

Potential and Sustained Faith

Even though all missionaries are entitled to the same heavenly endowments, they do not realize their full potential unless they learn to exercise faith on a sustained basis. Remember, by the process of faith, thoughts produce an effect as literal as physical exertion. Your thoughts, more than anything else, will be the determining factor in how many people you see join the Church during your mission, and for that matter, throughout your life. Missionaries who learn to put forth the necessary mental exertion daily are successful in cultivating the faith required to qualify for the power and force for righteousness that comes through faith.

Your missionary labors will lack direction and meaning unless you define very clearly in your mind what you want to accomplish and then train your mind to focus on your righteous desires. Unfortunately, some missionaries make very little effort to discipline their thoughts. They may exert some effort to avoid vulgar and obscene thoughts, but the Lord expects you to "cast away" all of your idle thoughts. (D&C 88:69.) This means that if your thoughts are not productive or edifying, you have the responsibility of replacing them with productive or edifying thoughts. (Read Alma 37:36,37.)

Once you are truly converted to faith as a principle of power, you will come to the realization that there is virtually no limit to what you can accomplish. You will find you can accomplish virtually anything you want to accomplish in righteousness. Your ability to memorize will be increased tenfold. You will be able to memorize as much in an hour as you did previously in ten. You will find you can baptize as many people in a month as you previously did in a year.

When you learn to exercise the faith required to release the powers of heaven, you will be able to consistently achieve righteous desires that require the Lord's help (e.g., teaching so many discussions a week, baptizing so many people a month.) You can measure this type of faith by the number of predetermined righteous desires you accomplish over a period of time.

When you are first striving to learn to use faith as a principle of power, you should gauge success by progress as well as attainment. For example, if you are presently able to memorize 30 lines of a discussion per day, and you set a goal of memorizing 50 lines per day, and you memorize only 40 lines the first day after you set the goal, you are starting to see the power of faith, and should recognize it as such.

As you are successful in using faith as a principle of power to achieve a righteous desire, repeat the process for another righteous desire, and then another, and another.

Check Your Understanding

The following activities will assist you in strengthening your understanding of faith.

1. Reread the following quotations from Joseph Smith regarding faith and analyze them in light of what you have read in this book. If possible, discuss them with someone else who is also reading this book.

   As faith is the moving cause of all actions in temporal concerns, so it is in spiritual.

   Faith is not only a principle of action, but of power also.

2. Read Alma 32:26-29 and, if possible, discuss the meaning of the

scripture with someone else.

3. Once you have read Alma 32:26-29, read and discuss the following adaptation:

> Now, as I said concerning faith, it is not a perfect knowledge, and so it is with your righteous desires. You cannot know of your ability to accomplish them first, unto perfection, any more than faith is a perfect knowledge. But behold, if you will awake and arouse your faculties even to an experimentation upon your ability to achieve your righteous desires with my help, and exercise a particle of faith—even if ye can no more than desire to achieve—let this desire work within you, even until you are willing to give place in your mind to think consistently about your righteous desire. Now we will compare this desire to a seed. If you give place that a seed may be planted in your heart, behold, if it be a true seed and a good seed, and if you do not cast it out by your unbelief, that you will resist the spirit of the Lord, behold, it will begin to swell within your breast, and when you feel this swelling motion you will begin to say to yourself, I can achieve it or I begin to have confidence in my ability to achieve it, for I begin to see how it is attainable. Now behold, would not this increase your faith? I say unto you, yea.

4. Read Ether 12:6 and, if possible, discuss the meaning of the scripture with someone else.

5. Once you have read and discussed Ether 12:6, read and discuss the following interpretation of this scripture:

> Faith is things which are hoped for (righteous desires) and not seen (you cannot see, on the basis of your own ability and circumstances, how these desires can be realized); therefore, dispute not because ye see not. For ye receive no witness (assurance from the Lord that he will open the way for your desires to be realized) until after the trial of your faith (exercising faith for a sustained period of time).

Throughout your mission you should continually ask yourself the following questions to evaluate your ability to draw on the powers of heaven.

1. Do I consistently analyze the role of faith in all my endeavors?

2. Am I functioning properly in terms of being worthy, having proper motives, being obedient, making constructive use of my time, avoiding inappropriate conversation, and directing all my thoughts to the work?

3. Do I understand the process necessary to draw on the powers of heaven?

4. Do I always seek inspiration in selecting righteous desires?

5. Do I set goals that require the Lord's help to be achieved?

6. Do I approach everything I desire to achieve with faith as a principle of power in mind?

7. When I plead my case before the Lord, do I explain my particular desire and my rationale in selecting it?

8. Do I consistently seek the Lord's help in achieving righteous desires I have selected rather than desires that grow out of a crisis in my life?

9. Are my daily prayers earnest and persuasive?

10. Am I able to control my thoughts and focus them on righteous desires?

11. Am I conscious of my thoughts?

12. When I pray or meditate, can I keep my mind from wandering?

13. Do I devote certain periods of time each day to meditation?

14. Throughout the day do I offer silent prayers seeking the assistance of the powers of heaven?

15. Am I able to consistently achieve predetermined righteous desires that require faith as a principle of power?

16. To what degree do I allow doubts and fears to occupy my mind?

17. Am I truly converted to faith as a principle of power?

18. Am I able to draw on the powers of heaven to assist me in every aspect of my missionary labors?

19. How many predetermined righteous desires did I accomplish in the last month?

20. Am I controlled by my circumstances?

Chapter 14

Desire Baptisms

As a missionary you need to consistently remind yourself that there are millions of people among the various sects and denominations throughout the world who are honest in heart. The Lord has promised that they will join the Church if they hear the message of the restored gospel taught properly: "...for mine elect hear my voice and harden not their hearts." (D&C 29:7.) Ultimately, The Church of Jesus Christ of Latter-day Saints will encompass the earth, and there will be wards and stakes organized throughout the world.

> This church will fill North and South America; it will fill the world. (Wilford Woodruff.)

> Zion will extend, eventually, all over this earth. There will be no nook or corner upon the earth but what will be in Zion. (Brigham Young.)

Consequently, there are good people living in every sector of the world who have been foreordained to join the Church and to serve in positions of leadership (e.g., General Authorities, Regional Representatives, stake presidents, bishops, Relief Society presidents). If you learn to function properly, perfect your performance, and desire baptisms, you will be instrumental in seeing many of the Lord's elect join the Church.

The Lord expects you to earnestly desire baptisms. Baptizing people must become the primary focus of your labors. Elder Bruce R. McConkie made the following statement in a mission presidents seminar:

The Lord wants people to be baptized. Our objective is to get people into the Church....

... We are not getting the results that we ought to get. We are not getting the number of baptisms that in my judgment the Lord expects us to get. To a degree, at least, we are grinding our wheels without going forward.

... Perhaps what is wrong is that we have not desired in faith with all our hearts to bring souls into the kingdom. Perhaps we have not made up our minds that we can and will bring people into the Church.

Baptizing is a matter of attitude, desire and feeling. We want converts, and we never say to a missionary, "Don't baptize unless." We always say: "You can baptize; there are choice, wonderful people out there; and here is how you do it." We give them an intelligent, affirmative approach; we instruct them in how to do it; and we motivate them. Then somehow or other the Lord does the rest, and they get people into the Church. "If thou canst believe, all things are possible to him that believeth." (Mark 9:23.) (Bruce R. McConkie, Mission Presidents Seminar, June 21, 1975.)

Missionaries will be much more successful in their labors if they will heed Elder McConkie's counsel.

Unless you truly desire to see good people join the Church, you will not have the incentive to totally dedicate yourself to the work. This is the only desire that will sustain you in your labors for two years. You have the promise that if you truly desire to succeed in your labors, the Lord will assist you in bringing people into the Church.

The Prophet Alma was aware of this promise, and it sustained him in his missionary labors. "I know that He (the Lord) granteth unto men according to their desire." (Alma 29:4.)

Alma's missionary labors provide an excellent example of the role of desire in missionary work. In the eighth year of the reign of the judges, Alma was the chief judge as well as the high priest (president) of the Church. The Church began to fail in its progress because the people began to be lifted up in their pride, to set their hearts upon riches and upon the vain things of the world. In an effort to correct the situation, Alma appointed someone else chief judge over the people so he could devote his time exclusively to the ministry.

Alma's strong desire to see people join the Church becomes very evident when the people in the city of Ammonihah reject his message. When Alma first attempted to preach to the people in Ammonihah, they would not listen because Satan had a great hold on their hearts. But Alma still desired to see them baptized. He prayed that the way would be prepared so that he could baptize them. The record says that he "labored much in the spirit, wrestling with God in mighty prayer, that he would pour out his Spirit upon the people who were in the city; that he would also grant that he might baptize them unto repentance." (Alma 8:10.)

Then, according to Alma's desire, the Lord prepared the way for the baptism of a very prominent and wealthy man, Amulek, his wife, his children, and his kinsfolk. (Alma 10:11.)

Following his conversion, Amulek joined Alma in the ministry with the result that many people in Ammonihah "began to repent, and to search the scriptures." (Alma 14:1.) Amulek continued to assist Alma in the ministry over the next several years: "And the establishment of the church became general throughout the land, in all the region round about, among all the people of the Nephites." (Alma 16:15.)

From Alma's account of his missionary labors, it is obvious that Amulek played a very important role in the establishment of the Church throughout the land. It appears that Alma's ultimate success in seeing thousands baptized would never have been realized if he had not desired with all his heart to baptize the people in Ammonihah even after they had rejected his message.

Later, when Alma undertook a mission to the Zoramites, he again prayed for success.

O Lord, wilt thou comfort my soul, and give unto me success....

O Lord, wilt thou grant unto us that we may have success in bringing them again unto thee in Christ. (Alma 31:32,34.)

Once again he convinced the Lord he was willing to pay any price to succeed.

...O Lord, wilt thou give me strength, that I may bear with mine infirmities...

O Lord, wilt thou grant unto me that I may have strength, that I may suffer with patience these afflictions which shall come upon me. (Alma 31:30,31.)

And again, the Lord granted according to his desires and gave him success in his labors.

We see this same pattern in the missionary labors of Ammon, one of the sons of Mosiah. Ammon's desire resulted in the conversion of a very influential man (King Lamoni), the way was opened, and thousands were baptized. It is important to realize that Ammon was not successful in his missionary labors until his desires had motivated him to be patient and long-suffering in his afflictions. He had experienced many afflictions. He had suffered much, both in body and in mind, such as hunger, thirst, and fatigue. Just as Alma had, so did Ammon "labor in the spirit." (Alma 17:5.)

In other words, he had to convince the Lord he wanted to baptize the Lamanites and was willing to pay any price in order to succeed; and then "the Lord... granted unto [him] according his prayers." (Alma 25:17.)

Modern-day missionaries have received the same promise. Elder Bruce R. McConkie has said:

> We have to ask the Lord for help; we have to seek converts; we have to desire baptisms; we have to know that we receive according to our desires, and if we desire to get such and such a thing, and have faith in the Lord, it is going to eventuate....
>
> ...In the day of wickedness just preceding our Lord's return there is going to be a great harvest of souls.
>
> We live in that day, the day when the harvest is ripe.
>
> We have deluded ourselves long enough with the thought that this is a day of gleaning only. This is not a day of gleaning but of harvest.
>
> ...Now, this work is going to succeed. That is absolutely guaranteed; it is the eternal decree of the Lord. (Mission Presidents Seminar, June 21, 1975.)

If missionaries cultivate a sincere desire to baptize people and convince the Lord they are willing to pay any price in terms of hard work, frustration, trials, or whatever, the Lord will grant their desires, and they will be instrumental in bringing many people into the Church. If you are laboring in an area where the Church is not well established, you should focus your desires on seeing people join the Church who will be capable of assuming positions of leadership.

Do not make the mistake of directing your efforts exclusively to the poor.

> Let us note that the kings and rulers and potentates and VIP's are not exempt from listening to this gospel, and we take the gospel to them and make special efforts for them. (Spencer W. Kimball, "Living the Gospel in the Home," *Ensign*, May 1978, p. 102.)

> This proclamation shall be made to all the kings of the world, to the four corners thereof, to the honorable president-elect, and the high-minded governors of the nation in which you live, and to all the nations of the earth scattered abroad.

> Let it be written in the spirit of meekness and by the power of the Holy Ghost, which shall be in you at the time of the writing of the same;

> For it shall be given you by the Holy Ghost to know my will concerning those kings and authorities, even what shall befall them in a time to come.

> For, behold, I am about to call upon them to give heed to the light and glory of Zion, for the set time has come to favor her.

> Call ye, therefore, upon them with loud proclamation, and with your testimony, fearing them not, for they are as grass, and all their glory as the

flower thereof which soon falleth, that they may be left also without excuse—

And that I may visit them in the day of visitation, when I shall unveil the face of my covering, to appoint the portion of the oppressor among hypocrites, where there is gnashing of teeth, if they reject my servants and my testimony which I have revealed unto them.

And again, I will visit and soften their hearts, many of them for your good, that ye may find grace in their eyes, that they may come to the light of truth, and the Gentiles to the exaltation or lifting up of Zion. (D&C 124:3-9.)

The establishment of branches and wards require leadership, and the full blessings of the gospel cannot be extended to people unless strong wards and branches are established.

Throughout your mission ask yourself the following questions:

1. Do I consistently remind myself that there are millions of people who are honest in heart who will join the church if taught properly?

2. Do I earnestly desire baptisms?

3. Has my desire to baptize good people become the primary focus of my labors?

4. Do I continuously remind myself that this is a day of harvest and not of gleaning?

Chapter 15

Set Baptismal Goals

Setting baptismal goals has an important place in missionary work. President Spencer W. Kimball said concerning baptismal goals:

> Well, now what we'd like to do, brethren and sisters, is to get back into the swing. We'd like to get back into baptizing many, many people.... What we want you to do is to establish *goals*. Now somebody also got mixed up and they thought a goal was spelled, "q-u-o-t-a," and it isn't, that's another word. Now there's a tremendous difference between a goal and a quota. A quota was what the mission president said. 'Now I want you all to get twenty baptisms,' or 'I want all of you to get forty baptisms.' That was a quota. But, when I, John Doe, say I'm going to baptize thirty people this month or ten people this month, that's a goal. That's my goal. It is self-imposed. *We hope that every one of you will have a goal and have a goal every month.* (Regional Representatives Seminar, Apr. 3, 1974.)

> ...We do not want stake and full-time mission presidents to establish "baptismal" quotas for missionaries. Rather, we expect them to inspire missionaries to set their own goals and to make them high enough to challenge their very best efforts and to work to achieve them. (Missionary Conference, Mar. 6, 1975.)

In a mission presidents seminar in June, 1976, President Ezra Taft Benson made the following remarks.

> New missionaries need to know exactly the purpose for being in the mission field which is to save souls, to baptize converts, to bring families into the church.

Goals and Faith

Once you have been successful in your effort to be totally dedicated for one month, you should set a goal to see at least one family join the Church by the end of the next month. Then proceed to exercise the faith that the powers of heaven will assist you in achieving your goal. After you are successful in seeing a baptismal goal realized, you should proceed to follow President Kimball's admonition and set a goal that you will see people join the Church each month you are in the mission field. A goal to baptize every month is essential to a productive mission.

Once you have established a firm goal to see people baptized every month you are in the mission field, you should systematically follow President Kimball's admonition to set a specific baptismal goal at the beginning of each month. Your monthly baptismal goal can be in terms of families or total baptisms. Remember it is impossible to exercise faith in your ability to achieve a baptismal goal until you make a very specific decision about how many people you desire to see join the Church each month.

Once you set a baptismal goal, you should then use faith as a principle of power in your effort to achieve your goal. This will insure that your baptismal goal will be the focus of your thoughts and efforts during the month. As you are successful in making your baptismal goal central to everything you think about, say, and do, your goal will be achieved.

It has been found that missionaries have only minimal success in bringing people into the Church even if they function properly unless they finally become committed to setting specific monthly baptismal goals. Once a missionary gains an understanding of the process of faith required to realize baptismal goals, he will consistently bring people into the Church every month of his mission. In contrast, missionaries who fail to come to an understanding of the process of faith required to bring people into the Church, and who do not become committed to setting baptismal goals, invariably have only minimal success in bringing people into the Church throughout their missions.

Once you realize how anxious the Lord is to use you to bring people into the Church, you should set a long-range baptismal goal. In setting this long-range goal, follow the guidelines provided by Elder McConkie.

> If you will ponder it in your mind, you will come up, in my judgment, with the conclusion that we could bring immeasurably more people into the church than we are now doing. We could fellowship more than we are now fellowshipping; in practice this could be five or ten or twenty times as many as we are now baptizing. Perhaps in due course it should be 24 times or 100 times as many as at present. (Mission Presidents Seminar, June 21, 1975.)

In other words, if the average missionary is having ten baptisms a year, your goal should be at least fifty baptisms a year. And if your faith is sufficient, you will enjoy ten or twenty times the average success of missionaries in your mission.

President Kimball has counseled missionaries not to discuss their long-range baptismal goals with others. This goal should be very private and discussed only with the Lord. This same privacy regarding the total number of people you see join the Church applies even after you return home.

You will find out that as you set baptismal goals, your ability to be diligent day in and day out throughout your mission will be much greater. You will have more incentive to get up and do those things the Lord requires of you on a daily basis. In contrast, if you do not set baptismal goals, you will find it extremely difficult to be diligent on a daily basis throughout your mission.

Once you perfect your ability to bring people into the Church, you will find you can bring as many people into the Church in one month as you did previously in six months. You will find it necessary to schedule more than one baptismal service a month. When you reach a point that you are holding more that one baptismal service a month, you should raise your long-range baptismal goal.

President Kimball's desire to see missionaries become more success-ful in bringing people into the Church will be realized when missionaries throughout the world function properly and systematically set baptismal goals on a monthly basis and then trust the Lord to help them achieve their goals. Remember, the Lord is limited in the help that he can extend to you unless you are willing to set baptismal goals. If you are not willing to set baptismal goals and then exercise the faith required to release the powers of heaven, you restrict the Lord and his ability to assist you in your labors. The most serious failing on the part of many missionaries with respect to baptisms is their failure to set specific baptismal goals each month and then consistently tell the Lord what assistance they will need to achieve their goal.

> Behold, I say unto you that whoso believeth in Christ, doubting nothing, whatsoever he shall ask the Father in the name of Christ it shall be granted him; and this promise is unto all, even unto the ends of the earth. (Mormon 9:21.)

After you set a baptismal goal, if you truly desire to see people join the Church, this desire will preoccupy your thoughts, and it will be the focus of your thoughts and efforts throughout the month. If you fail to truly cultivate a sincere desire to see people join the Church, you will find the goal will not occupy your thoughts, and you will not have the initiative to be diligent in your labors. If your baptismal goals are based on desire, they will consistently be realized.

Once you have set a baptismal goal, your next step is to plead your case before the Lord. Go to the Lord in earnest prayer; explain in detail your reasons for desiring to see people join the Church (e.g., leadership needs in the ward).

It is very important to explain in great detail why you want to see people baptized and what price you are willing to pay to realize your desires. Throughout history we see that the Lord is responsive to the requests of mortal men if they go to him in faith and can present a strong case for the blessing they are seeking. In a very literal sense you need to learn to reason with the Lord.

In your relationship with your Father in Heaven, you must ask in order to receive: "ask, and ye shall receive." (John 16:24.)

You should resolve to be specific in your requests and express very specifically your reasons for wanting to see people join the Church.

In your daily prayers consistently discuss the following points regarding your desire to see people join the Church. (1) your human frailties, (2) your dependence on the Lord to help you realize your desire to see people join the Church, (3) why you want to see people join the Church, and (4) the effort you are willing to put forth to qualify for the Lord's help.

You should be very specific in terms of how many hours you will work each week, not wasting time, avoiding inappropriate conversations, controlling your thoughts, etc. The commitments you make to the Lord should be reduced to writing and reviewed each day.

Remember when you are functioning properly, you have the right to ask the Lord to assist you in bringing people into the Church.

I, the Lord, am bound when ye do what I say; but when ye do not what I say, ye have no promise. (D&C 82:10.)

If you learn to function properly, set baptismal goals, and ask the Lord to assist you in achieving your goals, and then exercise the necessary faith that will make it possible for the Lord to assist you, you will see many more people join the Church than you would otherwise.

Goals Should Be Means, Not Ends

In no instance should the achievement of a baptismal goal mean you have "arrived" as a missionary. No matter how many baptismal goals you achieve on your mission, you must look ahead to new goals. Unless you adopt the point of view that baptismal goals are means and not ends, you will experience a letdown when you achieve a baptismal goal. The achievement of baptismal goals should be an ongoing process and not the culmination of an effort that does not lead to a sustained effort in achieving additional goals.

Example: *Goals as Ends*

Following an inspiring zone conference, Elders Smith and Jones set a goal to have four baptisms within 30 days. They met a choice family of four after 10 days of hard tracting, so they began to focus all their energies on the one family. The family accepted the baptismal challenge and were baptized the last day of the month. The elders' goal of four baptisms was realized. However, the two elders did not do another conscientious day of tracting after they met the family. Consequently, after the family was baptized, the elders did not have any other families they were teaching. After the choice family was baptized, the two elders found themselves sleeping in and not being very energetic about missionary work generally.

The previous example shows how the achievement of the goal to have four baptisms had an adverse effect on the two missionaries because they viewed the goal as an end and not as a means.

Example: *Goals as Means*

Elder Black received word from his mission president that he would be receiving a new elder to train. Elder Black then decided to formulate some goals for the first month they would be working together. He decided it would be very critical to the new missionary's training to see a family accept the gospel. So he set a goal to have at least one family come into the Church during the first month.

When the new elder arrived, the two elders approached their labors with real determination. Three days after the new elder arrived, they received a referral for a family who accepted the gospel immediately. The two elders were so excited to see the family accept the baptismal challenge that they resolved to work even harder as an expression of gratitude to the Lord. By the end of the month when the family was baptized, they were teaching three additional families who attended the baptismal service, and following the baptismal service two of the families expressed a desire to be baptized the following month.

In the above example, in the process of achieving a goal, the two elders caught the spirit of the work to an even greater degree and became more effective in their labors because they perceived their goal as a means and not as an end in and of itself.

Once you are truly converted to the process of systematically setting baptismal goals and then doing everything in your power to realize those goals, and exercising the faith necessary to release the powers of heaven, you will catch the vision that prompted President Kimball to ask the question: "Could we develop missionaries who could increase eight or twenty times the present production of converts?"

Throughout your mission you should consistently ask yourself the following questions:

1. Do I set my own goals and make them high enough to challenge my ability to achieve them?

2. Do I set specific monthly baptismal goals?

3. Am I exercising the faith necessary to consistently bring people into the Church every month?

4. Do I consistently tell the Lord what assistance I need to achieve my goals?

5. In my daily prayers do I discuss my frailties?

6. In my daily prayers do I discuss my dependence on the Lord's help in order to realize my desire to see people join the Church?

7. In my daily prayers do I discuss why I want to see people join the Church?

8. In my daily prayers, do I discuss the effort I am willing to put forth to qualify for the Lord's help?

9. Do I review the commitments I've made to my Heavenly Father each day?

10. Do I view my goals as means rather than as ends?

11. Am I doing everything in my power to realize my baptismal goals?

Chapter 16

Your Faith Will Be Tried

Each time you set a baptismal goal, you should realize that you will not be effective in bringing people into the Church unless you receive special endowments through the Spirit. You have the responsibility to determine what specific help you will need from the Lord to achieve your goal and then request the help. When you petition the Lord for special endowments and help, your faith will be tried.

Receiving Spiritual Endowments

From the beginning, the pattern followed by our Father in Heaven in granting major outpourings of the Spirit has been: (1) the faith of the person seeking the help will be tested and tried and (2) once the person has humbled himself and proven his faith by perseverance and sustained faithfulness, the special endowments and help are given in rich abundance.

It was not until Father Adam demonstrated his determination to be faithful to the commandments of the Lord that he received a rich outpouring of the Spirit (see Moses 5:4-12). We see this same pattern illustrated in the lives of other prophets of the Old Testament, such as Jacob, Abraham, and Moses. It is interesting to note that the Savior himself was not exempt from this pattern. (Matthew 1:11; Mosiah 3:7; Alma 7:11-12.)

> Though he were a son, yet learned he obedience by the things which he suffered. (Hebrews 5:8.)

Why Trials of Faith Are Necessary

It is necessary that someone who is seeking special blessings from the Lord undergo a period of proving, or a trial of faith to see if he will remain faithful in the face of opposition. If a missionary understands that his faith is going to be tried, it gives him a greater resolve to be persistent in time of opposition. As a missionary, you can endure your trial of faith, whatever it may be, by remaining faithful in the work, in spite of opposition, inconvenience, discomfort, or pain.

Your trial of faith serves three functions: (1) it lets the Lord know you really desire baptisms, (2) it is a means of purging you so that you become clean, pure, and spotless—literally free from the blood and sins of the world—and (3) it humbles you and brings you to the realization that you cannot rely on the "arm of flesh."

As you endure your trials of faith, you will literally become a new creature in Christ, and your body will be cleansed of all sin and renewed by the Spirit of the Lord. This is the rebirth and sanctification process.

It is extremely important that you understand that trials of faith are a necessary part of the sanctification process by which we are purified by the Spirit of God. (Read D&C 101:4-5.) Opposition plays a very important part in this process, for by overcoming opposition and enduring affliction, we are literally purged and made clean. When you endure opposition by serving the Lord, even through trials, to the utmost of your ability—no matter how limited that ability is—the grace of God is sufficient to intervene in your behalf, and you have the promise that you can become "perfect in Christ." (Read Moroni 10:32-33.) It is by this means that you can qualify for the Spirit of the Lord in spite of the limitations of the flesh.

The Nature of Trials of Faith

The nature of each trial of faith will be based on your particular temperament, disposition, and the special blessings you are seeking. The thing that will test one missionary's faith would not necessarily test another's. The thing that will test your faith early in your mission may not test your faith later.

Trials of faith will consistently bring you to the realization that you cannot succeed without the Lord's help. By yourself, you are extremely limited in bringing people into the Church. When you are humble, fully realizing that you cannot succeed without the Lord's help, and you submit yourself to your Father in Heaven and become earnest in your desire to see people join the Church, He will draw near to you. (See D&C 88:63.)

Trials of faith may come from companions. Trials of faith may come from the people you are trying to teach; perhaps they are cold, unfeeling, even cruel, as you attempt to teach them of their potential salvation. Maybe 730 days of early rising, poor food, and endless hours of tracting will be part of your trial of faith.

Trials of faith may also take other forms. It may be the death of a close relative at home, the divorce of parents, the sins of fellow missionaries. These, more than the inconveniences, unpleasantness, or pain that every missionary experiences to some degree, are the hard tests.

Satan is real, and his forces become very apparent during a mission. The efforts of the adversary are especially evident previous to significant events, such as when missionaries are about to start meeting with a particularly receptive family or when a choice family is approaching baptism. At such times the adversary may intensify his effort to get you to let down in some way. Also, when you are being considered for a position of leadership, the adversary may increase his efforts to get you to let down, so that you will be denied the opportunity of additional responsibilities. Missionaries in leadership positions may experience increased opposition just prior to situations in which they may have to deal with critical problems or helping other missionaries.

Be Patient in Afflictions

The Lord expects you, as a missionary, to "be patient in afflictions," not complaining about your problems or discomforts. (See D&C 31:9.) For example, when you write your parents, accentuate the positive aspects of the work, even if your companion is lazy, if most people slam doors in your face, if your district leader has misunderstood your intentions, or if the food has made you sick. The ability to endure patiently is a great virtue and will bring you maturity, stability, and spiritual strength.

> And if thou shouldst be cast into the pit, or into the hands of murderers, and the sentence of death passed upon thee; if thou be cast into the deep; if the billowing surge conspire against thee; if fierce winds become thine enemy; if the heavens gather blackness, and all the elements combine to hedge up the way; and above all, if the very jaws of hell shall gape open the mouth wide after thee, know thou, my son, that *all these things shall give thee experience, and shall be for thy good.*
>
> The Son of Man hath descended below them all. Art thou greater than he? (D&C 122:7, 8; italics added.)
>
> ...but we glory in tribulations also: knowing that tribulation worketh patience;
>
> And patience, experience; and experience, hope. (Romans 5:3,4.)
>
> ...for behold they were naked, and their skins were worn exceedingly because of being bound with strong cords. And they also had suffered hunger, thirst, and all kinds of afflictions; nevertheless they were patient in all their sufferings. (Alma 20:29.)

For verily I say unto you, blessed is he that keepeth my commandments, whether in life or in death; and *he that is faithful in tribulation, the reward of the same is greater in the kingdom of heaven.*

Ye cannot behold with your natural eyes, for the present time, the design of your God concerning those things which shall come hereafter, and the glory which shall follow after much tribulation.

For after much tribulation come the blessings. Wherefore the day cometh that ye shall be crowned with much glory; the hour is not yet, but is nigh at hand. (D&C 58:2-4; italics added.)

Examples of Men Who Endured Their Trials of Faith

One of the greatest examples of missionaries teaching by the Spirit is recorded in the book of Alma and involves the missionary labors of the sons of Mosiah. These men were responsible for the conversion of a large segment of the Lamanite population, even though the Lamanites were described as "a wild and a hardened and ferocious people" (Alma 17:14) and appeared as though they were not readily receptive to the gospel. The key to the mass conversion of the Lamanites was the Spirit of the Lord that accompanied the sons of Mosiah in their labors. Even in the limited account that we have of their missionary labors, it is evident that they experienced a trial of their faith.

... for they had many afflictions; they did suffer much, both in body and in mind, such as hunger, thirst and fatigue, and also much labor in the spirit.

... and they fasted much and prayed much that the Lord would grant unto them a portion of his Spirit to go with them, and abide with them, that they might be an instrument in the hands of God to bring, if it were possible, their brethren, the Lamanites, to the knowledge of the truth....

And the Lord said unto them also: Go forth among the Lamanites, thy brethren, and establish my word; yet ye shall be patient in long-suffering and afflictions, that ye may show forth good examples unto them in me, and I will make an instrument of thee in my hands unto the salvation of many souls. (Alma 17:5, 9, 11.)

The following quotation gives an excellent condensation of this entire experience.

And this is the account of Ammon and his brethren, their journeyings in the land of Nephi, their sufferings in the land, their sorrows, and their afflictions, and their incomprehensible joy ... (Alma 28:8.)

In other words, even though they suffered much, they ultimately experienced great joy and satisfaction in their labors because they endured their trial of faith.

One of the most successful missionaries in the history of the restored Church was Wilford Woodruff. You can probably recall hearing repeated references to the success Wilford Woodruff experienced during his missionary labors. However, most people fail to realize that he also experienced great hardships throughout his mission and that his faith was tried before he started to have success. The following excerpts from his own journal will give you some idea of the trial of faith to which he was subjected.

We dared not to go to houses and get food, so we picked and ate raw corn, and slept on the ground.

We had walked all day without anything to eat, and were very hungry and tired. Neither the minister nor his wife would give us anything to eat, nor let us stay overnight, because we were Mormons; and the only chance we had was to go twelve miles farther down the river to an Osage Indian trading post kept by a Frenchman named Jereu; and the wicked priest who would not give us a piece of bread lied to us about the road and sent us across the swamp, and we wallowed knee-deep in mud and water till ten o'clock at night in trying to follow the crooked river. We then left the swamp and put out into the prairies to lie in the grass for the night. (Matthias F. Cowley, *Wilford Woodruff*, pp. 47-48.)

These are but brief excerpts from Wilford Woodruff's journal that indicate in part the tremendous ordeal he encountered during the early months of one of his missions. Five months elapsed before he and his companion had a baptism. An interesting side note is that his companion finally became discouraged and returned home, leaving Wilford Woodruff alone for a period in the mission field. Shortly afterward, Brother Woodruff started to meet with success.

Today President Kimball is a classic example of someone who has endured various trials of faith. In the course of his life, he has endured many trials (Bell's palsy, chronic tonsilitis, evil spirits, recurring boils, heart attacks, cancer of the throat, open heart surgery).

Be Resolved

Each time you set a baptismal goal, you should resolve at the very outset that you will endure whatever trials of faith may confront you in order to prove to your Father in Heaven that you do truly desire to see people baptized. If you fail to endure the trials of faith you will encounter, you will not see your baptismal goals realized.

Maintain Faith in the Face of Opposition

Fortunately, there are several things you can do when your faith is being tried:

1. Reflect on this statement by President Kimball:

I have on occasion cited the need for many reservoirs in our lives to provide for our needs. I have said, "Some reservoirs are to store water. Some are to store food, as we do in our family welfare program and as Joseph did in the land of Egypt during the seven years of plenty." There should also be reservoirs of courage to overcome the floods of fear that put uncertainty in our lives; reservoirs of physical strength to help us meet the frequent burdens of work and illness; reservoirs of goodness; reservoirs of stamina; reservoirs of faith.

Yes, especially reservoirs of faith, so that when the world presses in upon us, we stand firm and strong; when the temptations of a decaying (and, I should add, increasingly permissive and wicked) world about us draw on our energies, sap our spiritual vitality, and seek to pull us down, we need a storage of faith that can carry youth, and later adults, over the dull, the difficult, the terrifying moments; disappointments; disillusionments; and years of adversity, want, confusion, and frustration.

2. Read and reflect upon the following scriptures:

   ...I do know that whosoever shall put their trust in God shall be supported in their trials, and their troubles, and their afflictions... (Alma 36:3.)

   Come unto me, all ye that labor and are heavy laden, and I will give you rest.

   Take my yoke upon you, and learn of me; for I am meek and lowly in heart: and ye shall find rest unto your souls.

   For my yoke is easy, and my burden is light. (Matthew 11:28-30.)

3. When you feel a need for a spiritual lift in times of disappointment or discouragement, read and reread Alma 17-26. If you will read these chapters prayerfully, you will be inspired and given the strength to endure your trials of faith.

4. Memorize the phrase "For after much tribulation come the blessings." (D&C 58:4.)

5. Identify a personal collection of favorite scriptures and quotations and read them when your faith is being tried. Suggestions: Alma 26:23-35; 2 Corinthians 1:4-7.

6. Reread this chapter.

7. Read the following scriptures: D&C 98:3; 68:6; 24:8; 31:9; 101:4-5; 88:63; 122:7-8; 58:2-4; 105:6; Moses 5:4-12; Alma 26:27, 31:30-31, 38; 7:11-12; 36:3; 17:14; 7:5,9,11; 28:8; 20:29; Mosiah 3:7; 23:21; Matthew 1:11; 11:28-30; Hebrews 5:8; Acts 5:38-42; Romans 5:3-4; 8:35-39; 2 Corinthians 6:4-6; John 16:33; Moroni 10:32-33.

Throughout your mission you should consistently ask yourself the following questions:

1. Am I resolved to be persistent in times of opposition?

2. Have I completely submitted myself to my Father in Heaven and become earnest in my desire to be blessed and sustained in my missionary labors?

3. Do I avoid complaining about problems or discomforts?

4. When I write letters home, do I accentuate the positive aspects of the work?

5. Do I have complete trust in my Heavenly Father and confidence that after tribulations come great blessings?

6. How well have I handled my recent trials of faith?

Chapter 17

Summary of Section 2

The following statement by President Spencer W. Kimball summarizes the importance of converting people to the restored gospel of Jesus Christ.

If there were no converts, the church would shrivel and die on the vine. But perhaps the greatest reason for missionary work is to give the world its chance to hear and accept the gospel. The scriptures are replete with commands and promises and calls and rewards for teaching the gospel. I use the word "command" deliberately for it seems to be an insistent directive from which we singly and collectively cannot escape. (Regional Representatives Seminar, Apr. 4, 1974.)

The prophet has made it very clear that it is up to the missionaries themselves whether or not they are successful in their efforts to baptize more people. The following are excerpts from talks he has given on this subject.

I have the faith that the Lord will open the doors once we have done everything in our power.

I can see no good reason why the Lord would open doors that we are not prepared to enter. Why should he break down the iron curtain or the bamboo curtain or any other curtain if we are unprepared to enter?

Millions of people are anxious and willing to learn if they can only hear the sound in their own tongue and in a manner that they can grasp and understand.

Millions of people will receive the gospel in large numbers if it is properly presented to them.

I feel that when we have done all in our power that the Lord will find a way to open the doors. That is my faith. Nothing is too hard for the Lord.

President Kimball has promised:

If we are in tune the spirit of the Lord will speak to us and guide us to those with whom we should share the gospel. (Regional Representatives Seminar, Apr. 3, 1975.)

An honest desire to see people baptized, coupled with goals, is one of the critical keys to seeing more people baptized each year. As you become earnest in your desire to see people join the Church, you must be resolved that you will endure the various trials of faith you experience. In the Lord's work there is no place for despair.

Chapter 18

Introduction to Section 3

One of the greatest concerns of many new missionaries is the challenge of learning to present the discussions. Yet presenting the discussions is one of the easiest aspects of missionary work. A much greater challenge is finding people to teach. Obviously, if a missionary can't get people to listen to his message, his opportunities to teach will be limited. Realizing the importance of this aspect of missionary work, President Kimball has said that *missionaries must become more effective in making themselves heard.*

If you contact 300 people per week, get return appointments with 10, and finally start the discussions with 5, you will most likely realize 1 or 2 baptisms for your effort. In contrast, if you become skilled in getting people to agree to listen to your message, get 100 return appointments for every 300 people you contact, and proceed to teach 60 of the 100, you could potentially realize 30-40 baptisms for your efforts.

If missionaries have the opportunity to *teach* more people, they will automatically *baptize* more people. This is why it is essential that you resolve to become increasingly effective in making yourself heard.

If used under inspiration the principles and procedures introduced in this section will be as effective for you as they have been for others in getting people to agree to listen to the message of the restored gospel. You should not attempt to use these principles and procedures unless you are functioning properly and qualify for the spirit of inspiration.

You should read and reread the chapters in this section until you are effective in making yourself heard because, unless you are effective in getting people to listen, your opportunities to teach families will be limited.

If you are serving as a senior companion, a district leader, a zone leader, or an assistant to the mission president, you should obtain a copy of the *Trainer's Manual* that accompanies this book. This manual will assist you in your efforts to train other missionaries.

Chapter 19

Trust the Lord
to Prepare the Way

As you approach your missionary labors, you need to consistently remind yourself of the Lord's promise that the hosts of heaven (angels) are given the responsibility to fulfill the various covenants the Lord makes with those who enter the ministry. (See Moroni 7:27-31.) Your faith will be strengthened if you are consistently mindful of the role of angels in assisting you in your missionary labors.

The Lord has promised, "Yea, I will open the hearts of the people, and they will receive you." (D&C 31:7.) You should exercise faith in this promise and daily plead with the Lord that he will go before you to prepare the hearts and minds of the people to accept the gospel. You should make every effort to consistently exercise faith in the organization of the priesthood on the other side of the veil, realizing that it exists as literally as the one on the earth, and that, according to your faith, those beyond the veil will assist you in your missionary labors.

> And whoso receiveth you, there I will be also, for I will go before your face. I will be on your right hand and on your left, and my Spirit shall be in your hearts, and mine angels round about you, to bear you up. (D&C 84:88.)

> Behold, I will go before you and be your rearward; and I will be in your midst, and you shall not be confounded. (D&C 49:27.)

The Spirit has power and by means of your faith will prompt people to be receptive to truth.

> And there was no inequality among them; *the Lord did pour out his Spirit*

*on all the face of the land to prepare the minds of the children of men, or to
prepare their hearts to receive the word* which should be taught among them
at the time of his coming—

   *That they might not be hardened against the word, that they might not be
unbelieving,* and go on to destruction, *but that they might receive the word*
with joy, and as a branch be grafted into the true vine, that they might enter
into the rest of the Lord their God. (Alma 16:16-17; italics added.)

And it came to pass that *the Lord did soften the heart of Ishmael,* and also
his household, insomuch that they took their journey with us down into the
wilderness to the tent of our father. (1 Nephi 7:5; italics added.)

And again, I will visit and soften their hearts, many of them for your good,
that ye may find grace in their eyes, that they may come to the light of truth,
and the Gentiles to the exaltation or lifting up of Zion. (D&C 124:9.)

Train your mind to think about things that will increase your faith in
this promise as you approach people for the first time (e.g., this person is
literally a child of God whose spirit was taught the gospel in the premortal
existence; the prophet and other Church leaders, as well as other members
of the Church, pray in your behalf every day; this person has ancestors in
the spirit world and they have ability to influence him.)

In your letters to your parents and loved ones at home, request that
they exercise faith and pray that the hearts and minds of the people will be
prepared to receive your message. Ask them to read Alma 16:16-17 and
then follow the counsel given in 3 Nephi 18:23-24 and Alma 6:6.

Unless you teach your parents otherwise, they will pray for you as a
missionary instead of for the people you call on. Help them to realize that
if they truly petition the Lord and exercise faith, their faith and prayers
will actually cause people to receive your message.

Above all, you should recognize the role of faith and inspiration in
getting people to agree to listen to your message. You must trust the
promises the Lord has made to those who are called to the ministry. He has
promised that if you truly love the people and are functioning properly you
will be inspired as you approach people regarding the gospel.

   And if thou wilt inquire, thou shalt know mysteries [e.g., what facet of the
gospel will appeal to a person, what to say to gain a person's confidence], . . .
that thou mayest bring many to the knowledge of the truth, yea, convince
them of the error of their ways. (D&C 6:11.)

   Therefore, verily I say unto you, lift up your voices unto this people; speak
the thoughts that I shall put into your hearts, and you shall not be confounded
before men; for it shall be given you in the very hour, yea, in the very moment,
what ye shall say. (D&C 100:5-6.)

You have the responsibility to desire to understand the "mysteries"—

the insights, all that is required to make it possible for you to touch the inner chords of a person's heart when you talk to him. You have the assurance that as you function properly and are sincere in your desires, the Spirit will cause the honest in heart to trust you, and they will have confidence in what you say. When they do, they will listen to the message of the restored gospel.

Before you leave your apartment, pray earnestly that the Spirit will bring to your mind what to say to cause people to listen to your message. The Lord knows the hearts and minds of the people. If you are in tune with the spirit of inspiration, the Lord will inspire you to know what to say when you meet people who are honest in heart.

As you approach a home or a person, offer a silent prayer that you will be inspired in what you say. Exercise faith consistently that the Spirit will touch and move people. The Spirit, more than anything else, will dispel people's apprehensions concerning your motives and cause them to trust you.

You should consistently remind yourself that the Church will be established throughout the world, so ultimately there will be wards and stakes organized in most, if not all, sectors of the world. You have the assurance that there are people foreordained to join the Church wherever you are assigned to labor. Your challenge is to seek them out.

Brigham Young has said that there are doubtless millions of just and honest people among the several religious denominations the world over who desire to know the right way. (Brigham Young, *Discourses of Brigham Young*, p. 319.)

> The greater portion of the inhabitants of the earth are inclined to do right. (Brigham Young, *Discourses of Brigham Young*, p. 423.)

> And ye are called to bring to pass the gathering of mine elect [those foreordained to accept the gospel]; for mine elect hear my voice and harden not their hearts. (D&C 29:7.)

You should not let the indifference of the majority deter your faith in this promise. If the Spirit is sustaining you in your labors, the honest in heart will respond favorably to your request to meet with them. You have the responsibility to maintain abiding faith in this promise.

Your faith will be strengthened if you will let the following statement of President Kimball guide you:

> Our goal should be to identify as soon as possible which of our Father's children are spiritually prepared to proceed all of the way into the kingdom. What you need to do is find out if they are the elect. . . . "My elect hear my voice and harden not their hearts." (D&C 29:7.) If they hear my voice and have

hearts open to the gospel, it will be evident immediately. If they won't listen, their hearts are hardened with skepticism or negative comments, they are not ready." (*The Ensign*, Oct. 1977, p. 6.)

This promise does not apply if you fail to qualify for the Spirit.

The promises discussed in this chapter are typical of numerous promises the Lord makes those serving as missionaries. You have the responsibility to become conversant with these promises. As you function properly, you will be able to exercise the faith required to see these promises fulfilled. Remember, faith is a gift of God granted to those who live righteously. The fulfillment of these promises will be in direct proportion to your dedication and faith.

Throughout your mission, ask yourself the following questions:

1. Do I exercise faith that the Lord will go before me and prepare the hearts and minds of people to accept the gospel?

2. Do I exercise enough faith in the organization of the priesthood on the other side of the veil to receive its assistance in my missionary labors?

3. Each morning before I leave the apartment, do I pray earnestly for the Spirit to bring to my mind what I should say to cause people to listen to my message?

4. As I approach a home or a person, do I offer a silent prayer that I will be inspired in what to say?

5. Do I exercise faith consistently that the Spirit will touch people and dispel their apprehensions regarding my motives?

6. Do I continually work at training my mind to think about things that will enhance my faith that the Lord will soften the hearts of people we meet?

7. Do I ask my parents and loved ones at home to exercise faith and pray that the hearts and minds of the people will be prepared to receive the gospel?

8. Do I have a general desire to understand the "mysteries," insights and knowledge necessary for me to touch the inner chords of a person's heart when I talk to him?

9. Do I consistently remind myself that the Church will be established throughout the world and that there are people foreordained to join the Church wherever I am assigned to labor?

10. Am I doing all I can to be entitled to the blessings and promises discussed in this chapter?

Chapter 20

You Must Understand the Hearts of Men

S ome people ask to be taught the gospel as a result of some contact with the Church (e.g., visitor's center, acquaintance who is a member). To a great extent, people who request to be taught the gospel already know it is true, and consequently they are receptive when the missionaries call on them. However, most people you approach regarding the gospel will have some apprehensions about your motives. This is especially true when you meet people during first-contacting or business-contacting. To a great extent it is true when you call on people who have been referred by members. When you approach people regarding the gospel, it is important that you understand the hearts of men. Depending on a person's frame of mind (his heart), he will respond to the gospel in basically one of two ways: (1) open-mindedly and (2) closed-mindedly.

Generally, if a person is in a closed frame of mind, he will reject new ideas. You will find that, until you dispel a person's apprehension regarding your motives, he will not listen with an open mind to what you have to say. Throughout the scriptures, *heart* and *mind* are used interchangeably. However, when the term *heart* is used in referring to the mind, it has reference to that part of the mind that provides a tie between our intellect and our inner feelings and our spirit. If a person's mind is closed when you talk to him, what you say to him does not reach his *heart*, or that part of his mind that allows his spirit to respond to your message. When this happens, the person's biases and preconceived notions, his suspicions about your motives, control his reaction to your message.

In contrast, if a person is open-minded and listens with his *heart*, your message will strike a familiar chord if the Spirit of the Lord is with you. Because all the inhabitants of the earth were taught the gospel in the premortal existence, each person's spirit is able to recognize the truth.

> The spirit which inhabits these tabernacles naturally loves truth, it naturally loves light and intelligence, it naturally loves virtue, God, and Godliness.... (Brigham Young, *Discourses of Brigham Young*, p. 422.)

When this happens, the person's spirit will prompt him to listen to your message. If a person is honest in heart, he will heed this prompting.

One of the greatest challenges you will face as a missionary is getting people to listen to the message of the restored gospel with an open mind.

One of the most serious mistakes missionaries make is assuming that if a person is closed-minded when they first start talking to him there is nothing they can do about it. Many people who are honest in heart have closed minds when they first come in contact with the gospel. It is normal to be suspicious of strangers.

In many instances those who appear least interested initially prove to be the most conscientious investigators. When a missionary has the Spirit and understands how to open a closed mind, he can be successful in getting many additional people to listen to the message of the restored gospel. Those who are honest in heart will respond to the message and join the Church.

You must be resolved to get as many people as possible to *listen* to your message. Some missionaries make the mistake of looking for the ideal investigator (one who has no Word of Wisdom problem, a believing frame of mind) and in the process overlook many good people. You should never assume that a doubtful initial response means that the person will never join the Church. Assume the attitude that until you have explored various alternatives for gaining an audience with a person, you cannot conclude that the person is not interested. Learn to be bold without being overbearing. (Alma 38:12.)

In this way you will meet the Lord's expectations of you, and then if people choose to reject your message, they will be held accountable before the Lord. In contrast, if you fail to consistently improve your ability to gain an audience with someone, you will be held accountable before the Lord.

As you become effective in dealing with people's objections and resolving their apprehensions, you will be effective in teaching the gospel. On the other hand, if you are not effective at getting people to listen to your message with an open mind, you will have few opportunities to give the discussions.

Your ability to get people to listen to your message with an open mind will be enhanced if you remember the following two things: (1) it is natural for people to be suspicious of the motives of a stranger and, consequently, most people that you call on for the first time will have closed minds; (2) once you qualify for the Spirit, your message will seem familiar to those you meet and their spirit will prompt them to listen to your message.

Throughout your mission ask yourself the following questions:

1. Do I consistently pray for the ability to understand the hearts of men?

2. When I speak to a person, do I exercise the faith necessary to strike a familiar chord in his "heart"?

3. Do I continually remind myself that people who are initially closed-minded, when approached properly, will become strong members of the Church?

4. Am I resolved to get as many people as possible to listen to our message?

5. Do I explore all the various alternatives possible for gaining an audience before I conclude that a person is not interested?

6. Am I bold but not overbearing?

7. Am I becoming skilled in using the principles and procedures discussed in this section in an effort to become effective in overcoming people's apprehensions?

Chapter 21

Perfect Your Initial Approaches

A basic part of missionary work is approaching people who do not know you. Generally, prior to their missions, missionaries have had very little experience approaching strangers. Consequently, some missionaries find it difficult to approach someone they do not know. However, to be effective as a missionary, you must become skilled in approaching people who do not know you. Even when you follow up on referrals, you will usually be calling on people you have not met previously. Obviously, when you are tracting (house-to-house contacting) or business contacting, you will be talking to new people all the time.

It has been found that if missionaries have the right attitude and are skillful in their initial approach, they are successful in finding people to teach when they do initial contacting. As a missionary you will meet people initially under a variety of circumstances: while tracting, at street meetings, during business contacting, at open houses, on busses, at zoos, in parks, etc. You should resolve to become effective in your ability to gain an audience with people who do not know you.

As a general rule you should do at least two hours of initial contacting every day. Initial contacts can be made in a variety of ways (i.e., tracting, house-to-house, business contacting, telephone contacting, etc.) The approaches used in a particular mission should be sensitive to the culture, etc., of the people. An approach that may prove very effective in one part of the world may not be effective elsewhere.

As you become skilled in the use of the principles discussed in this chapter and devote a specific amount of time each day to initial contacting, you will (1) experience the great joy of finding and baptizing families who would not have been found and baptized had you relied on referrals alone, (2) receive a great deal of growth in your ability to interact with people which will not only enhance your abilities as a missionary but will enhance your ability to succeed in future endeavors after your mission (i.e., business, marriage, school, Church service, etc.), (3) demonstrate to the Lord your desire to succeed in missionary work, (4) retain the Spirit of the Lord, which will enable you to teach the discussions with power, (5) enhance the confidence of members in you, thereby motivating them to provide you with referrals.

As you perfect your ability to use the following principles, you will be effective in gaining audiences with people who are honest in heart when you contact them for the first time.

Trust the Lord

The first chapter in this section discusses in detail the role of faith in getting people to agree to grant you an audience. Throughout your mission you should make an especially strong effort to increase your faith in the promises the Lord has made, that his Spirit will touch people, etc. Train yourself to always offer a mental prayer as you approach a house or office in which you ask the Lord to prompt the people to agree to talk to you.

You have the promise that when the Spirit is sustaining you in your labors, the honest in heart will be receptive to your message.

> Our goal should be to identify as soon as possible which of our Father's children are spiritually prepared to proceed all of the way into the kingdom. What you need to do is find out if they are elect—"my elect hear my voice and harden not their hearts." (D&C 29:7.) If they hear my voice and have hearts open to the gospel it will be evident immediately. If they will not listen, their hearts are hardened with skepticism or negative comments, they are not ready." (*Ensign*, Oct. 1977.)

Throughout your mission you should increase your faith in the promises the Lord has made that his Spirit will prepare the honest in heart to receive your message. "Yea, I will open the hearts of the people, and they will receive you...." (D&C 31:7.) "I will go before your face...." (D&C 84:88.) "Behold, I will go before you and be your rearward; and I will be in your midst, and ye shall not be confounded." (D&C 49:27.)

The Spirit will not only prepare people to receive your message, but it will also dispel people's apprehensions about your motives and will prompt them to grant you an audience.

Be Conscious of Your Appearance

Your appearance will determine, to a great extent, whether or not you gain an audience with people. In many instances, before you even speak, people will have already determined in their minds whether or not they will listen to you because of the image you portray. As a result, your ability to portray the proper image is crucial to your success. You should therefore be conscious of your poise at all times and maintain proper standards of personal cleanliness and grooming.

Many things determine your poise: your appearance, your voice, how you stand, etc. You should make every effort to insure that you handle yourself with poise when you are talking to people for the first time. As you talk with people, look them in the eye, smile, you should make certain that your hands are not in your pockets and that you refrain from nervous movements (e.g., shuffling your feet, wringing your hands, etc.). When you speak, speak confidently. Make sure the tone of your voice is natural.

Proper grooming entails all aspects of personal cleanliness (i.e., showering, shaving, hair cut and neatly combed, clothes clean and pressed, shoes shined, teeth brushed, etc.) You should resolve to do everything you can to make your appearance neat and presentable. As you do you will find people more inclined to invite you into their home, office, etc., to present your message.

Make Your Initial Statement Brief

In house-to-house contacting, when you first approach someone at the door, ask for permission to enter his home.

Examples:

"Hello. We are ministers. May we step in?"

"Hello, we are ministers and are sharing a message with those who are honest in heart. May we step in?"

"Good morning. We are ministers blessing the homes in the neighborhood. May we step in?"

"Good day. We are ministers acquainting ourselves with the families in the neighborhood. May we step in?"

It is important that your initial statement be brief. Generally, it is not advantageous to explain that you are missionaries or representatives of the Church of Jesus Christ of Latter-day Saints until you are in their home (or office in the case of business contacting.) You should not attempt to deliver a lengthy explanation of any kind at the doorstep. The distractions of the screen, etc. will interfere with your ability to communicate effectively.

These basic guidelines apply whether you are tracting house-to-house or business contacting. In every case you should briefly identify yourself and request an opportunity to talk to the person for a few moments.

In the process of gaining an audience, you should resolve to never be deceptive or resort to trickery of any kind. You must be genuinely honest as you approach people and ask for permission to enter their home.

Assume People Will Talk to You

As you approach people with the attitude that they will talk to you, you will have many more opportunities to talk to people. You will need to consistently maintain an attitude of assumption. An attitude of assumption is not only a frame of mind but is also evidenced by your tone of voice, and your physical movements as you talk to people.

In the case of house-to-house contacts after you make a brief statement regarding your intent, put your hand on the screen door and begin to move forward. If there is not a screen door, simply begin to move forward.

Become Skillful in Handling Objections

If the person voices an objection when you request permission to enter their home or to call on their home in the case of telephone contacting, you should say something to overcome the objection and again ask, "May we step in?" or "Could we please call on your home?"

You should become skilled at using the following principles which have proven effective in overcoming common objections.

1. Persuasion

Three of the most common objections people give are (1) they do not have time, (2) they belong to a church, and (3) they are not interested.

Persuasion is an effective way to overcome these common objections. For example, when people say they do not have time, let them know that your message will take only a few minutes.

Example:

Missionary: We are ministers from The Church of Jesus Christ of Latter-day Saints. May we step in and share an important message with you?

Person: I'm sorry, but I'm really busy.

Missionary: Our message only takes a few minutes. May we come in?

Person: I guess for a few minutes.

When people indicate they already belong to a church, let them know that your message is for people of all faiths.

Example:

Missionary: We are ministers calling on homes in the neighborhood. May we come in?

>Person: We already belong to a church.

>Missionary: Our message is for all people. May we step in for a few minutes?

>Person: All right.

When people say they are not interested, mention a facet of your message which will create an interest. Obviously, you will need to cultivate the ability to discern those things which will interest them.

Example:

>Missionary: We are ministers from The Church of Jesus Christ of Latter-day Saints. May we step in and share our message with you?

>Person: I'm not really interested, thank you.

>Missionary: Our message is for parents who are concerned about their children. It will bring happiness and additional blessings to your family. May we step in?

>Person: Well, I am interested in our family becoming closer. Come in.

As you use the principle of persuasion, you should be bold but not overbearing (Alma 38:12.) If people perceive your effort to use persuasion as being pushy, they will become defensive. You should therefore learn to rely on inspiration from the Spirit in responding to these common objections. As you do, you will be effective in overcoming the objections of many people.

2. Empathy

Empathy is a very effective way to overcome objections. You can express empathy regarding most objections people raise when you approach them about the gospel. When those who express objections feel that you understand their own objections and feelings completely, their objections will be dispelled.

Your ability to express empathy will be enhanced when you explain the reasons why you understand how they feel.

Example:

>Missionary: We are ministers in the area. May we come in and share an important message with you?

>Person: I'm sorry but I don't have time. My wife went shopping and left me with our six children.

>Missionary: I know what that's like. I'm the oldest in a family of ten and I know how hectic large families can be. Our message will only take a few minutes, though. May we come in?

Example:

Missionary: We are ministers calling on the homes in the neighborhood. May we come in?

Person: I wouldn't be interested.

Missionary: We can understand your apprehensions. I have to admit that if two strangers called on my home in Idaho, I would be a little apprehensive. But let us assure you that we're not trying to solicit donations. Our only purpose is to share the message of the living prophets with you. May we step in?

Person: I guess.

Example:

Missionary: We are ministers from The Church of Jesus Christ of Latter-day Saints. May we come in?

Person: I don't believe in God.

Missionary: I have to admit, if it were not for the gospel truths that have been revealed through prophets in our day, it would be hard for me to believe in God. I am certain that if you investigate these restored truths, you will come to believe in God. May we come in?

Person: Yes. Maybe you can succeed where my parents failed.

As you learn to express sincere empathy as the Spirit directs, you will be effective in getting many closed-minded people to listen to your message.

3. Honest Compliments

An honest compliment can be very effective in dealing with a person's objections. There are numerous things you can compliment people about: their feelings, their children, their yard, their desires, their honesty, their curiosity, the things they have done, the things they say and don't say, the way they treat you, etc.

In most instances, your compliments should be directed toward the person's objection. For example, if someone said he was a deacon in the Baptist Church and therefore would not be interested, you would not overcome his objection by merely complimenting him on his lovely home. You would overcome his objection by complimenting him on the fact that he was active in religion and let him know that your message has particular interest for people like him.

Example:

Missionary: We are ministers from The Church of Jesus Christ of Latter-day Saints. May we come in?

Person: I belong to the Baptist Church.

Missionary: Our message deals with Jesus Christ. We have found that members of the Baptist Church generally have a strong conviction of Christ's divinity. We find it very refreshing to talk to people who believe in Jesus Christ, especially in this age when many people do not believe in Christ. May we step in and share our message with you?

Person: Come in.

Example:

Missionary: We are ministers from The Church of Jesus Christ of Latter-day Saints and have a message to share with you concerning modern scripture. May we step in?

Person: The Bible states that there will not be any new scripture.

Missionary: From that statement, sir, I can tell you have studied the Bible. Most people do not even know what the Bible teaches. You are to be commended. On the surface it appears that what I said and the scripture you have referred to are not in agreement, but when you understand what the Lord has said concerning scripture, it becomes obvious there is no disagreement. May we come in and explain this to you?

Person: Yes, please do.

As you learn to pay people honest compliments under the direction of the Spirit, you will find you will have the opportunity to present the gospel message to many more people.

4. Curiosity

If the Spirit of the Lord is present when you are talking to someone for the first time, a simple statement that will arouse the person's curiosity can also serve as an effective way to overcome objections.

Example:

Missionary: We are ministers calling on people in the neighborhood. May we come in and share our message with you?

Person: What do you want from me?

Missionary: May we take a minute and explain why we do this kind of work? Most people are very surprised to learn that we are not paid to do missionary work, but actually do this at our own expense. May we step in and share our message with you?

Person: I see. Certainly.

Example:

Missionary: We are ministers and would like to share an important message with you. May we step in?

Person: Well, I think you'd be wasting your time and mine.

Missionary: What would you say if we told you we can guarantee you help in living a happier life?

Person: That is quite a guarantee. I guess I can use a little help in that department. Come in.

Example:

Missionary: We are ministers from The Church of Jesus Christ of Latter-day Saints. May we step in?

Person: Well, I'm really busy.

Missionary: May we take a minute and explain why we are called Mormons? We have found a few people in the area who do not understand why members of The Church of Jesus Christ of Latter-day Saints are called Mormons. May we step in?

Person: I have always wondered about that. Come in.

5. Humor

Humor can be an effective tool in overcoming objections. In order for your humor to be effective, it must be spontaneous, natural and tasteful. It should never be offensive to the Spirit, but should always befit a representative of the Savior.

Example:

Missionary: We are ministers from The Church of Jesus Christ of Latter-day Saints. May we come in?

Person: I wouldn't be interested.

Missionary: I'm sure glad you didn't invite us in.

Person: Why? (somewhat surprised)

Missionary: Well, I could smell your homemade bread and that would have made me homesick. I haven't had any homemade bread for over a year since I've been in the mission field.

Person: Well then, come in and have some. I insist.

Example:

Missionary: We are missionaries representing The Church of Jesus Christ of Latter-day Saints. May we come in?

Person: I don't think I'd be interested.

Missionary: I bet you wonder why two young men our age are wearing suits on a hot day like this.

Person: It is rather unusual. Most young men your age certainly wouldn't be doing this type of work.

Missionary: May we come in and explain why this work is so important to us and give you our message?

Person: Yes, come in.

Example:

Missionary: We are ministers calling on homes in the neighborhood. May we come in?

Person: I'm short on time today.

Missionary: I'll bet it is hard for you to believe that two young men our age are ministers, isn't it?

Person: You are very young. Why are you here instead of home with your families and going to college?

Missionary: Our message is very important. May we explain this as we share it with you?

Person: Come in—I'm curious to know.

6. Testimony

Sincere testimony can also be an effective way to overcome a person's objections. However, if you use it in an effort to overcome a person's objections, make certain your testimony is not trite and repetitious. As you bear an honest testimony, the witness of the Spirit will accompany it.

Learn to humbly tell people what your message will do for them as well as express your conviction of its truthfulness.

Example:

Missionary: We are ministers. May we come in and share our message with you?

Person: I don't have time today.

Missionary: We want you to know that the truths the Lord has revealed through modern-day prophets can make your life much fuller and happier.

Person: Do you really believe that your message could help me be happy?

Missionary: Yes, we sincerely do.

Person: Come in, then, and share it with me.

Example:

Missionary: We are ministers visiting the families in your neighborhood. May we come in?

Person: I'm not interested.

Missionary: We promise you that if you take the time to listen to our message, you will be amazed at what the Lord has revealed through modern prophets to increase the unity of your family.

Person: I do want the best for my family. Come in and tell me about it.

Offer to Leave a Blessing

If you call on a home and the person voices an objection and your effort to use persuasion, empathy, etc. fail to overcome the person's objection, offer to bless the home.

Example:

Missionary: We are ministers. May we come in?

Person: No, I am not interested.

Missionary: Our message will make your family happier and bring many wonderful blessings to your home.

Person: I'm sorry. We just aren't interested in your message.

Missionary: We want you to know that we respect your views. We would like to leave a blessing so that you will know that our intent was sincere and honest. May we step in and leave a blessing with you and your family?

Person: If that is all you wish to do, that would be all right. Come in.

You will find many people will agree to allow you to step in their home to bless it who would not agree to let you share a brief message with them.

Once you are in the home, request that the family kneel with you and your companion, and then one of you should bless the family. You should bless the home and family as the Spirit directs you.

When you conclude the blessing, stand and shake the person's hand and thank him for the opportunity to be in his home. If the Spirit has touched the person it will be very evident, and you will find it easy to get him to allow you to return. If the person has not been touched by your blessing, simply bid him good day and leave.

Summary

When you use any of the principles or procedures discussed in this chapter to overcome a person's objection, make your response to his objections *brief*.

If you say too much, people will perceive you as not sure of yourself. In contrast, as you learn to be brief, people will perceive you as being sure of yourself and will be much more inclined to listen to you.

As you perfect your ability to handle objections, you will become increasingly more effective in gaining an audience when you call on people for the first time.

Caution

The examples in this chapter should not be memorized as dialogues. When you love the people, are sincere and honest in what you say to them, and function properly, you will be inspired in what to say, the Spirit will bear witness to the truth of your message, and you will have the opportunity to teach the honest in heart the gospel. If you are not functioning properly, you should not attempt to use the principles discussed in this chapter. These principles are not effective unless they are used under inspiration.

Throughout your mission, ask yourself the following questions:

1. Am I doing everything I can to make my appearance neat and presentable?

2. Do I avoid attempting to deliver a lengthy explanation at doorsteps?

3. Are my motives genuine as I approach people and request an opportunity to talk to them?

4. Do I avoid trickery or deception of any kind as I approach people?

5. Do I rely on inspiration in responding to objections?

6. Are my responses to people's objections brief?

Chapter 22

Get People to Listen to Your Message

O nce you gain entrance to a home or a man's office or get someone to agree to talk to you for a few moments on the telephone, your next responsiblity is to get the person to agree to allow you to call on the person's home to share a message with the entire family. Your ability to get people to agree to listen to your message is critical to your success as a missionary.

You cannot be content to discuss the gospel with people in a general way. You must be resolved to have the opportunity to formally teach families the gospel. You must be wholehearted in your resolve to be effective in getting people to agree to let you return and share a message with the entire family. Otherwise you will find yourself talking to various people about the Church throughout the day, but not formally teaching families the gospel in the evenings.

Each time you have an opportunity to talk with someone and explain your purpose in contacting him, your conversation should generally cover the following points:

1. The simple *courtesies* of conversation. This would include a greeting, your name, and the name of the Church.

   Example:

   Missionary: We appreciate the privilege of coming into your home, Mr. Teichert. My name is Elder Tobler, and this is my companion Elder Simpson. We're representatives of The Church of Jesus Christ of Latter-day Saints.

2. The overcoming of any *apprehensions,* suspicions, or doubts that this potential investigator might have. Think! What might he have on his mind?

Some of the more common concerns people have are: their time (how long is this going to take?), money (are you selling anything?), why me?, etc. One good way to determine what these concerns are and to relieve them is to involve people in a two-way conversation.

Example:

Missionary: We realize you're very busy, and so we'll only take a few minutes. We want you to know that we're not selling anything. The reason we're here is to share with fathers who love their children a program designed to draw families closer together. Do you love your family, Mr. Teichert?

3. Once you have said something to put a person's mind at ease, you must *convince him you have something to offer.* As you learn to rely on your own ingenuity under inspiration for what to say at this point in your initial conversation with a person, you will be successful in sparking his interest to know more about your message. Creating this interest can be accomplished in various ways. You may want to use (a) a Book of Mormon approach, (b) the Family Home Evening program, (c) the Joseph Smith story, (d) the Savior. There are many ways to approach people. Of course, the message that best fits each individual or family should be used. *Meet their needs.* Ingenuity under the inspiration of the Holy Ghost will help you decide which message should be used. Effective use of your testimony will often convince people you have something to offer them that can bless their lives. As you testify, promise the people that your message will bless their lives, and be very specific in explaining how (e.g., you will have a much closer relationship with God, the harmony in your home will improve).

Example:

Missionary: Because of your love for your family, we know you'll be particularly interested in what we have to say. Our Heavenly Father has revealed through a living prophet a program designed to draw families closer together. Over the past fifty years it has proven to be an effective tool in maintaining love and harmony in the home.

The Family Home Evening is a regularly scheduled time in which family members get together and do things they enjoy. In most instances there's a lesson given by the father or one of the other family members.

The evening is filled with games, the sharing of talents, and refreshments.

The Family Home Evening program has had a powerful influence on my life. It has strengthened my love and appreciation for my parents. I know it will increase the love in your home and draw your family closer together.

In some instances you will say very little about your message when you first talk to someone. You will simply arrange to call back when you can meet with the entire family. Especially when you call at a home during the day and the father is not at home, you should explain that your purpose for calling on the home is to talk to the father and then proceed to make arrangements to call back when he will be home.

Generally the wife will ask why you want to talk to her husband, and you need to explain why.

Example:

Missionary: When will your husband be home so we can speak with him?

Person: Around 7:30, but why do you want to talk to him?

Missionary: We have a message which has been revealed by our Heavenly Father through modern-day prophets. It is of particular importance to fathers and we'd like to share it with him. We'll stop by at 8:00, or would a little later in the evening be more convenient?

4. *Arranging for an appointment.* Always assume the person will commit to an appointment (e.g., "We could call Tuesday at 7:00 or Wednesday at 7:30. Which of these times would be more convenient for you and your family?")

Along with this positive attitude, before you leave, make sure the appointment is confirmed in writing.

Example:

Missionary: We want very much to show you in your own home what a Family Home Evening is like. It will take only an hour. It will be a very special evening for your family. We're available Thursday evening at 7:00 or Friday at 7:30. Which would be the best time for you and your family?

Person: Thursday at 8:00.

Missionary: Great! We'll write that time down on this card with our names on it.

All the principles you have read about (i.e., faith, persuasion, empathy, etc.) for gaining entrance to someone's home or office can also be used when you are attempting to get the person to agree to an appointment.

The following are examples of missionaries arranging for a return appointment.

Example:

After a preliminary conversation, one of the missionaries says:

We could call back this evening at 5:30 or at 8:00. Which of these times would be most convenient for you and your family?

Person: I really don't think we would be interested.

Missionary: Our message is for parents who are concerned about the welfare of their children. You have certainly impressed us as a father who is concerned about his family. I can assure you the time will be well spent. May we call back?

Person: Why don't you come back at 8:00.

In the above example you note that the missionary used persuasion and honest compliments in overcoming the person's objection.

Example:

After a preliminary conversation, one of the missionaries says:

Would we be able to catch your husband home tomorrow evening at 7:00?

Person: I don't think there would be any point in calling back. We belong to a church.

Missionary: That's great that you belong to a church. Our message is for people of all denominations. Actually, the message is much more meaningful for people who are religious. May we call back and meet your husband?

Person: I guess it would be all right.

Missionary: All right. We will call back tomorrow evening at 7:00.

In the above example you will note that the missionary used persuasion and honest compliments in overcoming the person's objection.

Example:

After a preliminary conversation, one of the missionaries says:

Sir, as I look at our appointment book, I see that we could call on your home Thursday evening. Would that be convenient for you?

Person: I think you would be wasting your time. I have never been very religious.

Missionary: Sir, I have to admit that if it were not for my knowledge of the restored gospel of Jesus Christ and the truths that have been revealed through a modern prophet, I doubt that I would be very religious. You impress me as a man of integrity, and for that reason I know that you will find meaning in our message. May we call on your family Thursday?

Person: I guess it wouldn't hurt me. That would be all right.

Missionary: OK. We will stop at your home Thursday evening at 7:00. Thank you.

In the previous example the missionary uses empathy and honest compliments in overcoming the person's objection.

Example:

After a preliminary conversation, one of the missionaries says:

Missionary: Will you and your family be home Sunday afternoon?

Person: I'm afraid you would just be wasting your time.

Missionary: What would you say if we promised you that the message we have to share with you and your family would make your family happier? Would you be interested in a message that is guaranteed to make your family happier?

Person: Yes, I would.

Missionary: It has been our experience that people who share in the message of the restored gospel become much happier in their relationships as a family. Can we call back Sunday and explain this message to you and your family?

Person: Yes, if you can make me that kind of promise, you can.

In the previous example the missionary appealed to curiosity in overcoming the person's objection.

Example:

After a preliminary conversation, one of the missionaries says:

We would like very much to call back at a time that is convenient for you and your family and share with you the message of a modern prophet.

Person: We are generally very busy in the evenings as a family.

Missionary: Ma'am, I know that God lives, and he has spoken again to a modern prophet, and this message is the most important message your family will hear. It is the Lord's desire that you hear that message. May we call back and explain what has been revealed through a modern prophet?

Person: Yes, if you will make your visit brief.

In the above example the missionary used testimony in overcoming the person's objection.

If a person will not agree to a return appointment, you should express your testimony of the following:

1. The gospel of Jesus Christ has been restored to the earth through the Prophet Joseph Smith.

2. The message you have to share with the family would bless their lives significantly.

Example:

Missionary: Mr. Jones, before we leave, I know that the fulness of the gospel of Jesus Christ has been restored to the earth through a prophet by the name of Joseph Smith. The message that we've brought to you is the most important message you could ever hear. Through it, the lives of you and your family can be blessed significantly. Before we leave, may we leave a blessing on your home?

Before you leave a person's home or office, you should offer to leave a blessing. If the person agrees, the blessing is pronounced in the form of a prayer. It should be relatively brief and straightforward, expressing gratitude for the response of the person to the message of the restored

gospel. Ask a blessing upon the person and his family in the name of Jesus
Christ. A good example is found in Alma 7:27.

> And now, may the peace of God rest upon you, and upon your houses and
> lands, and upon your flocks and herds, and all that you possess, your women
> and your children, according to your faith and good works, from this time
> forth and forever. And thus I have spoken. Amen.

To be obedient to President Kimball's charge that missionaries
become more skillful in making themselves heard, you should consistently
strive to increase your effectiveness in getting people to agree to let you
return and share a message with the family. Perfect as many approaches as
you can. Make every effort to select approaches that will be appropriate
and meaningful. Most likely there will be some that your mission
president will want you to use specifically in designated areas.

Under no circumstances should the previous examples be memorized
as dialogues. When you truly love people, are sincere and honest in what
you say, and are living righteously, you are inspired in what to say.

> And if thou wilt inquire, thou shalt know mysteries (e.g., what facet of the
> gospel will appeal to a person, what you can say to gain a person's
> confidence)... that thou mayest find out mysteries, that thou mayest bring
> many to the knowledge of the truth, yea, convince them of the error of their
> ways. (D&C 6:11.)

> Therefore, verily I say unto you, lift up your voices unto this people; speak
> the thoughts that I shall put into your hearts, and you shall not be confounded
> before men; For it shall be given you in the very hour, yea, in the very moment,
> what ye shall say. (D&C 100:5,6.)

You have the promise that the Holy Ghost will bear witness to the
people as you talk to them.

> And I give unto you this promise, that inasmuch as ye do this (lift up your
> voice unto this people) the Holy Ghost shall be shed forth in bearing record
> unto all things whatsoever ye shall say. (D&C 100:8.)

You must honestly desire to understand the "mysteries," the insights,
etc., that will make it possible for you to reach the inner chords of the
person's heart with what you say. Remember, if you are in tune with the
Spirit and sincere in your desires, the Spirit will cause people to trust you,
and they will have confidence in what you say. They will also be willing to
meet with you and hear the message of the restored gospel.

Throughout your mission, ask yourself the following questions:

1. Am I consistent in my resolve to be effective in getting people to agree
   to let us return and share a message with the entire family?

2. Am I striving to perfect as many approaches as I can to increase my

effectiveness in getting people to agree to let us return and share a message with the family?

3. Am I expressing myself clearly in an understandable and logical way?

4. Am I experiencing inspiration as I am speaking to people for the first time?

5. Am I exercising faith that people will agree to a return appointment?

Chapter 23

Obtain Referrals
from Members

It has been found that if a member of the Church provides missionaries the name of an acquaintance, the probability that the person will join the Church is much higher than if the missionaries approach him during initial contacting without knowing his name. And the probability that the person will join the Church is enhanced even further if the member becomes involved in some way, such as inviting the person to join his family for a special home evening, or a barbeque, and having the meetings with the missionaries in the member's home.

In areas where the members are actively involved and committed to the work, the effort of the missionaries is greatly facilitated, and consequently many more people are baptized.

Even though members are consistently encouraged by Church leaders to be missionaries, many do not know how. To a great extent it is your responsibility to help them see how they can participate in missionary work. Once they experience the joy of seeing an aquaintance or a friend join the Church, they will have a greater inclination to go out of their way to be involved.

As with other aspects of missionary work, there are some basic guidelines in how to go about gaining the cooperation of members. As you follow these guidelines, you will be effective in gaining the support and cooperation of the members. Once you have their cooperation and support, you will be much more successful in bringing people into the

Church. Your mission leaders will provide you specific guidelines regarding how to work with ward mission leaders, stake missionaries, etc. The guidelines provided in this chapter are intended to be consistent with the various programs being followed in individual missions. It is your responsibility to adapt these guidelines, if necessary, so that they are totally compatible with programs in your particular mission.

Prove Yourself

You will be effective in getting members to provide you referrals or assist you in other ways only if they have confidence in your ability as a missionary. You should, therefore, resolve to do all you can to prove yourself worthy and capable of teaching and baptizing families.

A survey of members has shown that they tend to form strong opinions about missionaries, either good or bad. If you are keeping mission rules and working faithfully, they will have confidence in you. Members are discerning and perceptive in their association with missionaries. If they discern some lack on your part, they will not trust you to teach their friends.

Many members are reluctant to refer their close nonmember friends. Instead, they refer casual acquaintances, because it is safer. If the missionaries fail to properly approach and teach their referral, there has been nothing lost. They want their special friends to be taught by someone who will not fail. As you prove yourself by (1) functioning properly (2) finding, teaching, and baptizing people without the help of member referrals, and (3) using good judgment in the things you do and say around members, you will gain the confidence and trust of members. In return they will provide you with an abundance of choice referrals.

Function properly

Unless you are willing to function properly, you do not have any right to request referrals from members. Members generally are very tolerant of missionaries. They will treat you kindly, feed you, etc., even though they sense a lack of dedication on your part. Members seldom tell missionaries they lack confidence in them, but they will be very reluctant to give missionaries referrals if they feel missionaries are lax in the work.

Unfortunately, some missionaries take their cues from the wrong things. If the members are willing to feed them, they feel they have their support even when they are not obtaining referrals. You should consistently remind yourself that if the members are not providing you with referrals, *they may not* trust your ability to teach. And when this is the case, you should take inventory of yourself to determine why. Remember the Spirit is discernible. If you have the Spirit, the members will discern it.

So if you want the cooperation and support of the members, you must be willing to function properly.

As you function properly, you will have the Spirit. When you are called on to speak in various Church meetings, you will speak with power and authority, and the audience will be touched. If you do not have the Spirit, you will be inclined to rely on jokes, etc., when you speak, and there will be very little substance in your talks.

Once you are willing to pay the price in terms of total dedication and obedience, the Lord will prompt the members to cooperate with you. They will do everything in their power to assist you in your work. In contrast, if you fail to prove yourself to them and gain their respect, you can prod them, browbeat them, or beg them and still they will be reluctant to give you referrals.

Find, Teach, and Baptize People without the Help of Member Referrals

The best way to prove yourself is *not* to be totally dependent on the members for referrals. You will find the best way to gain the confidence of the members is to get out on your own (e.g., first contacting, etc.) and find, teach, and baptize people. As your investigators begin to attend Church meetings, prayerfully identify members in the ward to whom you will introduce your investigators. These should be member families whom you feel have comparable interests which will provide a natural inclination towards social ties as well as general fellowshipping. It is absolutely essential that your investigators establish strong social ties with one or more families or members of a ward while they are being taught. Surveys show that the conversion process is greatly facilitated when investigators have meaningful association with members. As the members see you succeeding on your own, they will have confidence in your ability to teach their friends and acquaintances.

Some missionaries make the mistake of assuming that it is the responsibility of members to provide them people to teach, and therefore fail to prove themselves to the members. Consequently these missionaries do not have anyone to teach. For this reason it is extremely important that you devote some time every day to finding new investigators on your own (through tracting, street meetings, business contacting, etc.).

As you begin to teach families you have met, immediately solicit the help of the members in friendshipping them. Generally your mission leaders will provide you with some specific guidelines on how to have members fellowship your investigators.

Use Good Judgment in What You Say and Do Around Members

When you are in the homes of members, be courteous and thoughtful. Show an interest in each child, and pay the family honest compliments. Avoid talking about things not related to missionary work or the gospel (e.g., politics, sports, current news).

Never watch television, even if members of the family do so while you are waiting to talk to the father. Never accept invitations to outings with the members. Your time with them should be devoted exclusively to missionary work. If you begin to socialize or fraternize with members, you will likely lose their respect and they will not trust you to teach their acquaintances.

> Too many missionaries are neutralized, and occasionally lost, (excommunicated) because of oversolicitous members, member sisters who 'mother' the missionaries, and socializing occurring between missionaries and members. Because of the importance of members and missionaries working effectively together on the member missionary program, it is vital that missionaries maintain the proper missionary image and have the reputation as great proselyting elders and not just 'good guys'. The greatest help members can be to a missionary is not to feed him, but to give him names of their friends so he can teach them with the spirit in their homes and challenge them, with the wonderful members helping to fellowship. (Ezra Taft Benson, Mission Presidents Seminar, June 21, 1975.)

If a member family has daughters in their teens, you should not talk to them, other than exchanging simple greetings, or involve yourself with them in any way.

If you eat a meal with members, use your best table manners and practice restraint in how much you eat. If you are called on to bless the food, bless the family, too. Above all else, restrict your visit to one hour or less.

Your conduct as you attend meetings, what you say and do around the chapel and the community, etc. will influence how much confidence the members have in your teaching ability. Members should see you as a mature agent of the Lord, not as a nice boy or as immature and naive. Only by using good judgment in your conduct at all times will you earn their respect.

Deal with members in a businesslike manner. Call on them by appointment, stipulating in advance how much time you take, so they know what to plan on.

How to Proceed

Once you have earned the respect of the members, prayerfully select five member families with whom to work. The number of member families you work with per month will be determined by the attitude of the members, and your time.

After you have prayerfully selected *some* member families, list them in the order in which you are going to work with them. You will not want to work with them all simultaneously, but should begin by working with the first family on your list. As you successfully progress with them, you can then begin working with the next family.

In obtaining referrals from member families, you will generally meet with the family three times. These visits should last no more than 30 minutes each.

Your First Visit

As you make your appointment with the father of the family you have selected, let him know that you can spend no more than thirty minutes with him and his family. If he invites you to dinner, thank him, but explain that you will *not* have time to eat.

Once you are in the home, you should do the following:

1. If the members are converts, ask them questions about their own conversion (e.g., the names of the missionaries that taught them, what aspect of the Gospel they found most appealing, how the Gospel has blessed their lives, etc.).

2. Let the family know that you are doing everything in your power to be successful (i.e., keeping mission rules, perfecting your discussions, working hard every day).

   Example:

   "Brother Clarke, we want you and your family to know that we're doing all that we can to qualify for the Spirit and be worthy of baptizing many families in this area. We're working as hard as we can to find families to teach and are doing all we can to perfect our teaching skills."

3. Commit the family to pray daily (individually and as a family) that the hearts of the people in the area will be softened so that they will be receptive to the gospel. In the April conference in 1978, President Kimball promised that if the members of the Church will pray night and morning, every day, the Lord will hear those prayers and he will soften the hearts of people so they will receive the missionaries. Help the family see the need to be specific in their prayers. For example, if the local branch or ward is in need of strong leaders or teachers, they should discuss this need with the Lord.

Example:

Elder Law: Even though we're teaching some special people, we need your help. We know that with your prayers and faith as a family we can be much more successful than we are now. Will you begin to pray as a family and ask our Heavenly Father to soften the hearts of the people in this area so they will be receptive to the gospel?

Bro. Clarke: We'd be glad to.

Elder Day: We appreciate your help. We were talking with the branch president last Sunday, and he mentioned the need for a scout master. Would you please ask our Heavenly Father specifically to guide us to the home of someone who can fulfill that need?

Bro. Clarke: We sure will.

4. Testify that you will be successful in bringing good families into the Church as the members in the area pray daily that the Lord will soften the hearts of the people. Remind them that we are commanded to pray for nonmembers. (Alma 6:6; 3 Nephi 18:22,23.).

Example:

Elder Day: We know that there are many great people whose hearts will be softened and who will join the Church because of your prayers. Our Heavenly Father has commanded us to pray for nonmembers. Sister Clarke, would you please read this scripture in Alma? (Alma 6:6.)

5. Leave the following references with the family and commit them to read and discuss them as a family: D&C 11:17; 18:15,16,44; 29:6,7; 31:7; 84:88; 105:26,27.

Example:

Elder Law: Bro. Clarke, we have a list of scriptures dealing with missionary work that we'd like you to read and discuss as a family. You may want to do so in your Family Home Evening. We're confident your faith and prayers will be enhanced by them. Will you read and discuss them as a family?

Bro. Clarke: Yes, we will.

6. Before you leave the home, offer to bless the family. If the father agrees, have the family kneel with you as one of you bless the family. The prayer that you offer should be a blessing, not merely a prayer. Bless them generally with health and the necessities of life. Then bless them to keep the commitments they have made that night with respect to praying that people in the area will become more receptive to the gospel, and bless them to read and discuss the designated scriptures.

Your Second Visit

A few days later, make an appointment to meet with the family again. When you make the appointment, stress that the matter you want to discuss with them will only take a few minutes. Otherwise they may think your motive is a free meal.

1. As you meet with the family for the second time, follow up by discussing the commitments they made during your previous visit (praying daily for the people in your area that their hearts will be softened, and reading and discussing the scriptures you left them).

If you have noticed you are having more opportunities to teach people in the area, tell the family what you have experienced. Discuss with them specific families you are now teaching and their potential contribution to the ward or branch.

If the family read and discussed the scriptures you left with them, ask them to comment on what they learned from them.

Example:

Elder Day: Bro. Clarke, how did you enjoy the scriptures we left you last week?

Bro. Clarke: They were very good.

Elder Law: Were you able to discuss them as a family?

Bro. Clarke: Yes. We did it for Family Home Evening as you suggested.

Elder Law: Were you able to pray every day for the people in our area that their hearts would be softened and that we would find someone who would make a great Elder's Quorum president?

Bro. Clarke: Yes, we did.

Elder Day: We knew you would. We have really noticed a difference in the response of people to our message this past week. Last Tuesday we had a Family Home Evening with the Sagger family. Brother Sagger was really positive and we have an appointment to teach his family the first discussion tomorrow evening. He's vice-president of the Gold Coast First National Bank down on Fairmont Avenue. We think he'd be a great Elder's Quorum president.

Elder Law: Brother Clarke, what did you learn from the scriptures we left you?

2. If the family has been conscientious in praying that people in the area will be responsive to the gospel, commit all members of the family to prayerfully consider the people they know and deal with who are not members, with the intent to determine through inspiration the individuals and families they feel would be most receptive to the gospel. Suggest that they especially consider people they know who have recently married, had a baby, or had a death in their family, or recently moved into the neighborhood.

Example:

Elder Day: We appreciate your prayers and we're sure they have had a positive influence on our success this past week. We're sure you all have friends who are not members of the Church. In your prayers this week as you continue to pray for the people in our area, will you seek guidance from our Heavenly Father and determine which of your friends would be most receptive to the gospel. Usually, if any of your friends have been recently married, had a baby, recently moved into the neighborhood, or had a death in their family, they will be especially receptive to our message. Will each one of you do that?

Family: Yes.

3. Promise them that, as they prayerfully seek the guidance of the Lord, they will be instrumental in bringing good people into the Church. Promise the family that they will be blessed for their efforts and will experience great joy in seeing others join the Church.

4. Leave a copy of "The Role of Members in Missionary Work," excerpts from talks given by President Kimball, found at the end of this chapter, and commit the family to read it and discuss it in their next home evening.

5. Before you leave the home, express your desire to bless the family, and if the father gives his permission, one of you do so. Again, bless the family in terms of health and strength and general well-being. Most importantly, bless the family in terms of the specific commitment they have made tonight to prayerfully determine who they know that will be receptive to the gospel.

6. Before you leave the home, make an appointment to return within the week to meet with the family for the third time. Again, stress that you will have only a few minutes and that you desire to meet with the entire family.

Your Third Visit

1. When you return a few days later, ask each member of the family who the Lord has impressed upon their minds as being the most inclined to be receptive to the gospel.

2. After you have obtained some names from the family, ask the father if you could kneel in prayer with his family and seek inspiration regarding the people they have referred. Tell him that he can offer the prayer or call on someone else. If he calls on you, the following should be part of your prayer: (1) gratitude for the family's willingness to provide you referrals, (2) a request that you can qualify yourself to teach the people, (3) a petition that the Spirit of the Lord will prepare the people to receive the gospel, and (4) an expression of your need to

be inspired in how to proceed.

3. Following the prayer, discuss with the member family how to proceed with each referral they have given you. Should they invite the person into their home to meet you, or should you contact the nonmember? What are the interests of the prospective contact? Should you attempt to teach the family in the home of the member or meet with them in their own home?

4. Before you leave, commit the family to pray every day about the people they have asked you to approach. *Promise the family that you will live worthy of the Spirit.* Then commit the family to consistently talk with other nonmembers about the Church, and make every effort to identify people who would be interested in the Church.

5. Assign the family to read and discuss the following scriptures: D&C 38:40-41; 88:81-82. Remind them that we are commanded to make every effort to share the gospel with people with whom we come in contact.

6. Be sure to let the family know you love and appreciate them; express your gratitude for their willingness to pray for your success, invite friends into their homes for you to teach, provide you referrals, and for whatever else they may have done to help.

7. Challenge them to set a goal regarding the number of people they will be instrumental in helping join the Church every year. Promise them that, if they will set such a goal and work toward it with faith and determined effort, it will be realized. They will have the joy every year of knowing they played some part in someone's conversion.

8. Before you leave, offer to leave a blessing on the home. If the father agrees, offer a prayer in which you bless the family and reiterate the promises you made previously regarding blessings and joys that come from seeing people join the Church.

Throughout your mission ask yourself the following questions:

1. Am I doing all I can to prove myself worthy and capable of teaching and baptizing families?

2. Am I willing to pay the price of total dedication and obedience in order to receive the cooperation and support of the members?

3. Am I having success independent of the help of members?

4. Do my companion and I prayerfully identify members of the ward whom we can introduce to our investigators to fellowship?

5. When I am in the homes of members, am I courteous and thoughtful?

6. When I am in the homes of members, do I avoid talking about things

not related to missionary work or the gospel?

7. Do I avoid socializing or fraternizing with members?
8. Do I deal with members in a businesslike manner?
9. Do members view me as a mature agent of the Lord?
10. Do I restrict my visits with members to one hour or less?
11. Whenever we teach a family referred by a member, do we not only keep the member informed of their progress but also involve him whenever possible in the conversion process of the referral?

The Role of Members in Missionary Work

Ever since President David O. McKay made the statement "Every member a missionary," the role of members in missionary work has received a great deal of emphasis. However, in spite of this emphasis, many members of the Church do not have a clear understanding of this responsibility. If more members did understand this responsibility and would act accordingly, there would be many more people baptized each year.

The following are excerpts from various talks given by President Spencer W. Kimball:

We are asking that our people include in their prayers that the Lord will soften the hearts and change the attitudes and make possible our selfless efforts to comply with his admonitions. Already we hear prayers in homes, firesides, committee meetings. We are delighted with that response. We ask the people to continue to implore the Lord to make the proselyting possible; then we are determined to do our part. (Regional Representative Seminar, Oct. 2, 1975.)

Brethren, do you always pray for the work, for the nations, for the leaders of nations, that we may have them open the gates for our missionaries ... to penetrate those great populations?

Do your children pray for this thing? Are they trained to pray thusly?

Let every man, woman and child and youth take this seriously. Pray for opening of doors. (Regional Representatives Seminar, Sept. 30, 1977.)

It is impractical for us to expect that 19,000 missionaries alone can warn the millions in the world. Members must be finders. The valuable time of our teaching missionaries is too often spent in "finding."

It is the responsibility of the members to provide the stake and full-time missionaries with the names of individuals and families to teach. Sometimes we forget that it is better to risk a little ruffling in the relationship of a friend than it is to deprive him of eternal life by keeping silent. (Regional Representatives Seminar, Apr. 3, 1975.)

It should be clear to us that usually we must warn our neighbors. Before we can warn them properly, our neighbors must experience our genuine friendship and fellowship. We want members to entreat neighbors, not to scold them or scare them.

What we need are not more quotas but fewer qualms about sharing the gospel. We hope our members will not simply go through the motions, but will keep this requirement of sharing the gospel.

Someone has said that the only true form of slavery is "service without joy." (Regional Representatives Seminar, Sept. 30, 1976.)

Our first line of defense is our young missionaries, scattered abroad in this world. These are 19-year old young men and a few young women who, at their own expense and that of their families, after having been prepared, now proselyte for two years, with the understanding that it is not a two-year mission; it is an eternal mission. It not only includes all their mortal lives, but their spiritual lives after their demise when they will continue to preach the gospel. (Regional Representatives Seminar, Sept. 30, 1977.)

The following are excerpts from a talk given by President Spencer W. Kimball on April 3, 1975:

...there are two keys to productive missionary work—(1) family-to-family friendshipping (when a member family shares the gospel with a nonmember family) and (2) cooperation between members and the missionaries to reach people.

Members should shoulder this responsibility. Every member knows of nonmembers he or she can refer to the missionaries. Every father, mother, and youth in this church should share the gospel by giving a Book of Morman, telling the account of the Prophet Joseph Smith, or inviting our acquaintances to a special meeting. If we are in tune, the spirit of the Lord will speak to us and guide us to those with whom we should share the gospel. The Lord will help us if we will but listen.

...Several decades ago when President David O. McKay presided over the church, he gave impetus to the missionary work in the stakes of Zion. He coined the term, "Every member a missionary," and it is obvious that would be a giant step toward the accomplishment of our directives, with 3.5 million member missionaries. However, if only two million of the Latter-day Saints energetically and fully accepted the challenge of President McKay to work with the full-time missionaries, or separate from them as seemed wise, certainly we could extend our efforts and "lengthen our stride" and greatly increase the conversions and build the kingdom and eventually knock at every door. That would be only about 2,000 to each missionary, but the ratio would rapidly change if we really did this.

If we could get all of the baptized members of the church to accept the challenge, we would have some 10,000 missionary members in the Phillipines proselyting instead of 336. In the 21 stakes in South America we would have over 100,000 missionaries to supplement the work of the 2,300 full-time missionaries.

With five stakes in the German area in Europe, we would have probably 15,000 additional missionaries to complement the efforts of the seven or eight hundred full-time missionaries, and so we move on around the globe and find probably two million devoted local missionaries to bring to the total proselyting effort the local culture, the local language, and the gospel in its fullness.

...could we bring concerted action to a "lengthening stride" movement that would bring into the missionary activity the good members of the Church the world around. The approach and the attack will need to be planned very carefully. We will need to impress upon stake, ward, and branch leaders around the globe their opportunity and responsibility. There will be need for strong, well-organized stake, ward, and district missions. It cannot be left to a mere suggestion, and a comprehensive score must be kept as a stimulant to the workers. Such a special, organized, developed program could bring many other of the blessings of the Church to more people as we have said.

The work by the membership of the Church who have testimonies themselves is boundless. Numerous people of the church in the past few years have brought to the baptismal font a total of many thousands of converts. This can continue to be done, and the work of the proselyting missionaries full time can be greatly increased.

A woman in Uruguay claims that she has brought to the waters of baptism 82 people since her own baptism.

Thousands of members have brought in one, five, or ten.

In our latest South American tour we found a taxi driver, new in the Church, who states that he has brought in over 200 souls. He himself is a Seventy and carries in his taxicab ten or twelve copies of the Book of Mormon and every day approaches everyone who will listen. (Regional Representatives Seminar, Apr. 3, 1975.)

From the scriptures we learn that members have two basic responsibilites with respect to missionary work:

1. Fast and pray for nonmembers. (Alma 6:6; 3 Nephi 18:22,23.) In this regard they should be as specific as possible, praying that the Spirit of the Lord will prepare people in the area to receive the message of the restored gospel. (Read D&C 11:17; 18:15, 16, 44; 29:6, 7; 84:88; 11:17.)

2. Warn and testify in their conversations with nonmember acquaintances. (D&C 88:81-82; 38:40,41.) By so doing they cause people to become interested in the Church and get them to agree to meet with local or full-time missionaries.

It is interesting to note that members do *not* have the responsibility to teach the gospel. The responsibility to teach rests with those who are called and set apart specifically to do missionary work. However, many members excuse themselves from missionary work because they do not have the time to teach nonmembers. And yet that is not what the Lord requires of members—he requires members to fast and pray regarding nonmembers and to testify and warn them. These are things every member is capable of, so members are without excuse if we fail in this responsibility.

In addition to these two basic requirements, the Church leaders have encouraged members to support missionary work financially. This can be done through local quorums or the central missionary fund.* Generally, money from the central missionary fund is used to support native missionaries in developing countries.

------

* Anyone desiring to contribute to this fund should make a check or money order payable to the LDS Church and mail it to the Central Missionary Fund, Missionary Department, Church Office Building, 50 East North Temple, Salt Lake City, Utah 84150.

Chapter 24

Obtain Referrals
from Your Investigators

Once your investigators catch the spirit of the message of the restored gospel, they are a primary source for referrals. How you go about obtaining referrals from your investigators is limited only by your ingenuity.

Examples:

1. Brother Brown, I sense you feel good about the message of the restored gospel we have shared with you. If you could have anyone with you this evening to share this experience, who would it be?

2. Brother Brown, of your neighbors and acquaintances, which do you feel are seeking truth?

3. As you make plans for your baptism, you should begin to decide what friends you want to invite to your baptismal service.

4. The ward is having dinner at the chapel this Friday. Can you think of a friend or neighbor you would like to invite to go with you?

5. As you have discussed our visits with your friends, which ones have shown the most interest in the things we have taught you?

6. Brother Brown, as you prepare for your baptism, you should be aware of an additional commandment the Lord has given. We are commanded to share the message of the restored gospel with our neighbors and friends. We'd like to have you and your family begin to pray regarding those relatives, friends and acquaintances you would like us to call on to share the message of the restored gospel.

An Effective Approach

One of the most effective approaches for obtaining referrals from investigators has been developed by David W. Ferrel, a former Mission President in Ecuador. There are seven basic parts to the approach.

1. *The Baptismal Commitment.* When the missionary says to the investigator, "We invite you and your family to be ready for baptism into The Church of Jesus Christ of Latter-day Saints on Saturday. Will you prepare for that date?" and gets a positive response, the missionary then proceeds by saying, "A baptismal service is a sacred, special, and sensitive time in a person's life. You will no doubt want to have your loved ones and special friends present at the baptismal service." The missionary then proceeds to enumerate the following:

1. Parents of the investigator
2. Aunts and uncles and their children
3. Brothers and sisters and their families
4. Special friends whom he told he was taking lessons from the Mormons

The missionary strives to suggest about five potential teaching units (families), who are particularly close to the investigator, for invitation to the baptismal service. Then the missionary says, *"Brother Brown, do you wish to invite them, or shall we? ... we'd love to!"* (These can be the most enjoyable and easiest door approaches that he will ever make.)

2. *Invitation to the Five Potential Teaching Units.* The missionaries knock at the door. A person answers. The missionaries know the person's name already and also know the spouse by name even though the spouse may not be present. You introduce yourself as Elder or Sister and companion, saying, "I'm sure you know who we are." (By the smile on the face, you do not have to explain the obvious.) Then say (for example), "Your brother, his wife and children are receiving the missionary discussions—a series of seven presentations on the things that we believe in. They plan to be baptized a week from Saturday. They would like to invite you, your husband and children to be present at their baptismal service. We plan to meet at their home Saturday, at 3:30 in the afternoon and go together, all of us, to the service at 5:00. We'll be inviting several other members of the family to attend." The missionary then indicates, "I'm sure you'll need to talk to your spouse, so we'll call back in a couple of days to confirm arrangements; but, *can we indicate at this point to your brother whom we are teaching that you are able to attend?"*

3. *Home of the Investigator.* Missionaries return and give a full and glowing (if true) report of visits with (1) Grandma and Grandpa, (2) aunt and uncle, (3) sister and brother-in-law, (4) the people

downstairs, and (5) the family of the man at work. The missionary tells the investigator that he should be prepared because these people will probably ask him questions about what he is doing and what he is learning.

4. *Second Visit to the Five Families that the Missionary is Lacing to the First Investigator Family.* The missionary says (to the aunt and uncle), "Hi, ...! We had the most fantastic discussion with your nephew and his family last night on a subject that we call Eternal Progression. I know that may not mean much to you, but we talked about (1) where you came from before you were born, (2) why you are here in this life, and (3) where you will go after this life. It was absolutely exciting. Normally we stay only 45 minutes, but we were with them for an hour and a half last night. Why don't you ask them questions about it? By the way, did you talk to your spouse? Is everything all set for Saturday at 3:30 P.M. at the home of your nephew? By the way, one of us will call for you on Saturday to accompany you to their home."

5. *Helping Investigators during the Extremely Important Last 72 Hours before the Baptismal Service.* (Missionaries should understand that things always tend to go wrong during the last 72 hours before the baptism.) The missionaries give another full report of conversations with friends of the investigator. The missionaries ask the investigator, "Which two families out of the five should we invite to your home next Tuesday (after baptism) to hear the same discussion that we gave to you two and one-half weeks ago—Grandma and Grandpa and your aunt and uncle?" The investigator might respond, "Grandma and Grandpa, yes, but not my aunt and uncle. I'd really prefer my sister and her family, though, because last night we had a three-hour conversation about Joseph Smith, eternal progression, and the commandments. They said that they'd like to stop smoking."

6. *The Day of the Baptismal Service.* The missionaries arrange to split with members (seventies or stake missionaries).

Morning. One missionary and a member call on the friends (five families) of the current investigator during the morning hours; making quick visits to indicate the time that they will be by during the afternoon and to make sure that everything is set. The other missionary and a member call on the family to be baptized first thing Saturday morning to answer questions, to explain details, and to resolve obstacles that will come up (i.e., (1) white clothes do not fit, (2) baby daughter is sick and someone from the Relief Society will have to be called in to watch the child, or (3) the father cannot get off work, and the missionary will have to drop by the

place of employment to talk with the boss and invite him to come, etc.).
This often consumes the morning hours.

Afternoon. One missionary and a member companion call for the
friends of the investigator to be baptized. The other companion is at the
home and resolving obstacles that have come up that could prevent
baptism. Friends and relatives arrive about 4:15 (the missionaries knew
that it would be that way from the very beginning). Finally everyone leaves
together for the chapel by bus, taxi, on foot, etc. One or more of the five
families will not show up. It is always that way, for they have "self-selected
themselves out." Missionaries do not mind, because they want to know
who has the greatest interest. However, *missionaries must always check,*
because sometimes the absent family is the most golden, and a giant
obstacle has arisen.

The missionaries have pre-planned the baptismal service because
they want the service to be spiritual and impressive. (The missionaries'
next investigators depend on the quality of the baptismal service!) After
the service (Saturday night and Sunday, until Sunday night), the
missionaries ask those who attended: (1) *"What did you think?"* (2) "How
did you feel?" Sometime before Sunday night the missionaries invite the
two families out of the group who are to come to the home of the new
member to receive discussion "C". The missionaries who have made their
selection in prayerful consideration with the newly baptized family say, for
example, *"Your grandson, his wife and the children want to invite you to
their home Tuesday at 8:00 for a little visit, a light refreshment, and then
afterwards, a presentation. They have also invited us to their home
Tuesday night to give to all of you the same presentation that we gave to
them two and one-half weeks ago. We'll call by to pick you up at 7:15."*
Then the missionaries repeat the process with the married sister and her
family. They talk about the baptismal service and then say, "Your brother,
his family ... want to invite you ... and they have invited us to their ...
We'll call by for you at 7:40 with Grandma and Grandpa."

Most teaching units (families) will contain 2-3 baptism age individuals.
Assuming that there are 2 baptizable aged individuals per teaching unit
implies that 10 are preparing for baptism, which usually results in 6 being
baptized on the scheduled baptismal date with up to 2 others being
baptized about a week later. Then the cycle starts all over.

All other variations that come to the minds of the missionaries in
righteousness are acceptable. This whole process serves to stimulate the
prayerful, thinking and seeking missionary, and helps him to be more
effective in his calling and to magnify and multiply himself in his
stewardship.

Missionaries should realize they are laying the foundation for next month's program as they teach this month's investigators.

This procedure helps resolve the problem of hills and valleys in baptisms in which missionaries finish giving the discussions to their investigators, baptize them, and then have no one else to teach until six weeks later. The cycle is shortened to about three weeks or less.

Cautions

If you intend to use the approach developed by President Ferrel, you should keep the following points in mind: (1) Baptismal services should be planned carefully, and great care should be taken to insure that the talks given are appropriate. Every effort should be made to insure the service is a special occasion in the lives of the investigators. (2) The C discussion may not be the most appropriate discussion in some parts of the world or with particular families. You should be very prayerful in deciding on the discussion to be presented first to a family. (3) This particular approach is intended principally for missionaries who are willing to work hard, give approximately 20 discussions per week, are accustomed to baptizing at least one or two people per month. The approach is intended to provide missionaries guidelines and should not be used verbatim.

Throughout your mission ask yourself the following questions:

1. Are we using our investigators as a primary source for referrals?

2. Are we using ingenuity under inspiration in effectively obtaining all the referrals possible from our investigators?

3. Are our baptismal services being planned and conducted in such a way that each one will be a positive experience for the nonmenbers who attend?

4. Are we teaching our investigators how to get their friends interested in the gospel?

Chapter 25

Trust Your Own Ingenuity

Once you are in the mission field, learn to trust your own ingenuity (cleverness, originality) in what you say when you approach people about the gospel and in how to create opportunities to talk to people about the Church. Remember, you are entitled to inspiration. If you live for it and seek it, the Lord will bring ideas and approaches to your mind. Your own ingenuity in creating opportunities to talk to people is extremely important in making yourself heard. Your mission leaders will provide you with some suggestions and ways you can create opportunities to talk with people; however, the thing you should remember is that they are only suggestions and in no way represent the only ways there are. You have the responsibility to seek inspiration regarding how you can become more effective in getting opportunities to talk with people about the gospel.

An entire book could be written on the host of approaches missionaries have used over the years. The following examples are only a few of literally hundreds of approaches missionaries have used.

Contacting Groups

Your success as a missionary is directly related to the amount of exposure you receive. Many baptisms have resulted from teaching large groups of people. Entire congregations have been baptized. The following are only a few ways in which missionaries have successfully approached groups of people.

1. Taught a weekly class at a university during a time segment called "free hour".

2. Attended local churches and met ministers and members of congregations. In many instances missionaries have received invitations to speak to various religious groups.

3. Set up a tent and display at a local fair in town.

4. Spoke to a group of police.

5. Presented the Family Home Evening program to local clubs, Lions, Rotary, and Jaycees; then went into each of the homes of club members and presented a Family Home Evening.

6. Presented (health missionaries) a weekly health puppet show on TV.

7. Presented daily sermonettes over local TV.

8. Set up Family Home Evening displays in libraries and the history of the Book of Mormon displays on college campuses.

9. Recruited members of the community to be on a half-hour TV show during which children talked about their families.

10. Wrote weekly newspaper articles for the religious section.

11. Gave filmstrip presentations to junior high and high school classes.

12. Set up displays in shopping malls.

13. Contacted the mayor of a city and had him declare a Family Unity Week. Got the entire ward involved in displays, had a TV show of a family having a home evening, published newspaper articles, had Family Day at a park sponsored by the Church. Held entertainment, with games, refreshments, and received many referrals.

14. Obtained permission from the mission president to have neighborhood primaries on a military base for nonmembers, which resulted in the conversion of six families over a two-month period.

15. Visited mortuaries and made themselves available to give funeral sermons at no cost.

Contacting Families

A large percentage of missionaries find families to teach by going from house to house, visiting businesses, and meeting people on the street. Though these are good ways to find people to teach, you should be careful, that you don't get caught in the rut of mechanically going from door to door and business to business greeting people with one or two memorized approaches. You should resolve to use ingenuity under inspiration. As you do, you will find this type of contacting to be one of the most exciting aspects of your mission. The following are examples of ways in which missionaries have successfully found families to teach.

1. Sang songs like "Love at Home" at doorsteps and street corners.

2. Contacted bank presidents. Made flipcharts to present the Family Home Evening program and the Book of Mormon.

3. Found out the names of the people before knocking on their doors.

4. Visited the children's ward at the hospital and got to know the children. Then when they met the parents, they secured an appointment to visit their home after their child returned home.

5. Had a ward tracting day. Trained the members in how to approach people and then spent a Saturday tracting an area.

6. Contacted people over the phone if a companion was ever ill.

7. Created pamphlets announcing general conference to be broadcast on the local TV station. Invited people to watch the Tabernacle Choir and the prophet on TV. After conference, talked with the people about their impressions of the program.

Getting Your Own Referrals

There are many ways in which you can obtain referrals of people who will be receptive to the gospel. You are not limited to referrals from members, investigators, and visitor centers. The following are only a few ways in which missionaries have obtained their own referrals.

1. Checked obituaries and called on families who had had a recent death in their family.

2. Checked announcements of new births and called on families who had recently had a baby.

3. Called on recently married people.

4. Checked with utility companies or city officials and obtained names of people who had recently moved into the area.

5. When business contacting, secured a list of employees whom the president felt would be interested in your message.

6. When tracting, asked people if they knew of anyone who was new in the area, had recently had a death, birth, or marriage in the family.

7. Had a person's four-generation group sheet sent to him and used the names of relatives as referrals by finding similar names in the phone book and calling on their homes.

8. Read the local newspaper for noteworthy events and then knocked on the door of persons involved, using the information gained from the newspaper.

9. Looked through old censuses, found large families, and then contacted them.

Preparation Day Contacting

Some missionaries consider their preparation day a day to rest from missionary work. Nothing could be farther from the truth. As you use ingenuity under inspiration in finding people, you will not only gain an excitement and joy, but you will catch the vision of your calling as a missionary. As you do, you will take advantage of every opportunity throughout your preparation day to find people to teach. The following are some examples of ways in which missionaries used their preparation day in this way.

1. Approached people at the laundry, including the owner.

2. When grocery shopping, asked advice from people and then told them who they were and got an appointment to visit their family.

3. Went to a Little League ball game. Met parents, discussed their children with them, and gained an appointment to teach them.

4. Established a father and son weight-lifting club by teaching at the police boys' club every Monday morning.

Holiday Contacting

Throughout the year, there are special occasions which lend themselves to unique ways of approaching people. The following are a few examples:

1. Make Family Home Evening "gift certificates" at Christmas time to use in the door approaches when families are very busy, and also let members give them to nonmenber friends as gifts.

2. Set up an exhibit on eternal life in the cemetery on Memorial Day.

3. At Christmas time, create a special presentation on the life of the Savior and make it available to religious groups.

4. During the Fourth of July, go to the park dressed as Paul Revere and Thomas Jefferson. Enter family picnic groups and tell children stories of the American Revolution. Approach the parents afterwards.

5. Send Christmas cards to selected nonmembers and offer to give a special Christmas presentation to their families.

Caution

An important part of using ingenuity in finding people is making sure that your decisions are made under inspiration. You should be prayerful regarding the ways you select to find people to teach. Throughout your mission as you select various ways to approach people, ask yourself the following questions:

1. Is the approach the most productive way of finding people to teach?

2. Is my major reason for selecting this approach to find people to teach, or am I doing it for my own entertainment?

3. Will this type of approach enhance the dignity of my calling?

4. Have I been prayerful about the approach I've selected?

Leave a Blessing

In some parts of the world it is effective to use your desire to bless the home as your initial approach, especially if the father is home. This approach has proven very successful in touching hearts and opening the minds of many people.

It is completely in accord with the scriptures. The Lord has declared that your first responsibility is to leave the Lord's peace and to bless the home.

> And into whatsoever house ye enter, first say, Peace be to this house.
>
> And if the son of peace be there, your peace shall rest upon it: if not, it shall turn to you again. (Luke 10:5,6.)
>
> Yea, let all those take their journey, as I have commanded them, going from house to house, and from village to village, and from city to city.
>
> And in whatsoever house ye enter, and they receive you, leave your blessing upon that house. (D&C 75:18, 19.)

Your second responsibility is to testify that the gospel of Jesus Christ has been restored to the earth through the Prophet Joseph Smith. However, if you use a request to bless the home as your initial approach, you must be certain you have the Spirit of the Lord as your companion. This more than any of the suggested approaches requires that it be used under inspiration to be effective.

In this way you will meet the Lord's expectations of you, and if people choose to reject your message, they will be held accountable before the Lord. In contrast, if you fail to consistently improve your ability to gain an audience with someone, you will be held accountable before the Lord.

If you use the approach, when you first get inside the house, it is a very critical moment. At that moment you must put the father in his rightful place as head of that home. You do this by asking him to introduce you to his family. There is nothing a father would rather do than introduce his family to you. Fathers love their families. Fathers love to show their families off to the world. Most fathers will go into all the rooms of the house, in the back yard, upstairs, and all around to find all the members of their families to introduce them to you. Let him introduce them to you one by one.

Do your best to remember their names. As you are introduced to them, say each first name as you hear it. Later, after you have left their house, write their names down so that you can remember them. People like to be called by their names, and it will be very impressive to them if you can say their names when you go back to visit them.

In many cases, failure takes place after the family is introduced. At this point you should not start a conversation with them, which is what many missionaries are inclined to do.

As soon as you have been introduced to the family, you should address the father and say, *"Our purpose in being here is to leave the Savior's peace and a blessing in your home. Will you kneel with us so that we may do that?"* By the time you have said the last word, you should already be on your knees. If you hesitate to kneel as you say the last of these words, it will leave an opening for debate. Don't give the father and his family a chance to question whether or not they are going to kneel with you. If you kneel, they automatically will kneel with you.

You don't have to ask permission to bless them after you are in the house. If you analyze the dialogue you used at the door, you will realize that you asked permission to bless them when you asked to come into their home. The fact that they have allowed you to come in has already given you permission.

Although, as a part of this blessing you bless their house, that is not the real purpose of your visit. Your purpose is to bless the people who live in the house. By calling a blessing from heaven upon their house, you are only blessing them indirectly.

As soon as you get on your knees, you begin the blessing by saying, *"In the name of Jesus Christ, and by the power of the Holy Priesthood which I bear."* Do not use the word *Melchizedek*. They will not understand what that word means, and it will frighten them. Rather, you say, *"By the power of the Holy Priesthood which I bear."*

Then you bless the house itself. You bless the house that it will be protected from the elements and be a place of safety. You bless it that it will be a place where the Spirit of the Lord can dwell, a place where righteous things can happen, and a place where fond memories can be built. There are other things which you will think of as you bless the house.

Next, you bless the father separately. Bless him that he will have health and strength, that he will have the ability to provide his family with all that they need, and that he will have love for his wife and children, that they will understand him, and that he will understand them. Bless him that he will be a good example to all who know him, bringing dignity and honor into the lives of his family. There are many other things that you will think of as you bless the father.

Then you bless the mother that she will have health and strength, that she will know how to care for her children, that she will love, honor, and respect her husband, and that she will always be a shining light and example of righteousness to her children. You will think of many other things to bless a mother with.

Next, you bless collectively all who live in that house. You should close the blessing by asking the Lord to seal all these things upon them, and to give them special desires to want to know what is true and to have the ability to understand it when they hear it. Then you end the prayer in the name of Jesus Christ.

As you stand up, you will discover many different kinds of people. Some will be in tears. Others will not take you seriously and will mock what you have done. There will be all kinds of reactions.

At this point you are entitled to know if the Lord wants to teach the gospel to the family. This is the separating moment. This is the moment that the Spirit will touch you and touch them so that you both know if the gospel should be taught in the home.

After you have invoked blessings from on high upon these people, if the Spirit has touched their hearts through you, you will know it and they will know it. If not, you will also know it, and there will be no need for you to pursue the teaching process with that family.

If the Spirit testifies to you that this family should be taught the gospel, you should express a desire to teach them.

Example:

Missionary: We are so happy that the Lord has sent us here to teach the truths of this gospel to you. It has been a privilege for us to come into your home, and to have had the opportunity of meeting you and your family. We feel that the Lord wants you to hear his truths. We are his messengers sent to teach those truths. We would like to come back into your home to tell you what it is that the Lord wants his children to do while upon this earth. Would _____ (give a time) be all right for us to return to talk with you for about forty-five minutes?" (Have an alternative time ready.)

Be sure that you return to teach that family within forty-eight hours after you have given the blessing to them. Forty-eight hours should be a maximum time. If you wait longer, your chances for success with them diminsh because they will have had time to talk to their friends and neighbors and their ministers or priests. They will get advice from the world of Satan, and much of the spirit that you carried into their home will be lost before you get back. You carry the Spirit of the Lord with you. You leave it in their home when you are there for the first time. You want it to be strong enough to remain there until you get back. You should get back as soon as you can so that Satan's influence will not rob them of the spirit you left there.

If you teach them another lesson right after that blessing, it will, in most cases, be anticlimactic. The blessing was the most spiritual thing that has ever happened inside the walls of their home. You should not do anything that would be anticlimactic to that great event. The Spirit needs to work with them. They need to have an opportunity to think about what you did and how important it is in their lives.

You have to go to their homes with faith that the blessing you give them and the power you call down from on high into their home will have effect in their lives. You should expect the plan to work. You should surely expect that, if you bless them to have desires to hear the gospel, they will want you to come back and teach it to them. This is the way the Lord has asked us to do it.

In addition you should ask yourself the following questions relating to your ability to use ingenuity under inspiration:

1. Do I use ingenuity in the ways I create opportunities to talk to people about the Church?

2. Do I seek inspiration regarding how I can become more effective in getting opportunities to talk to people about the gospel?

3. Are my companion and I successfully avoiding the rut of mechanically going from door to door expressing one or two memorized approaches?

4. Am I successfully making initial contacting one of the most exciting aspects of my mission?

Chapter 26

Summary of Section 3

Perfecting your ability to make yourself heard should be one of your primary focuses when you first arrive in the mission field. Once the Lord is convinced you are doing everything you can to make yourself heard, he will prepare the way so that you will have the opportunity to teach people who are honest in heart. The Lord knows the heart and intent of people, and if your faith is sufficient to allow him the opportunity to assist you, he will help you find numerous ways to contact people who will be receptive to your message. You must remember that faith and effort must be combined in order to make yourself heard. One without the other will fail.

Chapter 27

Introduction to Section 4

I t is disappointing enough when people refuse to give you an audience to discuss the gospel, but when you teach a family the discussions and they are not converted, it is even more disappointing. In the process of teaching a family, you grow to love them and it is very traumatic when they do not join the Church. President Kimball has said that *missionaries must become more skillful in making themselves believed.* Over the years there has been a great deal of discussion as to what is the most effective way to do missionary work. Some feel missionaries should not be required to follow any predetermined plan. At the other end of the continuum are those who feel missionaries should follow a specified dialogue verbatim. The pros and cons of these two points of view have been thoroughly considered. For the past several years there has been a leaning toward verbatim dialogues. However, surveys conducted by the Missionary Department and others show that missionaries are not effective if they rely exclusively on memorized dialogues. The general consensus now is that, in addition to a basic dialogue, missionaries must be able to use various teaching principles under inspiration.

The Savior's ministry among the Nephites supports the idea that missionaries should not try to rely on memorized dialogues alone. His example provides an excellent standard for determining to what extent you should rely on a memorized dialogue and provides a clear indication of the type of activities that should occur when you are teaching people the gospel.

Some of the Savior's message to the Nephites was apparently determined in advance. It was not a memorized dialogue, but was rather a carefully preplanned message to meet the specific needs of the Nephites. The Savior's example suggests that a substantial part of what missionaries say when they meet with investigators should be preplanned with the specific needs of the investigators in mind, not memorized as a dialogue.

Another part of the Savior's message to the Nephites was given almost verbatim to both the Nephites and the people in Jerusalem. Most likely this portion of his message was also given verbatim to the other inhabitants of the earth visited by the Savior.

From this part of the Savior's ministry to the Nephites, we can conclude that some aspects of the gospel are so basic and fundamental that they should be given virtually verbatim to all people and should be memorized, read aloud to an investigator or presented on a tape.

However, a large part of the Savior's message to the Nephites came as a direct result of the people's response to what he said and his ability to discern how they were reacting as he went along. From the scriptural account it is obvious that this part of his message was neither pre-planned nor memorized. It is interesting to note that this substantial part of the Savior's message to the Nephites during his first visit came after he had told them he was going to depart so they could better prepare themselves to understand his message, and was a direct result of his ability to discern their desires.

Even though verbatim dialogues have an important place in missionary work, from the Savior's ministry among the Nephites we can conclude that missionaries will never be totally effective in their labors if they try to rely entirely on them. From his example it is apparent that, when you meet with a family, your presentation should consist of various activities, *not* of merely reciting a memorized dialogue.

This section deals with those principles, procedures, and activities that will significantly influence whether or not people believe your message. As you learn to comply with these principles and become skillful in using, under inspiration, the various proselyting principles discussed in this section, you will be effective in getting people to believe your message.

As was the case with the proselyting principles discussed in the last section, you will not be able to use those discussed in this section unless you are functioning properly as a missionary. If you attempt to use them without the support of the Spirit, you will fail.

Obviously, non-English speaking missionaries will not be able to use these principles and procedures unless they are fairly fluent in their mission languages. Consequently, if a non-English speaking missionary intends to use the proselyting principles and procedures discussed in this section, he must become fluent in his mission language.

Once you are in the field, you will realize that what you say apart from the formal discussions influences a person's conversion more than the discussions themselves. Most likely you will not see the full relevance of the proselyting principles discussed in this section until after you have been in the field a few months. Once you begin to see the role of these principles in the conversion process, you will realize that you will never be very effective in getting people to believe your message until you learn to use at least some of the proselyting principles discussed in this section.

The chapters in this section should be prayerfully read at least once a month for the first six months of your mission, and then at least once every two months.

Chapter 28

Seek the Gifts of the Spirit

Your ability to make yourself believed will be enhanced significantly by cultivating various gifts of the Spirit. You have the responsibility to earnestly seek certain gifts of the Spirit.

...seek ye earnestly the best gifts, always remembering for what they are given. (D&C 46:8.)

Behold, thou has a gift, or thou shalt have a gift if thou wilt desire of me in faith, with an honest heart, believing in the power of Jesus Christ, or in my power which speaketh unto thee. (D&C 11:10.)

And I would exhort you, my beloved brethren, that ye remember that he is the same yesterday, today, and forever, and that all these gifts of which I have spoken, which are spiritual, never will be done away, even as long as the world shall stand, only according to the unbelief of the children of men. (Moroni 10:19.)

Because many things the Lord requires of us during this mortal existence exceed our capabilities, the gifts of the Spirit are available so that we will be equal to the tasks the Lord requires of us. The Lord has said that the gifts of the Spirit are given "of God unto men, to profit them." (Moroni 10:8.) The various gifts of the Spirit are at your disposal to assist you in your missionary labors if you will but seek them.

God is the same today as He was yesterday.... (He) is willing to bestow these gifts upon His children. I know that God is willing to heal the sick, that He is willing to bestow the gift of discerning of spirits, the gift of wisdom, of knowledge and of prophecy, and other gifts that may be needed. (G. Q. Cannon, *Millenial Star,* Apr. 16, 1894, p. 260.)

The Lord has said that he desires to grant missionaries a special endowment and blessing if they are faithful. (See D&C 105:11, 12.)

The gifts of the Spirit appear to be virtually unlimited—they seem to grow out of specific needs—thus it would be impossible to try to list them all. There are, however, certain gifts that are crucial to your success as a missionary, gifts that should be cultivated by all missionaries.

Cultivate the Power to Convince People of the Restoration

As a missionary you should especially seek the gift of the Spirit that will give you the power to convince people that the gospel of Jesus Christ has been restored to the earth.

> And it shall come to pass, when the Lord seeth fit in his wisdom that they shall minister unto all the scattered tribes of Israel, and unto all nations, kindreds, tongues and people, and shall bring out of them unto Jesus many souls, that their desire may be fulfilled, and also because of the convincing power of God which is in them. (3 Ne. 28:29.)

Once you successfully gain this gift of the Spirit through a prayer of faith (D&C 42:14), you will be able to teach with power and authority and people will accept the gospel.

> ...they had given themselves to much prayer, and fasting; therefore they had the spirit of prophecy, and the spirit of revelation, and when they taught, they taught with power and authority of God. (Alma 17:3.)

Teaching under the inspiration of the Spirit more than anything else is the key to making yourself believed. The Spirit performs various functions when you are teaching: (1) The Spirit will inspire you as to what to say, (2) the Spirit will attest to the heart and mind of the person of the validity of your message, (3) the Spirit will facilitate the understanding of your investigators, and (4) the Spirit will motivate your investigators to repent, etc.

Thirty years before the birth of the Savior, the Nephites were "ripening for destruction." Their laws had become corrupted to the point that they "could not be governed by the law nor justice, save it were to their destruction." Nephi, who was the chief judge of the people, became "weary because of their iniquity; and he yielded up the judgment seat and took it upon himself to preach the word of God" for the rest of his life. He and his brother Lehi became two of the greatest missionaries who have ever lived. The power they had to convince people of the truthfulness of the gospel had a significant influence on their success.

> Therefore they did speak unto the great astonishment of the Lamanites, *to the convincing of them,* insomuch that there were eight thousand of the Lamanites who were in the land of Zarahemla and round about baptized unto

repentance, and were convinced of the wickedness of the traditions of their fathers. (Helaman 5:19; italics added.)

Helaman and his brethren experienced the same success as a result of this gift.

Therefore, Helaman and his brethren went forth, and did declare the word of God *with much power unto the convincing of many people* of their wickedness, which did cause them to repent of their sins and to be baptized unto the Lord their God. (Alma 62:45; italics added.)

As you do all you can to prepare yourself to teach (i.e., live the gospel, learn the discussions, study the scriptures) and exercise the faith necessary to cultivate this particular gift, you will have "the power of God unto the convincing of men." (D&C 11:21.)

Cultivate the Gift of Discernment

As a member of the Church of Jesus Christ of Latter-day Saints, you have been given the basic gift of the Holy Ghost. (Moroni 7:12-18; D&C 63:41.) You are endowed with the ability to discern between good and evil, whether or not a person is righteous (D&C 101:95; Malachi 3:18; 3 Nephi 24:18), and when the Spirit of God is being manifest. (D&C 46:23; 1 Corinthians 12:10.) If you are desirous and earnestly seek it and strive to cultivate it, you will be endowed with even greater discernment. As you successfully cultivate this keener discernment, "the thoughts and intents of the heart" of people will be revealed to your mind. (D&C 33:1; Hebrews 4:12.)

The Lord expects you to earnestly seek the gift of discernment. (Read D&C 11:10; Moroni 10:19.) Throughout your mission consistently remind yourself that this gift is given "of God unto men, to profit them." (Moroni 10:8.) It is at your disposal to assist you in the work if you seek it. Through it you can discern thoughts, motives, attitudes, character, intent, beliefs, etc. Obviously, if you cultivate the gift of discernment, your effectiveness as a missionary will be greatly enhanced. You should resolve to earnestly seek the gift of discernment.

You need the Spirit of the Almighty to look through a man and discern what is in his heart, while his face smiles upon you and words flow as smoothly as oil. (*Journal of Discourses* 3:225.)

By means of the gift of discernment, "the mind will be enlightened so that we shall see, know and understand things as they are." (*Journal of Discourses* 13:336.) Brigham Young spoke often about this gift:

I rejoice in the privilege of meeting with the Saints, in hearing them speak, and in enjoying the influence that is within and around them. That influence opens to my understanding the true position of those who are endeavoring to serve their God. I do not require to hear them speak to enable me to know their feelings. Is it not also your experience that, when you meet persons in the streets, in your houses, in your offices, or in the workshops, more or less an influence attends them which conveys more than words can.... This knowledge is obtained through that invisible influence which attends intelligent beings, and betrays the atmosphere in which they delight to live. (*Journal of Discourses* 8:57.)

Cultivate the Gift of Charity

We are admonished to seek charity, "which is the greatest gift of all," and we are admonished to pray for this gift with all the energy of our hearts. (Moroni 7:48.) Moroni exhorts us to cleave (to adhere, to cling) unto charity. He also teaches that if, in the final analysis, a man does not have charity, "he is nothing."

> Wherefore, my beloved brethren, if ye have not charity, ye are nothing, for charity never faileth. Wherefore, cleave unto charity, which is the greatest of all, for all things must fail. (Moroni 7:46.)

Until you develop a Christlike love for the people you are called to teach, you will not experience much success. Your efforts will be as "sounding brass, or a tinkling symbol." (1 Corinthians 13:1.) In other words, when you teach, your words will not touch the hearts of the people. People can discern whether or not you love them. Once you have charity, people will listen to your message, commit to live the principles of the gospel, and enter the waters of baptism. As a result, you have the responsibility to "pray unto the Father with all the energy of heart, that ye may be filled with this love...." (Moroni 7:48.)

A person who has charity will be long-suffering and kind, will not envy, will not be puffed up, will serve the interests of others, will not be easily provoked, will not think about evil things, will rejoice in the truth, will bear patiently the infirmities and afflictions of this mortal life, will believe all the gospel truths, will hope for the realization of the promises made in the holy scriptures, and will endure all things without wavering in his commitment to the Lord Jesus Christ.

You have the responsibility to study the scriptures to learn of the various gifts of the Spirit that can assist you in your missionary labors, and then prayerfully seek insight regarding these gifts. Once you understand a particular gift of the Spirit that you feel would make you more effective as a missionary, you then should earnestly seek it until you receive it. If you are not functioning properly as a missionary you will not qualify for the gifts of the Spirit.

> How many of you ... are seeking for these gifts that God has promised to bestow? How many of you, when you bow before your Heavenly Father in

your family circle or in your secret places, contend for these gifts to be bestowed upon you? How many of you ask the Father, in the name of Jesus Christ, to manifest Himself to you through these powers and these gifts? Or do you go along day by day like a door turning on its hinges, without exercising any faith whatever; content to be baptized and be members of the Church, and to rest there, thinking that your salvation is secure because you have done this?...

If any of us is imperfect, it is our duty to pray for the gift that will make us perfect. Have I imperfections? I am full of them. What is my duty? To pray God to give me the gifts that will correct these imperfections. If I am an angry man, it is my duty to pray for charity, which suffereth long and is kind. Am I an envious man? It is my duty to seek for charity, which envieth not. So with all the gifts of the Gospel. They are intended for this purpose. No man ought to say, "Oh, I cannot help this; it is my nature." He is not justified in it, for the reason that God has promised to give strength to correct these things, and to give gifts that will eradicate them. (George Q. Cannon, *Millenial Star*, Apr. 16, 1894, p. 260.)

The gifts of the Spirit will be yours as you (1) desire them, (2) ask the Lord to grant them to you, (3) function properly, and (4) exercise the necessary faith.

Behold, thou hast a gift, or thou shalt have a gift if thou wilt desire of me in faith, with an honest heart, believing in the power of Jesus Christ, or in my power which speaketh unto thee. (D&C 11:10.)

Throughout your mission, ask yourself the following questions:

1. Am I earnestly seeking the gifts of the Spirit that will help me be equal to the tasks that the Lord requires of me?

2 Am I seeking to cultivate the power to convince people of the restoration?

3 Am I endowed with the ability to discern between good and evil, whether or not people are righteous, and when the Spirit of God is being manifest?

4. Am I praying for the gift of charity with all the energy of my heart?

5. Am I studying the scriptures to learn of the various gifts of the Spirit that are available to assist me in my labors?

6. Do I prayerfully seek insight regarding the gifts of the Spirit?

Chapter 29

Qualify for Inspiration

The missionary discussions are designed to help missionaries teach people the gospel. It is very important that the teaching system of the missionary program be uniform. You have the responsibility of becoming totally conversant with the message all missionaries are presenting. Your success, however, will be limited if you rely primarily on memorized dialogues. In order for you to become an effective teacher, you must learn to adapt the discussions under inspiration to meet the specific interests and needs of your investigators.

For example, you should not teach an older couple whose children have all moved away the same way you'd teach a couple who have seven children under ten. You should not teach a Harvard graduate the same way you teach a person who hasn't completed the fifth grade. You should not teach a Catholic family the same way you teach a Baptist family. You need to qualify for inspiration relating to the needs of families and then adapt your presentation accordingly in order that those you teach will have every opportunity to gain a testimony of the restoration of the gospel.

Obtaining Inspiration through Mental Preparation

Each time you are scheduled to present a discussion, devote at least half an hour to intense mental preparation, during which time you formulate questions you will ask, things you will say to make your message appealing, etc. As you do, you will obtain the inspiration necessary to meet the specific needs of those you teach. The time you spend in mental

163

preparation should be spent in determining those things you will teach the family and how you will teach them. Train your mind to think through the various topics introduced in this section and determine how each relates to the discussion you are teaching, where particular principles contained in this chapter can be used, and how you should use them.

Through inspiration you will be able to determine three things: (1) Those aspects of the gospel that will be most appealing to your investigators. (2) Those aspects of the gospel your investigators will have reservations about. In many instances, these reservations will be the result of something the person has read or heard about the Church that is not true. Unless you are discerning and insightful in knowing what these reservations are and then deal with them effectively as the Spirit directs, these reservations can interfere with the person's conversion. (3) The parts of the discussion that need to be changed to enable you to communicate clearly.

Unless you train yourself to prepare mentally, you will not be effective when you present a discussion. Merely reciting a discussion to your companion does not qualify you for inspiration. In contrast, as you train yourself to prepare mentally as well as spiritually for every discussion you give, and heed the promptings of the Spirit, you will be effective when you present the discussions. You will receive a great deal of inspiration regarding the family you plan to teach during the half hour you devote to mental preparation.

There is no one best way to prepare mentally to give a discussion. Some missionaries are very effective in referring to comments or questions investigators have made previously as they present a discussion. Others are effective in determining ways that they can compliment their investigators as they are presenting a particular discussion. Others find that thinking through very carefully how they will systematically review what has been taught previously is a good way to adapt or introduce a particular discussion. Because the initial warmup conversation is critical to the success of a discussion, some missionaries focus their mental preparation primarily on what they will say initially prior to the presentation of the formal discussion.

Throughout each day there are times when you can mentally prepare (e.g., while you are shaving, traveling) which will not detract from other important missionary labors. The time you spend in mental preparation will not only help you obtain inspiration regarding what and how you should teach, but will help you be more receptive to inspiration during the presentation of the discussion itself. You will find you will not be very receptive to inspiration when you are teaching if you fail to devote at least one-half hour to mental preparation for each discussion you give. This mental preparation will have as much influence on the investigator's conversion as what you say during the discussion.

Inspiration and Functioning Properly

If you are not functioning properly, you will not have sufficient control over your mind to mentally rehearse how you intend to give a discussion. It is impossible to adapt a discussion under inspiration unless you are worthy in every way. Unless you are willing to function properly, the discussions you give will not touch the hearts of your investigators unless they are basically converted already. When a person is basically converted, it does not require much preparation to bring him into the Church. However, if the people you are teaching are not basically converted when you start to teach them, your mental preparation will be a major factor in their conversion.

You should train your mind to engage in this type of mental preparation each time you are going to have a teaching opportunity, whether it be speaking in a meeting, talking to civic groups, presenting a discussion, etc. In addition, you should make it a policy on your preparation day to devote a substantial amount of time to reflecting and thinking about the families you are teaching as well as the problems you are facing in your particular field of labor. Likewise, when you are attending district and zone conferences, you should orient yourself to reflect and think about your investigators. Do not make the mistake of divorcing your investigators from your mind when you are engaged in other missionary activities.

Throughout your mission ask yourself the following questions:

1. Am I totally conversant with the discussions?

2. Do I adapt the discussions to meet the specific interests and needs of investigators?

3. Am I able to determine those aspects of the gospel that will be most appealing to our investigators?

4. Am I able to determine those aspects of the gospel that those we teach have reservations about?

5. Am I able to determine those parts of the discussion that need to be changed in order for me to be able to communicate clearly?

6. Am I fluent in my mission language?

7. When I memorize the discussions, do I make certain that I understand what I am memorizing?

8. When I am attending district and zone conferences, do I orient myself to reflect and think about our investigators?

9. Do I make it a policy on preparation day to devote a substantial amount of time to reflecting and thinking about the families I'm teaching?

Chapter 30

Direct Your Message to the Father

As a missionary, you have a responsibility to teach and baptize entire families. President A. Theodore Tuttle has said, "The problem we face in the conversion process is to bring whole families into the Church." The father is the key to teaching and baptizing families. Whenever you baptize a father, you will baptize the entire family. On the other hand, if you fail to baptize a father, you will divide a family you were sent to unite for time and eternity. It is therefore very important that you learn how to approach fathers in the most effective manner to insure their conversion. The following guidelines will assist you in this process.

1. Get Your Message to the Father.

As missionaries proselyte, they find that one of the primary hindrances to bringing a family into the kingdom is the fact that they meet the mother at the door and approach her instead of the father. You should not approach her directly, but should set the stage for getting the message to the father. What you say on your initial visit will have a great influence on your effectiveness in teaching the entire family in subsequent visits. (Note: When you are first contacting and you find fathers at home, it is appropriate to present a message at that time rather than asking for a return appointment. The following principles will assist you in getting the message to the father.)

In your initial approach, state that you have come to see the father and ask if he is at home. Merely talking to a wife without mentioning her husband will make it more difficult when you meet the husband later. You should direct your initial approach toward the father by stating that you have come to speak with him (e.g., "Good morning. We're ministers and would like to speak with your husband. Is he at home?").

If the father is at home, ask permission to enter and speak with him. Example:

> Missionary: Good morning. We're ministers and would like to speak with your husband. Is he in?
>
> Person: Yes, he is.
>
> Missionary: May we come in and speak with him?

If the father is not at home, express your regret and secure a return appointment. In such cases, explain that your message is vital and has a particular appeal to fathers. Then make an appointment to meet him together with the mother and the family at an appropriate time when he is at home.

Example:

> Person: I'm sorry, he's at work.
>
> Missionary: When will he be at home so that we can speak with him?
>
> Person: He'll be home at 7:30.
>
> Missionary: Fine. We'll come by around 8:00—or is there another time that will be more convenient for you?

Make the Father the Focal Point.

From the first moment you walk into a home, it is important that you focus your attention on the father. The majority of your comments, questions, and teaching should be directed at him. As you do this, he will be receptive to your message, and you will prepare him throughout the entire discussion to accept the responsibility as the head of his home to lead his family in prayer.

Example:

> Missionary: Mr. Jones, it's good to meet you. We suppose your wife told you that we came to see you this morning. We are happy, honored, and privileged to be in your home tonight because the message we have for your family is designed particularly for you and will have great appeal.
>
> How do you do, Mrs. Jones. It's nice to see you again.

2. Commit the Father to Lead His Family in Prayer on the Very First Visit.

Nothing will motivate a father to change his life more than prayer. When you get him to pray, you can expect some changes in his life. The question is: How do you get him to pray? Your success in having a man lead his family in prayer is dependent upon how you handle the first visit (e.g., discussion, family home evening). As you do the following, you will succeed in getting fathers to pray.

At the conclusion of the discussion, ask the father for permission to have prayer with him and his family.

Example:

Missionary: Mr. Jones, you've heard some unusual and some interesting things tonight, haven't you?

Father: Yes, I really have.

Missionary: You have heard us say several times that we know these things to be true. Is that right?

Father: Yes, that's what you said.

Missionary: Mr. Jones, this isn't private information. You, too, can know that what we have told you is absolutely true, but you have to find out exactly the same way we did. And that is through prayer. Would you object to our having prayer with you and your family before we leave your home this evening?

Father: No, I wouldn't object, I think it is a good idea.

(Note: You are not asking the father to pray; you are asking permission to pray with his family.)

Obviously, you do not expect him to object to having prayer. You have just presented an effective family home evening or taught a discussion to the family, and the father and other members of the family will be on a high spiritual level and receptive to the suggestion of family prayer.

Once the father agrees to your having prayer with his family, explain that sometimes there is a little reluctance to offer vocal prayer simply because it is new. Let him know that you can understand this, but that, nevertheless, the Lord expects families to kneel in prayer.

Example:

Missionary: Mr. Jones, we realize that it is natural for people to be a little reluctant to pray vocally because it is a new experience, but the Lord expects families to kneel in prayer together often.

As missionaries, you must realize that there are many people in the world who are not accustomed to praying vocally because, in many cases, they don't know how.

Teach the father the elements of prayer.

Example:

Missionary: Mr. Jones, the scriptures teach us a very simple and beautiful way to approach our Heavenly Father in prayer. There are basically four steps.

1. Since we are talking to our Heavenly Father, we begin by saying, "Our Heavenly Father" or "Our Father in Heaven."

2. Next, we thank him for our blessings. What are some of the things you are grateful for, Mr. Jones?

Father: Response.

3. Missionary: We then ask him for what we need most. You mentioned you wanted to ask our Heavenly Father (repeat what he wanted to ask). Is that right?

Father: Response.

4. Missionary: We always pray in the name of Jesus Christ; therefore, at the end of the prayer we say, "In the name of Jesus Christ, Amen." Why do you think we pray in the name of Jesus Christ, Mr. Jones?

Father: Response.

Commit the father to pray. It is critical that you commit the father to pray at the conclusion of the visit. There is a proper way to lead the father to pray, and it must be accomplished.

If the father is reluctant to pray, use the principles of getting commitments until he eventually agrees to offer the prayer. (Note: It is important that you not only use the techniques for getting commitments, but that you apply the principles of love, faith, discernment, and boldness.)

Fathers will pray when you follow the steps correctly. Some fathers may say that they will offer the prayer next time. The possibility of there being a next time is minimal. If you fail to commit the father to pray on this first visit, you will probably never have an opportunity to baptize him. You should therefore resolve to be bold in committing the father to pray at the conclusion of your first visit.

Example:

Missionary: Mr. Jones, we want you to know that our Heavenly Father loves you and it is his desire that you pray about the things we've discussed this evening. Will you kneel with us and offer a prayer?

Father: I'd rather not; I've never prayed before.

Missionary: Mr. Jones, I can understand why you would feel uncomfortable praying. I know I'd probably feel the same way if I'd never prayed before. Our Heavenly Father understands how difficult it is, but he still wants you to pray. He'll help you and sustain you as you offer the prayer this evening. As you pray, your children will be able to follow your example in the future, and, as a family, you will receive the guidance and blessings of our Heavenly Father in your daily lives. Will you kneel with us now and offer the prayer?

Father: Yes, I will.

Once the father has agreed to offer the prayer, help him briefly review the steps of prayer.

Example:

Missionary: Mr. Jones, would you briefly review for us the four steps to prayer that we just talked about?

Father: Yes, I will. (He lists the four steps.)

Once you have reviewed the steps of prayer, kneel down in front of the family and invite them to kneel with you.

At this point, the father is ready to pray. His family is kneeling, the missionaries are kneeling, and everyone is ready for the prayer. Fold your arms and bow your head. As you do it properly, the father will lead his family in prayer.

Exercise faith that the father will pray. Your faith will have a major influence at this critical point. Through mental exertion throughout the day before you meet with the family, conditioned upon your dedication as a missionary, you can invoke the Spirit of the Lord to sustain the father as he prays and touch the hearts of the entire family.

3. After the prayer, compliment the father on the prayer he offered and express your personal feelings for the family (e.g., love, appreciation).

Example:

Missionary: Brother Jones, do you mean to tell me that was your first vocal prayer?

Father: Yes.

Missionary: Well, that was a marvelous prayer, and the Lord heard it and will answer it. We really appreciate the privilege of coming into your home and sharing our message with you. You have a special family. As a result of our discussion with you and your family this evening, we have developed a real love for all of you.

If you consistently follow these guidelines in your efforts to get the father to pray, you will be able to say, as Elder Gene R. Cook has said:

I would tell you that I don't know how many brethren I've ... [committed to pray]. I guess that it would be in the thousands, but I have never had one single man, not one time, who would not kneel down and pray with me in a discussion.... I bear my testimony that as a man approaches it in a refined manner with the spirit of the Lord, in humility, that another man will kneel down and pray. (Mission President's Seminar)

4. Testify, using the principles of testimony found in this section.

As you approach the father in this manner with the Spirit of the Lord, with proper humility and sufficient faith, the father and family will be spiritually prepared for your testimony. As you bear personal testimony of the specific things you have talked about in your discussion, the Holy

Ghost will testify to their hearts.

5. *Commit the father and the other members of the family to make the things you've taught a matter of personal prayer.*

In subsequent visits, consistently direct your message to the father and systematically commit him to (1) pray with his family daily, (2) teach his children to pray vocally, (3) have a blessing on the food at each meal, and (4) pray for special occasions as a family (e.g., when a family member leaves on a trip; when there is a death, birth, or emergency in the family; when the father is considering a change of employment; when a child in the family has a special need).

As you perfect your performance in directing your message to the father, you will be making one of the most significant steps in teaching an entire family the message of the restoration, and you will baptize many more families.

Throughout your mission, ask yourself the following questions:

1. As I work at finding people to teach, am I making every effort to find fathers?

2. As I teach, do I direct the majority of my questions and teaching toward the father?

3. Am I resolved to commit fathers to pray after the first presentation?

4. In the process of committing the father to pray, do I exercise the faith sufficient to invoke the Spirit of the Lord to sustain him as he prays and touch the hearts of the entire family?

Chapter 31

Make Effective Use of Your Testimony

There is a right and a wrong way to present gospel truths, and it is important that you present them the right way. As a result of your previous life-orientation, your natural tendency is probably to cite facts or evidence in an attempt to get someone to accept your point of view. We use this method of persuasion when we talk about cars, sports, politics, scientific facts, and the like. Yet it is not effective when you are teaching the gospel. Citing facts as evidence does not convert people. A person must provide his own evidence that the gospel is true, and this evidence comes only as he lives it—as he experiments upon the Savior's words to see if it is true. (Read Alma 32:27-28.)

> If any man will do his will, he shall know of the doctrine, whether it be of God, or whether I speak of myself. (John 7:17.)

Your responsibility as a missionary is to get people to study and pray about the message of the restored gospel, not to prove that it is true.

Use Facts and Evidence Wisely

Once a person is converted, facts and evidence can be very appealing. As a result, when missionaries hear such support for gospel truths, they find it very persuasive and are prone to think nonmembers will respond in the same way. However, you must realize that facts and evidences are too often counterproductive when you are teaching investigators who are not converted. When you cite facts to convince people that the gospel is true, it puts the burden of proof on you. Consequently, the investigator will not realize his responsibility to pray about your message. As a missionary, you should talk about (1) how people can know the gospel is true and (2) the *fruits* of the gospel—what the gospel will do for the people—not the *proofs* of the gospel.

> Evidence may be collected to fill a library, but there will never be a real convert to the Church who will get his knowledge of the truth by any source other than the witness of the Spirit. (Willard A. Ashton.)

You must understand that you have no obligation to "prove" the gospel to be true. The Lord has sent you forth to *declare* the gospel, *not* to *prove* it. People are converted and convinced by the witness of the Spirit, not by facts. (Read D&C 100:7-8.) Hence, you must learn to trust the power of your testimony and the Holy Spirit to convert people.

Teach with the Spirit

In order to teach with testimony, you must have the Spirit of the Lord with you.

> Men are not converted by eloquence or oratory; they are convinced when they are satisfied that you have the truth and the Spirit of God. (Joseph F. Smith, *Gospel Doctrine*, p. 357.)

Unless you are consistently complying with the laws and principles that govern the Spirit, you will not be blessed with the Spirit. The Spirit of God cannot be feigned. You cannot invoke it by changing the tone of your voice or by being affected in your mannerisms or speech. If you are teaching with the Spirit, you will speak and act naturally. You will feel comfortable in using your regular vocabulary, with the exception of slang.

> In the mission field, as in our daily lives, it is best to be natural, rational—neither given to exaggeration of spiritual gifts nor to destructive affectation in act or language. It is best to develop simplicity of speech, earnestness of manner, humility of spirit, and a feeling of love for our fellows, thereby cultivating that well-balanced common sense in our lives that shall command the respect and admiration of the honest in heart, and insure the continual presence and aid of the Spirit of God. (Joseph F. Smith, *Gospel Doctrine*, p. 360.)

Some people are sufficiently in tune with the Spirit of the Lord that they will discern the truthfulness of the gospel even if you do not have the Spirit. And, in some instances, you may teach people who are basically converted before you give them the discussions. However, many honest people will not respond to the message of the restored gospel unless your testimony is conveyed to their hearts by the power of the Holy Ghost. Hence, it is essential that you qualify for the Spirit and understand that the power and influence of the Holy Spirit are real. (Read 2 Nephi 33:1; D&C 5:16; 6:14-16, 22-24; 8:2; 9:8, 9.)

When you have the Spirit of God, you will speak with power and authority, and the Spirit will bear witness to people that you are speaking the truth. Unless you have felt the witness of the Spirit when someone was speaking, you will have difficulty understanding how it bears witness to "the hearts of the children of men." Following are examples of how the Spirit bears witness:

> Now when they heard this, they were pricked in their heart, and said unto Peter and to the rest of the apostles, Men and brethren, what shall we do? (Acts 2:37.)

> And they said one to another, Did not our heart burn within us, while he talked with us by the way, and while he opened to us the scriptures? (Luke 24:32.)

When you are teaching with the Holy Spirit *a witness of the Spirit will be borne to everyone you talk to.* (D&C 100:8.) How they respond to this witness will be dependent on many factors. But "it will be just as well with you, as though all men embraced the gospel." (*History of the Church,* 1:468-469.) In other words, it is your responsibility to be living in righteousness so that the Spirit can bear witness through you of the truthfulness of your message. Your faith coupled with the Spirit can cause the truthfulness of the gospel to be revealed with power to the heart of an investigator, but he, once he has experienced this witness of the spirit, must then exercise his free agency to accept or reject the Savior of the world and his gospel. (Read 1 Nephi 17:45; 2 Nephi 33:1,2; Alma 12:9-11.)

Principles for Teaching with Testimony

As you give a family a discussion, you will have numerous opportunities to teach with testimony. There is more to teaching with testimony than merely saying you know the Church is true. Brief interjections of testimony that you make during a discussion are a major determinant in whether or not the family joins the Church. So you need to become skillful in what you say when you interject your testimony during a discussion. The following suggestions will help you make effective use of your testimony.

1. Personalize Your Testimony

The power of your testimony will be greatly enhanced if it is personalized. You can personalize your testimony in various ways.

a. Express your love for God and the Savior of the world.

Example:

"I'm grateful for the knowledge I have that God is literally my Father in Heaven. As he has answered my prayers, and as I have read and pondered his counsel contained in the scriptures, I have gained a great love for him. I want you to know that I love my Heavenly Father with all my heart, and because of my love for Him and the Savior, I'm here bringing the message of the restoration into your home.

b. Explain how the particular aspects of the gospel that you are presenting have helped you individually.

Example:

"I know in my own life that if I hadn't had a testimony of the importance of keeping the Sabbath day holy, I would not have the understanding of the scriptures that I now have. As I have attended Sunday School and Sacrament Meeting, and have participated in other Sunday functions, I have gained a testimony and an understanding of those things we have been teaching you."

c. Express your gratitude.

In your expression of gratitude you should explain how your life is fuller and richer as a result of the gospel. Don't be inhibited in expressing your feelings about the gospel, your parents, the family you are teaching. Your feelings are an integral part of your testimony.

d. Discuss the steps you took or experiences you had that resulted in your conviction of a particular truth or principle.

Example:

"I have a sure knowledge that the Savior lives. He gave his life in order that you and I might have the privilege of repenting of our weaknesses and return to the presence of our Heavenly Father. I also know that he is the head of the Church of Jesus Christ of Latter-day Saints. I have obtained this knowledge through prayerfully reading *The Book of Mormon,* keeping his commandments, and listening to his special witnesses testify of his divinity."

e. Discuss in detail what you experienced when you received your personal conviction of a particular truth or principle, and what you have felt or experienced through a witness of the Spirit.

And this is not all. Do ye not suppose that I know of these things myself? Behold, I testify unto you that I do know that these things whereof I have spoken are true. And how do ye suppose that I know of their surety?

Behold, I say unto you they are made known unto me by the Holy Spirit of God. Behold, I have fasted and prayed many days that I might know these things of myself. And now I do know of myself that they are true; for the Lord God hath made them manifest unto me by his Holy Spirit; and this is the spirit of revelation which is in me. (Alma 5:45,46.)

f. As you talk about things you did and experienced in the process of acquiring your testimony of a particular point, be as specific as possible.

Example:

Missionary: I know that Spencer W. Kimball is a prophet of God. When he was called to be the Lord's prophet, I listened to him speak and while he was speaking the spirit of the Holy Ghost bore witness to my heart that he was truly a prophet of God. Every time I have heard him speak since, that knowledge has been strengthened by that same warm, peaceful feeling you've felt during our discussions.

g. Help those you teach see the parallel between the way people responded to truth anciently and the way people respond today to the truths you are teaching.

As you draw the parallel, help them also realize that only the honest in heart responded to the truths taught by the Savior, his apostles, and prophets anciently, and in like manner, only the honest in heart respond positively to the particular message you are teaching.

Example:

Missionary: Mr. Taylor, I want you to know that I know that God speaks to a prophet today just as he spoke to prophets anciently. When the Lord called Noah to be a prophet, the people rejected him. They failed to listen to his message. They didn't sense the importance of sincerely attempting to find out if he was a prophet. Throughout history, only the honest in heart have recognized the Lord's prophets. The same is true today. Only the honest in heart recognize that Spencer W. Kimball is a prophet. I know that there is a prophet living today. He is just as much a prophet as Noah, Moses, or Abraham.

Whenever your investigators respond positively to a truth you are teaching, commend them for being honest in heart and help them identify with the honest in heart who responded to the Savior's message.

Example:

Missionary: Are you sincere in wanting to follow the Savior?

Bro. Harris: Yes, I am.

Missionary: Do you feel that a person can truly follow the Savior without keeping His commandments?

Bro. Harris: No, I don't.

Missionary: Your answer demonstrates to us that you are genuine in your desire to follow the Savior. During his ministry there were many who wanted to follow him without keeping his commandments. There was the rich man who asked him what he needed to do to enter the kingdom of God. When the Savior finally told him to sell all he had and give it to the poor, he couldn't do it. Only the honest in heart truly followed the Savior by keeping his commandments. If you had lived back then, you would have been one of the few who truly followed the Savior. We're grateful for being able to teach the fullness of the gospel to someone like you.

2. If people you teach are prone to request proof or evidence, tell them there is nothing you can do or say to prove the truths you are declaring.

Bear your testimony and explain to them that if they will study and earnestly pray to their Father in Heaven for inspiration and understanding, the truthfulness of your message will be manifested to them by the Spirit.

Example:

Mr. Jones: How can you prove that Joseph Smith saw the Father and the Son?

Missionary: Mr. Jones, there is nothing I can do to prove to you that Joseph saw the Father and Son, but I promise you in the name of the Lord Jesus Christ, as you read the story of Joseph Smith and then ask the Lord in earnest prayer if the story is true, the Lord will reveal to your heart that the story is true. Will you put our claim to this test?

Mr. Jones: Yes, I will.

Missionary: I want you to know, Mr. Jones, that I applied the same test, and the Lord revealed to my heart through the power of the Holy Ghost that his claim of seeing the Father and the Son is a true account. I know it to be true beyond a shadow of a doubt.

3. Help the people you teach realize that the only way they can know the truthfulness of your message is by the witness of the Holy Ghost.

As you teach people the gospel you have the responsibility of helping them realize that they cannot rely on their physical senses (i.e., sight, hearing, touch) for a testimony because they are vulnerable to deception. It is absolutely essential that people understand that if it were not for the witness of the Spirit, they could not know that the Bible is the word of God, or that God lives or that Jesus is the Christ, or that there is life after death, or any other spiritual truth.

Example:

Missionary: Tonight we've taught you some important truths. We've taught you that our Heavenly Father has called a living prophet to guide and teach us today. We've discussed the *Book of Mormon* and the need for Priesthood authority. I know that these things are true. The only way you can know the truthfulness of these things is by the witness of the Holy Ghost. It is by the witness of the spirit that you know that God lives, that Jesus is the Christ, that the Bible is the word of God. In like manner, the only way you can know that the things we are teaching you are true is by that same witness.

As a missionary you should be able to bear testimony of each of the points of doctrine covered in the discussions. In addition, you can testify of things other than gospel doctrine. For example, you can express your conviction that God loves the family, that it is God's desire to bless the family. You can make use of your testimony by expressing your conviction that your investigators will receive specific blessings as they comply with gospel truths.

Examples:

> Missionary: I know that as you consistently read the Book of Mormon and pray regarding its validity, God will reveal the truthfulness of the book to your heart. I know for an absolute certainty that as you comply with the principle of tithing, the Lord will honor his promise and you will be prospered in many ways that you presently cannot understand. I know without any reservation that as you live the Word of Wisdom, the promises specified in the Doctrine and Covenants will be fulfilled in your life.

Obtain and Strengthen Your Own Testimony

As a missionary you have the responsibility of doing all you can to obtain a testimony of those truths you teach people. It is important that you realize that people you teach are discerning. If you were to testify of a principle or truth of the gospel without a testimony of it, your words would not touch their hearts. President Joseph F. Smith said that "a testimony of the truth is more than a mere assent of the mind, it is a conviction of the heart, a knowledge that fills the whole soul of its recipient." (*Gospel Doctrine*, p. 364.) As you develop this type of testimony of the things you teach, you will be able to testify using the principles discussed previously and convince people of the truthfulness of your message.

The power of testimony is a tremendous tool and it is essential that you learn to use it effectively as a missionary. As you do so, you will make yourself believed, and you will convert people to the gospel of Jesus Christ. You should learn to be bold in the use of your testimony. As you read scripture, you should make it a point to analyze the various ways that missionaries of old have used the power of testimony in their proselyting endeavors.

When you make effective use of your testimony, you leave people without excuse if they do not accept the gospel of Jesus Christ. If you fail in this regard, as was declared by Jacob, the blood and sins of the people you teach will be on your head. You do not discharge your responsibility by merely presenting a discussion. Your responsibility has not been discharged unless you have borne solemn witness of the truthfulness of the gospel of Jesus Christ and had that witness confirmed by the witness of the Spirit. When people fail to accept the gospel of Jesus Christ, one of two things will happen on judgment day: either you will be indicted for your failure to teach with testimony, or your testimony will stand as a witness against the people who rejected your witness.

There are two ways that you can generally determine whether you are teaching with the Spirit. First, the people will understand what you are saying, and, second, even if people do not accept your message, they will be subdued and will not be inclined to be argumentative.

Throughout your mission you should ask yourself the following questions:

1. Am I guilty of attempting to cite facts or evidence in attempting to get someone to accept the truths we're teaching?

2. Am I doing all I can to get people to study and pray about the message of the restored gospel?

3. As a missionary, do I teach people the ways they can come to know that the gospel is true?

4. As a missionary, do I continually let people know what the gospel will do for them?

5. Do I trust the power of my testimony and the Holy Spirit to convert people?

6. Do I have the Spirit of the Lord with me?

7. Am I consistently complying with the laws and principles that govern the Spirit?

8. As I testify, do I speak and act naturally?

9. Am I ever guilty of attempting to feign the Spirit by changing the tone of my voice?

10. Am I exercising the faith necessary to allow the truthfulness of the gospel to be revealed with power to the hearts of those I teach?

11. Am I able to genuinely bear testimony of each of the points of doctrine and gospel principles covered in the discussions?

12. Am I bold in the use of my testimony?

13. As I read the scriptures, do I analyze the various ways that the missionaries of old used the power of testimony in their proselyting endeavors?

14. Do I continually evaluate each teaching situation to determine whether or not I was successful in teaching with the Spirit?

Chapter 32

Follow the Savior's Example

President Joseph F. Smith admonished missionaries to teach as nearly as they can after the manner of the Master. (*Gospel Doctrine*, p. 364.) In order to do this, you must become very conversant with the life and ministry of the Savior. As you do, you will see where his ministry provides specific guidelines for teaching the gospel.

Even though a substantial part of the Savior's message to the Nephites was a verbatim presentation, inspiration and discernment played a very important role in his missionary labors with the Nephites. You likewise will be effective in getting people to believe your message when inspiration and discernment determine to a great extent what you say when you are meeting with a family. This will require that you not only become skilled in presenting the discussions, but also become skilled in handling the other activities that should occur when you meet with the family.

As you begin to meet with people, it will become very obvious that presenting the formal discussion (the part of your message that is memorized, presented on a tape, or read) only constitutes a part of your total presentation. As was explained in the introduction to this section, when you meet with a family your presentation will consist of various activities, not just merely reciting memorized dialogue.

This chapter will discuss various activities that are involved when you make a presentation. If these activities are consistently covered under inspiration each time you meet with a family, you will be much more effective in getting people to believe your message.

Prepare the Family for the Discussion

What you say to prepare a family for a discussion is not a memorized dialogue; however, it should be prayerfully thought out in advance and be adapted to the particular family. What you say will be influenced by several things: the number of times you have met with the family, how they have responded to the message of the restored gospel, the questions they ask, etc.

Inspiration is the key. You will qualify for this inspiration if you are obedient and dedicated and then train yourself to focus your mind frequently on the investigating family before you meet with them to present a discussion. Learn to focus your mind specifically on what to say to them and then rehearse it several times in your mind. By the time you arrive at the home, you should know what you plan to say to prepare the family to be taught. However, your preplanning should not be so rigid that you become insensitive to inspiration as you meet with them.

In most instances the following points should be covered:

1. *Show a genuine interest in the family.* This can be accomplished by asking various members of the family questions about their interests, activities, achievements, etc.

2. *Express gratitude for the opportunity to meet with the family.*

   Example:

   "Mr. Brown, it is a pleasure for us to meet with you and your family. We are grateful for this opportunity."

3. *Compliment the family.* The Savior repeatedly commended the Nephites.

   Example:

   "Mr. Jones, it is refreshing to meet a family as wholesome and good as yours—we want to commend you. Your children are a real tribute to you and your wife."

4. *Each time you meet with a family, express your personal conviction of the following:*

   —that God lives,

   —that Jesus is the Christ,

   —that the gospel of Jesus Christ has been restored to the earth.

Each time you meet with a family, you should discuss God's love and desires for the family.

Example:

> "Mr. Brown, God loves you and your family. He is pleased with your effort to live righteously. It is God's desire that you enjoy all of the blessings that come to those who are a part of his Church and kingdom."

5. *Frequently promise your investigators that God will reveal to them that your message is true.*

   Note: Chapter 33 in this section provides specific guidelines in how to do this.

Express your dependence on the Spirit and request permission to have your companion offer an opening prayer, or have the father pray if he has prayed with you several times previously.

Example:

> "As we meet with you, we sense very keenly our dependence on the Spirit of the Lord. We have found that without His Spirit we cannot convey an understanding of the beautiful truths we desire to share with you. If it meets with your approval, I'd like to ask my companion to offer an opening prayer. Would that be permissible, Mr. Brown?"

As a general rule, you should take no more than five minutes to prepare the family for the discussion.

Follow Up On Commitments

You follow up on previous commitments each time you meet with a family after the first discussion. Basic to the conversion process is the willingness of members of the family to pray, read, etc. For this reason, at the conclusion of every discussion, you commit them to do specific things. Follow-up is very critical to the committing process. It is essential on subsequent visits that you ask the family if they carried out their commitments. (Note: Maintain a careful record of the things the family members have agreed to do. Otherwise, you will not be able to remember what was agreed upon.)

Introduce the Discussion

What you say to introduce a discussion is not memorized. The purpose of what you say is threefold:

1. To create a desire in the family to know more about the restored gospel of Jesus Christ.

2. To make them aware that, as a result of modern-day revelation, basic doctrines taught by Jesus Christ have been revealed in their fullness once again.

3. To determine whether the family is ready to receive the discussion.

   In most instances you should talk about God's desire for his children to know and accept truth and should ask questions to assess your investigator's reaction to concepts you have introduced previously.

Example:

Missionary: The Spirit of God prompts men's desire to know where they come from. Mr. Brown, have you ever had a desire to know where you came from?

Mr. Brown: Yes.

Missionary: Because God has always wanted his children to know where they came from, he has revealed basic truths about our origins through prophets. When the Savior was on the earth, he taught his disciples that they lived with God as spirits before they were born into this world. Evidence of this basic truth is found in the New Testament. (Read and discuss the following scriptures: Hebrews 12:9; Acts 17:28,29; Job 38:7.)

Missionary: Do you believe you existed as a spirit prior to this mortal existence?

Mr. Brown: Yes, I do.

Missionary: Do you believe that God is the father of your spirit?

Mr. Brown: Yes.

Missionary: How does this knowledge help you understand why we refer to God as our Father in heaven?

Mr. Brown: Well, from these scriptures we learn that he is the Father of our spirits.

Missionary: Mr. Brown, if it were not for the witness of the Spirit, you could not know that God is the Father of your spirit. Your knowledge that God is literally your Father in Heaven has been revealed to you through the Spirit. We want you to know that we know with absolute certainty that God lives and is our Father and that we lived with him as premortal spirits prior to this earthly existence.

Mr. Brown, do you feel that the knowledge that God is literally the Father of your spirit is critical to your salvation?

Mr. Brown: Very definitely.

Missionary: Prior to modern-day revelation to the Prophet Joseph Smith this beautiful doctrine was lost to the world. I am personally grateful that God has seen fit to reveal many glorious truths in this day and age that enhance our ability to love and worship him.

For example, by appearing to Joseph Smith, God established that he was a glorified being with a body of flesh and bone. Prior to his appearance to Joseph Smith, the churches of the world taught that God was without body, parts, or passions. Obviously, knowing that God lives as a glorified person makes it much easier to approach him in prayer. This knowledge is basic to an understanding of the purpose of this life.

This evening we want to share with you and your family a beautiful message regarding the purpose of this life. This message will help you understand even more fully your relationship with your Father in Heaven.

If the family is ready to receive the discussion, give it. If not, follow the direction of the Spirit in determining how to proceed. In most instances you should seek to learn what reservations the family has and try to overcome them. However, in some situations you will be prompted to challenge the family to read and pray before your next visit instead of having the discussion. You have the responsibility to live so you can be inspired in what you say if you feel that a family is not ready for the message.

Present the Discussion

If the family is ready to receive a discussion, present it. It will probably be a verbatim presentation, such as a taped message, reading a specific message with the family, a flipchart presentation, a filmstrip, or a dialogue you have memorized. This kind of presentation will insure that the basic doctrines of the Church are presented in a uniform way. Throughout the discussion, each missionary should bear his personal testimony of the doctrines and principles introduced, with particular emphasis on how he gained his conviction of their truthfulness, and how they have influenced his life.

Assess the Family's Response to Your Message

As you are presenting a discussion, you have the responsibility to assess the family's reponse to your message. Chapter 34 provides specific guidelines for assessing a family's response to your message, and Chapter 35 provides you guidelines in dealing with questions investigators ask.

Stress Modern-Day Revelation

You have the responsibility to remind people consistently that your message is from God and was revealed through a modern-day prophet. Continually express your gratitude and appreciation to the Lord for revealing the gospel of Jesus Christ. By the time you have the family ready to be baptized, they should be expressing their gratitude and appreciation when they pray to the Lord for restoring the gospel through Joseph Smith. Chapters 36 and 40 provide specific guidelines on how to carry out your responsibility of stressing modern-day revelation. You are expected to be conversant with the scriptures introduced in Chapter 36 so that you will be able to refer to them as you tie everything you teach to modern-day revelation.

Help the Family Understand the Workings of the Spirit.

When you are teaching a family the gospel, the Spirit will be manifest on many occasions. You have the responsibility to help the family recognize and understand the workings of the Spirit. Chapter 33 provides specific guidelines in how this is accomplished.

Commit the Family

As you teach a family, you should commit them to all of the things specified for the discussion (e.g., praying as a family, reading and studying the scriptures, attending church, repenting) and promise them specific blessings if they do what you ask them to do. As the need arises, you should carefully teach them how to fast, pray, pay tithing, keep the Word of Wisdom, and otherwise live the gospel. Do *not* assume they have a clear understanding of concepts like morality, keeping the Sabbath day holy, and the like. You have the responsibility to teach them carefully how to comply with the Lord's commandments.

In most instances, you should commit the father before you commit the other members of the family. Chapter 37 provides guidelines to follow when you are committing your investigators.

Summarize Your Message

Always provide the family a summary in writing of what has been covered, including scriptures cited and other related scriptures. Reading assignments and commitments should also be written out. A commitment is strengthened when it is reduced to writing. Some parts of this summary can be prepared before you meet with the family and then can be finalized by one of the missionaries while you are meeting with the family. Before you leave you should commit the family to prayerfully review the summary of the discussion and read all the scriptural references.

Discuss Membership in the Kingdom of God

Each time you meet with a family you should follow the guidelines in Chapter 38 and consistently discuss the blessings that come from membership in the Savior's true church.

Commend and Compliment Your Investigators

As you are teaching people the gospel, it is important to commend people for their ability to understand the gospel of Jesus Christ, repent, pray, exercise faith, etc. In addition, you should consistently commend the people for other achievements (their pretty flower garden, close family unity), and character traits (honesty, thoughtfulness). You should always strive to see the good in the people you teach and express your confidence that they can live up to the Lord's expectation of those who join his Church. Chapter 40 provides specific guidelines for expressing love and appreciation to your investigators.

Bless the Family

Once you are successful in getting the father and the other members of the family to pray at the conclusion of a discussion, you should then request that you be allowed to bless the family. In many ways, people are more receptive to what is said or taught in a prayer than in a direct conversation: " ... their hearts were open and they did understand in their hearts the words which He prayed." (3 Nephi 19:22.) Chapter 39 provides specific guidelines for blessing your investigators.

Following this blessing of the family, you should shake the father's hand and express your feelings (appreciation and love) for the family. Generally, this is the ideal time to make arrangements to meet with the family again.

Obtain Referrals

After an investigator family has caught the spirit of the message of the restored gospel, use the guidelines provided in Chapter 24 to obtain referrals from them.

Summary

A review of the Savior's ministry among the Nephites shows these basic activities discussed in this chapter that should be considered when you meet with your investigators which are evidenced in his ministry.

1. The Savior bore his testimony to the Nephites. (See 3 Nephi 11:35.)

2. The Savior tied his message to God the Eternal Father. (See 3 Nephi 15:15-19 and 16:3.)

3. The Savior promised the Nephites that God would reveal to them that his message was true. (See 3 Nephi 11:32-36.)

4. The Savior asked the Nephites if they had any questions regarding his message. (See 3 Nephi 17:1-9.)

5. The Savior provided the Nephites the "big picture" so that they could see how their dispensation tied in to all other dispensations. (See 3 Nephi 26:1-5.)

6. Even though Jesus was the Savior of the world, he taught the Nephites from the scriptures. (See 3 Nephi 23:6.)

7. Jesus committed the Nephites to study the scriptures and promised them they would find evidence of the things he had taught them. (See 3 Nephi 23:1-5.)

8. The Savior stressed the need for modern-day revelation. (See 3 Nephi 23:6-14; 24:25.)

9. The Savior helped the Nephites understand the workings of the

spirit. (See 3 Nephi 17:5, 15, 17; 19:13-15, 25, 33.)

10. The Savior committed the Nephites to do various things—i.e. to ponder and pray about his message: (see 3 Nephi 17:3), to fast (3 Nephi 13:16-18), to read the scriptures (3 Nephi 23:1, 5), to pray as a family (3 Nephi 18:18-21)— and he consistently promised the people specific blessings if they were willing to embrace the gospel of Jesus Christ. (3 Nephi 11:21, 33; 18:11.) Also he carefully taught them how to fast and pray *before* he committed them to do it.

11. The Savior committed the Nephites to maintain a record of his teachings (write the things which I have told you), and review them (give heed) often. (See 3 Nephi 23:4.)

12. When the Savior was teaching the Nephites, he repeatedly talked about baptism. He stressed the following points: 3 Nephi 11:21, 22, the necessity of authority; 3 Nephi 11:20-26, proper manner; 3 Nephi 11:38, requirement for salvation; 3 Nephi 11:37, qualifications.

13. The Savior frequently made reference to the Nephites' membership in his church and talked about the blessings and opportunities they would enjoy as members. (For example, he promised them that they would be the recipients of the gift of the Holy Ghost following their baptism (3 Nephi 11:35; 12:1) and that the devil would not have power over them (3 Nephi 8:11).

14. The Savior prayed for the Nephites and blessed them. After he had blessed the sick, lame, blind, dumb, and afflicted in any manner among them, he offered a special blessing in their behalf. (See 3 Nephi 17:13-17 and 3 Nephi 19:25-34.) He even wept for them because of his great love and compassion for them. (See 3 Nephi 17:20, 21.) He blessed their children. (See 3 Nephi 17:21-24.) The Savior consistently offered personal prayers in behalf of the people. His prayers were not general or repetitious. His prayers in behalf of the people impressed them as much as anything he did.

15. The Savior consistently commended the Nephites regarding their faith, etc. The following are examples:

> I see that your faith is sufficient that I should heal you. (3 Nephi 17:8.)

> Blessed are ye because of your faith. (3 Nephi 17:20.)

> And it came to pass that when Jesus had made an end of praying, he came again to the disciples and said unto them:

> So great faith have I never seen among all the Jews; wherefore I could not show unto them so great miracles, because of their unbelief. Verily I say unto you, there are none of them that have seen so great things as you have seen; neither have they heard so great things as ye have heard. (3 Nephi 9:35, 36.)

And now, behold, my joy is great even unto fullness, because of you, and also this generation; yea, and even the Father rejoiceth and also the holy angels, because of you and this generation; for none of them are lost. (3 Nephi 27:30.)

16. When the Savior was teaching the Nephites, he committed them to pray for people who had not accepted the gospel, to teach others the things he had taught them, and in their association with non-members, to do things they had seen him do. (See 3 Nephi 18:22-25; 23:14.) The people the Savior had been teaching were so impressed with what they had experienced that after he ascended to heaven, they labored exceedingly all night to tell other people about their experience with Jesus and to encourage them to be there the following day so that they could see him. (See 4 Nephi 19:1, 3.) Consequently, the Savior was able to teach many more people the gospel.

General Instructions

The expression of testimony should occur at appropriate times throughout the presentation. You will find you can make use of your testimony in conjunction with every activity discussed in this chapter. Testimony is especially important when you are preparing a family for a discussion, presenting a discussion, assessing understanding, responding to questions, and committing your investigators. Without doubt, effective use of your testimony will prompt people to accept your message more than anything else. You should make it a policy to analyze every presentation you make to determine if you made use of your testimony as you handle the various activities discussed in this chapter.

In addition to presenting the regular discussions, you need to become insightful in what you say when you call on the family between regular discussions (e.g., to remind them of church meetings and socials, to drop off something for them to read, to invite them to participate in a home evening with a member of the ward, or to conduct a home evening with the investigator family.)

Frequent contact with your investigators is one of the keys to conversion. You should conscientiously seek inspiration regarding what you say and what you do when you call on a family between the regular discussions.

Do not assume your investigators understand everything you have taught them even if they are converted. If possible present the discussions again after people are baptized. As you do, make every effort to get them to explain the principles and doctrines in their own words and to express their convictions.

As you go through the discussions again, commit them to do

additional reading in the *Book of Mormon, A Marvelous Work and A Wonder*, and *The Articles of Faith.* If the family has children over eight years of age, as you go through the discussions the second time, adapt them to the children and direct your questions to the children.

Throughout your mission ask yourself the following questions:

1. Am I doing all I can to follow the example of the Savior as I teach the gospel to others?

2. Do I maintain a careful record of the commitments my investigators make?

3. Am I living in such a way that I can be inspired in what I say if I feel that a family is not ready for the message?

4. Do I consistently remind people that my message is from God and was revealed through a modern-day prophet?

5. Do I assess my investigator's responses to the truths I teach?

6. Do I stress modern-day revelation when I teach?

7. Do I help those I teach understand the workings of the Spirit?

8. Do I commit my investigators to do those things which will result in their conversion?

9. Do I consistently discuss membership in the Kingdom of God when I teach?

10. Do I bless those I teach?

11. Do I express my love and appreciation for those I teach?

12. Am I effective in obtaining referrals from my investigators?

Chapter 33

Understand and Teach the Workings of the Spirit

As you teach people the gospel you have the responsibility to help them understand the workings of the Spirit. You do so by (1) explaining the witness of the Spirit, (2) explaining the role of the Spirit in revealing understanding of gospel truths, (3) helping them recognize the presence or absence of the Spirit, and (4) encouraging your investigators to express appreciation.

Explain the Witness of the Spirit

As you teach people the gospel, it is important that they understand that the witness of the Spirit is the Lord's way of letting them know something is true. People outside the Church generally do not have any conceptual understanding regarding the witness of the Spirit. You have the responsibility to systematically teach people that the witness of the Spirit is the way the Lord confirms that something is true, right, or good.

It is absolutely essential that your investigators understand that they cannot rely on their physical senses (sight, hearing, touch, taste, feel) or on their intellectual powers in determining if your message has been revealed from God. They must realize that God confirms or verifies all truth by means of the witness of the Spirit. Explain to them that if this means of knowing did not exist, there would be no way mortal men could know that God lives, that Jesus is the Christ, that there is life after death, that certain men are prophets of God, or that anything else you teach is true.

Generally you should cover the following points when you are teaching an investigator about the witness of the Spirit.

1. *Establish a need for the witness of the Spirit.*

Example:

Missionary: The New Testament teaches us a very critical concept regarding truth. Following the Savior's resurrection and ascension to heaven the disciples testified that the Savior had been resurrected and had visited them. In contrast, the Roman guards had been bribed to testify that the disciples of the Savior had taken the body from the tomb. Mr. Hill, if you were living at that time and heard those two conflicting testimonies, which story would appear more plausible?

Mr. Hill: The testimony that the body had been taken from the tomb.

Missionary: It was only by the witness of the Spirit that those who were assembled that day who were honest in heart received conviction that the testimony of the disciples was true.

2. *Refer to the Savior's promise that the Holy Ghost will testify of the things associated with him.*

Example:

Missionary: Mr. Hill, would you open your Bible to Acts 2 and read verse 37?

Mr. Hill: (Reads the verse.)

Missionary: When the Savior was on the earth, he promised that the Holy Ghost would testify of him. Mr. Hill, would you turn to John 14:26 and read that verse?

Mr. Hill: (Reads the verse.)

3. *Explain how a person can recognize the witness of the Spirit.*

Example:

Missionary: It is by means of the witness of the Spirit that we are able to determine if something is true that is claimed to be associated with the Savior of the world. Mr. Hill, we have been called by a living prophet and have been given the Lord's authority to teach you divine truths. We promise you that the Holy Ghost will reveal to your heart and mind that our message is true. The Spirit will reveal that the message we declare is, in fact, revealed of God. Mr. Hill, do you believe the Savior's promise that the Holy Ghost will testify of those things associated with him?

Mr. Hill: Yes, I do.

4. *Commit your investigators to rely on the witness of the Spirit to determine if your message is true.*

Example:

Missionary: Mr. Hill, as you are prayerful regarding our message and rely on the witness of the Spirit in determining its truthfulness, is there any way we could deceive you?

Mr. Hill: No, I don't think so.

Missionary: As we now proceed to teach you truths that have been restored through a living prophet in this day and age, we ask you to look into your own heart and mind in your effort to discern and feel whether our message is true. Then, most importantly, turn to your Father in Heaven in prayer asking him to confirm through the witness of the Spirit that our message is true. Will you do that?

Mr. Hill: Yes, I will.

In the following example the missionaries have been door-to-door contacting. They have gained entrance into a home. Mr. Hill has expressed an interest in knowing more about God speaking through a prophet today. The dialogue is an example of how they could help Mr. Hill understand the role of the Spirit as it relates to his knowing the truthfulness of their message. As you read this example, determine where they use the four points discussed previously.

Example:

Missionary: Mr. Hill, we appreciate the fact that you were not expecting us to stop by, so we will not take more than 20 minutes of your time.

As ministers of The Church of Jesus Christ of Latter-day Saints we are personal representatives of the Lord Jesus Christ. He has a special message for you and has sent us hundreds of miles to deliver it. We would like to invite our Heavenly Father's Spirit here today. Would it be all right if we had a word of prayer?

Mr. Hill: Response.

Missionary: Would it be all right if Elder Jones says the prayer?

2nd Missionary: (Says the prayer. In the prayer he asks for the Holy Ghost to bear witness. Also he pronounces a blessing of peace on the home. Luke 10:5-6.)

Missionary: Mr. Hill, do you have a Bible?

Mr. Hill: Response.

Missionary: We have been called by a living prophet and have been given the Lord's authority to teach these truths. The way that you can know that these things are true is by the power of the Holy Ghost. In your Bible (motions for him to hand him his Bible) the Lord tells us what the purpose of the Holy Ghost is (missionary turns to John 15:26). Will you please read verse 26?

Mr. Hill: (Reads verse 26.)

Missionary: Mr. Hill, do you know who the Comforter is? (If he is unsure, the missionary should read John 14:26.) Who does the Lord say the Comforter is?

Mr. Hill: The Holy Ghost.

Missionary: And what does the Lord say the Holy Ghost will do?

Mr. Hill: Testify of him. (Make certain that Mr. Hill understands that the Holy Ghost will testify of Jesus Christ.)

Missionary: The Holy Ghost bears witness to us that God lives and that Jesus Christ lives and is his Son. It is very important that you know how to recognize the witness of the Holy Ghost. The Lord has revealed the following explanation regarding how the Holy Ghost bears witness of the truth.

Yea, behold, I will tell you in your mind and in your heart, by the Holy Ghost, which shall come upon you and which shall dwell in your heart. (D&C 8:2.)

This is how the Holy Ghost operates, Mr. Hill, by impressions in the mind and feelings in the heart. Feelings will come to you like warmth and peace and will give you assurance. The feelings of confidence will come to you after you have the opportunity to study these things out in your mind. Then you'll gain faith—then a sure knowledge.

Mr. Hill, we can liken the Holy Ghost to the wind. We can feel the wind beat against us, but we can't see it. We can liken the Holy Ghost to the love that you have for your family. If I said, "Mr. Hill, show me the love that you have for your family—put it right here in my hands—you couldn't do it, could you? It's the same with Holy Ghost. We can feel it—it is a real thing, just as the wind is real, just as the love that you have for your family is real—but we can't see it. At one time William Shakespeare said, "To thine own self be true." What does this mean to you, Mr. Hill?

Mr. Hill: It means to be true to myself, to the feelings inside of me.

Missionary: That's right. Being true to ourselves means to accept truth as it is. Mr. and Mrs. Hill, today we would like you to be particularly sensitive to the feelings you have inside of you because this is the way the Holy Ghost communicates to you. Before we begin, let's go over one more thing about the Holy Ghost. The Lord has told us a sure way to recognize the Holy Ghost. (Missionary quotes D&C 9:7-9.)

Mr. Hill, as we deliver the message the Lord has sent us to deliver, study these things out in your mind and ask our Heavenly Father if these things are true. What does the Lord say will happen if they are true?

Mr. Hill: He says that we will have a good warm feeling, or a burning in our bosom.

(If the missionary feels so impressed, he may also bring in what the Lord said to Oliver Cowdery in section 6, verse 23, of the Doctrine and Covenants.

"Did I not speak peace unto your mind concerning the matter? What greater witness can you have than from God?")

Missionary: Mr. Hill, we are going to have a sacred experience today. (The missionary gives them portions of the first page of the first concept:" Throughout history whenever the Lord has had important truths to communicate to his children ... Joseph Smith, then still a young man was living in the state of New York.")

Now my companion is going to tell you what happened to Joseph Smith, written in Joseph Smith's own words. As he relates this story to you, ask yourself this one question: Is what he is saying true?

2nd Missionary: (Quotes the Joseph Smith story. "There was in the place...." The purpose of this visit is to deliver you this wonderful message and explain how you can know that it is true.)

Missionary: I, too, know that God has once again opened the heavens in our day and that he and his Son Jesus Christ appeared to Joseph Smith that beautiful spring morning. Now, Mr. Hill, I wasn't there in that grove of trees, but I know just as surely as I am sitting here that it happened.

(The missionary gives the second concept in detail to allow the investigator the opportunity to really feel the things that happened to Joseph Smith. "Mr. Hill, suppose you put yourself in the position.... As a result of this and similar other experiences you might write something like this:

"And now, after the many testimonies which have been given of him, this is the testimony, last of all, which we give of him: that he lives! For we saw him, even on the right hand of God; and we heard the voice bearing record that he is the Only Begotten of the Father. [D&C 76:22,23.]"

The missionary may feel impressed to have Mr. Hill read this.)

Mr. Hill, I testify to you in the name of Jesus Christ that the things which I just quoted to you are true. Joseph Smith did not say, "I am God," nor did he say, "I am Jesus Christ." He only stated that he wanted to add his testimony to all the other testimonies that have been given of Jesus Christ, such as the Bible and the words of the apostles. He knows that Christ lives because he saw him standing even on the right hand of the Father, and he heard the voice of the Father bearing record that he (Jesus Christ) was the Only Begotten of the Father.

2nd Missionary: Mr. Hill, I bear you my witness in the name of Jesus Christ that what you have just read is true. God the Father and Jesus Christ did visit the Prophet Joseph Smith. Mr. Hill, how do you feel in your heart right now?

Mr. Hill: Response.

2nd Missionary: (If there are any other members of the family in the room, ask them the same question.) Mr. Hill, do you know what these good feelings are?

Mr. Hill: The Holy Ghost. (Help Mr. Hill to recognize the Holy Ghost and its purpose—this recognition needs to be reinforced.)

2nd Missionary: Mr. Hill, have you ever had a salesman come to your door and try to sell you something?

Mr. Hill: Response.

2nd Missionary: What type of feeling did you have?

Mr. Hill: I wanted to get rid of him.

2nd Missionary: Do you have that feeling now?

Mr. Hill: No

2nd Missionary: Why?

Mr. Hill: Because the Holy Ghost is here.

2nd Missionary: Mr. Hill, why do you feel the Lord has sent the Holy Ghost to your home today?

Mr. Hill: To let me know that these things are true.

2nd Missionary: And what do you feel the Lord wants you to do?

Mr. Hill: To learn more about these things.

2nd Missionary: Mr. Hill, if you come to know that these things are true, would you become a member of the Lord's church (by being baptized)?

Mr. Hill: Sure, if I come to know that they are true.

2nd Missionary: I testify in the name of Jesus Christ that the feeling that you are feeling right now is the power of the Holy Ghost bearing witness to your soul that the things that we are sharing with you are true.

Missionary: Mr. Hill, the Lord gives us a special promise that when we bear testimony in his name, the Holy Ghost is shed forth. I know that the Spirit of the Lord is here today. It really feels good, doesn't it? Mr. Hill, what was the question that Joseph Smith asked when he went into the grove of trees to pray? What did he want to know?

Mr. Hill: Response.

Missionary: Answering his question, the Lord told Joseph Smith to join none of the churches, and he explained why. He said that they all had a form of godliness, but they taught the doctrines of men and were not of God. The Savior told Joseph Smith that the church he had established in the meridian of time was not on the earth. (At this point the missionary explains the apostasy to the degree that he feels is necessary.)

Mr. Hill, how does this help you to understand why the churches today teach so many different doctrines?

Mr. Hill: Response.

Missionary: Mr. Hill, the Spirit which has been in your home tonight will stay for a short while and then leave. It will return as we come into your home again and share the message of the restoration of the gospel of Jesus Christ. It will also return as you ponder the things that we have shared with you. To help you remember what we have talked about, we would like to leave with you this pamphlet that deals with the things that happened to Joseph Smith. It goes into a little greater detail than what we have today, and as we return we would like to share that with you. Would Tuesday at 7:00 or Wednesday at 8:00 be better for you?

Mr. Hill: Response.

Missionary: Mr. Hill, would it be all right if we left with a word of prayer?

Mr. Hill: Yes.

Missionary: (Says the prayer. If at all possible have the family gather around and have them kneel. In the prayer pronounce a blessing upon the family collectively and individually.)

If you are successful in teaching the honest in heart how they will be able to know your message has been revealed from God, they will now be inclined to want you to prove your message. They will rely on the witness of the Spirit as the means of determining whether or not your message is true. People who are not honest in heart will not be inclined to rely on the witness of the Spirit. As a missionary you have the responsibility to exercise faith in the promise the Lord has made that the Holy Ghost will testify to the heart and mind of people that your message is true. If you lack faith you restrict the Spirit, and people will not experience a strong witness of the Spirit as you are teaching them.

5. *Explain the role of the Spirit in revealing understanding of gospel truths.*

As you are teaching people the gospel, it is important that they realize that when they understand a gospel truth, they have been spiritually enlightened.

Which things also we speak, not in the words which man's wisdom teacheth, but which the Holy Ghost teacheth; comparing spiritual things with spiritual.

But the natural man receiveth not the things of the Spirit of God: for they are foolishness unto him: neither can he know them, because they are spiritually discerned. (1 Corinthians 2:13-14.)

And now because of their unbelief they could not understand the word of God; and their hearts were hardened. (Mosiah 26:3.)

Understanding is the first stage of a testimony. Most missionaries realize that people they teach will gain a testimony only through the witness of the Spirit. However, very few realize that people's ability to understand the truths of the gospel is also dependent upon the Spirit. President Joseph F. Smith taught that the role of the Holy Ghost is two-fold—one, to "reveal the things of the Father to man" (in other words, to bring to the minds of people an understanding of truth), and two, to "bear witness in our hearts." (*Gospel Doctrine,* p. 59.)

You must realize that people will not fully understand the truths you present unless their understanding is quickened through the influence of the Holy Ghost.

The Holy Spirit ... is the influence of Deity, ... which proceeds forth from the presence of God ... to quicken the understanding of men. (*Gospel Doctrine,* p. 60.)

By the power of the Spirit our eyes were opened and our understandings were enlightened, so as to see and understand the things of God. (D&C 76:12.)

But there is a spirit in man: and the inspiration of the Almighty giveth them understanding. (Job 32:8.)

As your investigators come to an understanding of a particular gospel truth, help them realize that this understanding has come through the Spirit of God, that the Spirit has literally facilitated their ability to comprehend the gospel of Jesus Christ. Understanding is a basic aspect of testimony. If a person is enlightened and understands a basic gospel truth, he has experienced a witness of that truth in the process of being enlightened.

Example:

Missionary: Mr. Hill, this evening we have discussed a basic gospel truth with you and your family. Is there any doubt in your mind that Jesus Christ lives today with a glorified body of flesh and bone?

Mr. Hill: None whatsoever.

Missionary: So when you read the account in Luke 24:36-39, it is your understanding that, when Jesus appeared as a resurrected being, he had a body of flesh and bone.

Mr. Hill: He told his disciples to handle his body of flesh and bone.

Missionary: You are absolutely right, Mr. Hill, and you must realize that your understanding of this beautiful truth has come to you through inspiration from the Holy Spirit. The prophet Job taught:

There is a spirit in man and the inspiration of the Almighty giveth them understanding. (Job 32:8.)

Do you have a sense of gratitude to the Lord for bringing this understanding to your mind?

Mr. Hill: Yes, I do.

6. *Help those you teach recognize the presence or absence of the Spirit.*

As long as you are functioning properly, the Spirit will generally be manifest when you meet with a family. As you teach them, help them become aware of the presence of the Spirit by getting them to express what they feel. They need to know that the warm, special feeling they experience when you are in their home is caused by the Spirit of the Lord. They must not attribute this "good" feeling to your presence, but must realize that it would not be there if the Spirit of the Lord did not sustain you in your labors. Help them understand that this is the way the Lord lets them know your message is from God. The presence of the Spirit is confirmation that your message is true.

It is very important for you to realize that as missionaries, you and your companion, through exercising faith, can draw upon the powers of heaven and literally invoke the Spirit of the Holy Ghost to help your investigators understand the truths you are teaching, and testify of the truthfulness of your message.

When the Spirit is present and touches the hearts of those you are teaching, you can help them recognize the presence of the Spirit in three ways:

a. You can have them describe what they feel and tell them that the feeling is the Spirit of the Lord letting them know that what you are teaching them is true.

> Example:
>
> Missionary: Mr. Hill, would you please describe for us the feeling you have in your heart right now?
>
> Mr. Hill: I have a warm peaceful feeling—a kind of tingling inside.
>
> Missionary: Mr. Hill, that feeling is the spirit of the Lord testifying to you that what we've just taught you is true.

b. You can let them know that what they are feeling is the Spirit of the Lord before you have them describe their feelings.

> Example:
>
> Missionary: Mr. Hill, I know that Joseph Smith truly was a prophet. As we've taught you these things today, the feeling that you have in your heart is the Holy Ghost letting you know that what we've taught you is true. Would you please describe for us what you're feeling right now?

c. Ask people to "watch" for the Spirit. You should orient your investigators so they are "looking" for indicators that the Spirit of the Lord is being manifest.

> Example:
>
> Missionary: As we speak of these sacred things and the Spirit begins to testify to you, Mr. Hill, we would appreciate it if you would watch for and recognize this feeling of warmth and comfort that will come to your heart. This is the Lord's way of letting you know our message is true. May we remind you, Mr. Hill, that Christ is the Prince of Peace and that he does speak peace to a person's mind. Not uneasiness, nor doubts, nor misgivings, but peace. You can be assured that when the Spirit of the Lord is present it will bring a feeling of peace to your heart and mind.

In some instances the Spirit will be noticeably absent when you meet with a family. When this proves to be the case, you should discuss the problem openly with your investigators and then take steps to correct it. There is no point in trying to continue with your presentation if the Spirit is not present.

The absence of the Spirit can be caused by a number of things (i.e., lack of preparation on the part of the missionaries, a lack of unity between missionaries, the investigators may have read or heard something about the Church that has disturbed them.) It is your responsibility to be sufficiently discerning to be aware of the presence or absence of the Spirit when you are meeting with an investigator. When the Spirit is absent from a meeting, how you handle the situation is determined by the situation. You must handle it as the Spirit directs. Without inspiration you will be unable to cope with a situation where the Spirit is absent. For this reason the following examples include only the response of the missionary to the problem, not the steps they would take to correct it.

Example:

Missionary: Mr. Hill, we have been instructed by our Heavenly Father that we are not to teach without the Holy Spirit. In our past meetings we've been able to teach you and your family because the Spirit has been present. Tonight the Spirit is not present, and without the Spirit you would not be able to understand the truths we've prepared to teach. Has something happened to you recently to cause you to view our message differently?

Example:

Missionary: Mr. Pratt, we really appreciate the privilege of coming into your home tonight. For some reason, we don't feel comfortable about beginning our presentation. We simply don't feel the Spirit of the Lord. Do you recognize the difference in what you're feeling now and what you felt two days ago when we talked about the prophet Joseph Smith?

Mr. Pratt: Yes—there really is a difference.

Missionary: Has anything happened since we were last here to cause this change?

(Note: If you discern that the reason the Spirit is not present is because of you, you have the responsibility of solving the problem before you teach. If the problem cannot be solved before you are to teach a family, you should reschedule your appointment for another time.)

Occasionally, the Spirit will be present when you start to present a discussion and then will withdraw at some point in the presentation. When this happens, you should discuss the problem openly and take steps to correct it.

Example:

Missionary: Brother Patch, you apparently don't feel comfortable with something we've said or done, because the Spirit of the Lord has withdrawn. Would you please tell us what you are feeling right now?

Mr. Patch: Response.

Example:

Missionary: Brother Tony, for some reason the Spirit of the Lord has left us. We really can't proceed any further with our discussion without that Spirit.

Have we said something that bothers you?

Brother Tony: Response.

As you help your investigators realize that their understanding of truth has come from the Spirit and help them recognize the presence or absence of the Spirit, they will be able to discern its workings even when you are not with them. For example, when they study the *Book of Mormon* and the Spirit opens to their understanding the truth and meaning of what they are reading, they will realize that their understanding comes from the Spirit. When they attend church and the Spirit is present as a member speaks, they will realize that the feeling they have is the Spirit. Conversely, when they encounter situations in which the Spirit is absent (e.g., when someone gives them anti-Mormon literature, when friends try to discourage their being taught the gospel), they will be able to recognize its absence.

The strongest witness of the Spirit will usually be manifest while you are teaching people. If you fail to help them recognize that witness, they will continue to seek for an answer from the Lord after they have received it. In such cases, many people never realize their prayers have been answered, and then consequently fail to join the Church. As you help your investigators understand the workings of the Spirit, they will gain a spiritually rooted testimony and will be able to recognize the Spirit when it directs them and bears witness to them.

Encourage Your Investigators to Express Appreciation

Once people are aware that they have been enlightened by the Spirit, it is important that you help them express gratitude vocally and in prayer.

When people express gratitude for the role of the Spirit in helping them understand various gospel truths, conviction of these truths will be enhanced. In contrast, if they fail to recognize the role of the Spirit in helping them understand various gospel truths, and if they proceed to seek a further manifestation of the Spirit, more often than not they will not receive any additional manifestation of the Spirit. It is, therefore, essential that you help people realize that no one can understand any of the truths of the gospel of Jesus Christ unless they are enlightened by the Spirit. If someone understands a gospel truth as you present it, that person's understanding is evidence that the Spirit has enlightened his mind—and understanding is the foundation of testimony.

As people acknowledge the role of the Spirit in helping them understand the discussions and associate the "good" feeling they experience when you meet with them with the Spirit of the Lord, they will develop a sense of gratitude for the Lord's hand in their conversion. In contrast, if they fail to recognize the role of the Spirit in their experience with you, they will not trust their convictions, and it will be difficult to commit them to baptism.

Example:

> Missionary: Brother Smart, as we've taught you tonight, we have been blessed with an understanding of some very important truths, truths that have been lost to the world for centuries. As we've discussed these truths, the Spirit of the Lord has been present. Through that spirit, you have not only been able to understand the truths, but you have had a spiritual witness that they are true. You have received this guidance and understanding because of the Lord's love for you. Would you take a minute and let us know how you feel about our Heavenly Father and the blessing of having the guidance of the Spirit of the Lord in learning these truths?

When you become successful in helping your investigators understand the workings of the Spirit, you will be much more effective in your efforts to bring people into the Church. Even more important, the people you see join the Church will be truly converted. This understanding of the workings of the Spirit will make it easier for them to cope with the adjustments they will face after they join the Church.

Throughout your mission ask yourself the following questions:

1. Do those I teach understand the witness of the Spirit?

2. Do those I teach understand the role of the Spirit in revealing understanding of gospel truths?

3. Do I help those I teach recognize the presence or absence of the Spirit?

4. Am I exercising faith sufficient to draw upon the powers of heaven and invoke the Spirit of the Holy Ghost to help our investigators understand the truths we teach?

5. Do I encourage our investigators to express appreciation for the blessings that come into their lives as a result of the Spirit of the Lord?

Chapter 34

Check for Understanding and Conviction

As you are teaching you need to systematically determine two things: (1) does the person *understand* the doctrines and concepts you have introduced and (2) does the person *accept* the doctrines you have introduced. Relying exclusively on the answers to questions in the discussions will not adequately assess understanding and conviction. You must learn to ask additional questions that will help you check for understanding and conviction.

Assessing Understanding

You have the responsibility of presenting the truths of the gospel in such a way that those you teach can understand them. You cannot assume that just because you have said something, the person listening understands. You must continually check for understanding as you teach your investigators. The following guidelines will help you ask questions which will adequately assess understanding.

1. Once you have taught a concept, doctrine, etc., *ask your investigator if he understands.*

Examples:

After teaching Mr. Taylor about the restoration of the priesthood, you ask: "Mr. Taylor, the restoration of the priesthood is difficult for many to understand. Do you understand what the priesthood is?"

After teaching Mr. Green about the coming forth of the Book of Mormon, you ask, "Mr. Green, do you clearly understand what the Book of Mormon is?"

After having Mr. Patch read I Peter 4:6, you ask, "Mr. Patch, do you understand the meaning of this scripture?"

After teaching Mr. Crofts about baptism for the dead, you discern that he is confused. "I sense, Mr. Crofts, that something we said has confused you. Do you have some questions about baptism for the dead?"

2. *Ask your investigator(s) to summarize the concept you taught them in their own words.*

Examples:

After having Mr. Downs read Moroni 10:3-5, you ask, "Mr. Downs, what is the Lord's promise to us if we read the Book of Mormon, ponder it, and pray?"

After teaching the D-2 concept concerning the purpose of mortal life, you ask, "In your own words, what are some of the reasons we came to this earth?"

Note: Each time you determine that your investigators understand a critical concept or doctrine, remind them that their understanding has been received through inspiration.

Assessing Conviction

It is very important to get the people you are teaching to express themselves regarding their feelings, beliefs, and acceptance of the doctrines you are teaching them. The following suggestions will help you ask questions which will assess conviction.

1. *Ask your investigators if they believe the concept you have taught them is consistent with the teachings of the Savior.* In those sectors of the world where the Bible is accepted as the revealed word of God, it is absolutely essential that your investigators realize that the doctrines and teachings you are introducing are totally consistent with the teachings of the Savior.

Examples:

You have just taught Mr. Butler that the Father and Son are separate and distinct persons, each with a glorified and perfected body of flesh and bones. You ask, "Mr. Butler, as you think about this great truth that has been revealed again through modern-day prophets, do you feel it is consistent with the Savior's teachings during his mortal ministry?"

You have just taught the doctrine that God measures our love and faith in him by how well we keep his commandments and that no one can ever be saved in his kingdom without showing his faith by obeying the Lord's commandments. You ask, "Do you feel that this is consistent with the teachings of the Savior?"

Note: These types of questions only apply in those sectors of the world where the people accept Jesus as the Christ or the Bible as being the revealed word of God.

2. *Ask questions which will allow your investigators to express their feelings.*

Examples:

You have just taught Mr. Jenkins that no one can be saved in the Lord's kingdom without keeping the commandments. You ask, "What are your feelings about the importance of keeping the commandments?"

After teaching your investigator that our Heavenly Father has provided a way for all his children to hear the gospel before the resurrection, you ask: "Would you please express for us your feelings about our Heavenly Father's plan for all of his children to hear the gospel at some time before the resurrection?"

After teaching Mr. and Mrs. Dixon that mankind rejected the gospel which resulted in the loss of truth and authority from the earth, you ask: "Mr. Dixon, what do you believe are some of the evidences that the apostacy foretold by Christ and the apostles came to pass?" "Mrs. Dixon, how do you feel about this Apostasy from truth?"

3. *Ask questions to assess belief.* As you are presenting a discussion, you should consistently ask specific questions to determine if your investigators believe what you are teaching.

The following are sample questions that could be asked following a discussion of eternal progression:

Do you believe that it is God's desire that we become more like him?

Do you believe the revealed word of God that one of the basic purposes of this life is for each of us to obtain a body so that we can experience a perfect joy?

Do you believe that God expects us to walk by faith in this life?

Do you believe that our love and faith in God can be measured by how well we keep his commandments?

Do you believe the Lord's declaration that no one can be saved in His kingdom without showing faith by obeying God's commandments?

Do you have a desire to keep God's commandments?

Do you believe that all mankind will be literally resurrected as a result of the atonement of the Lord Jesus Christ?

Do you believe that the resurrection is literal—that the spirit and the body will be reunited as was the case with the Savior's spirit and body following his crucifixion?

Do you believe the revealed words of God that we cannot be reunited with our Father in Heaven unless we are willing to keep the Lord's commandments?

Do you believe the revealed word of God that a way has been provided whereby all the inhabitants of the earth who have never heard of the Lord Jesus Christ in this life will have an opportunity to hear and accept the gospel in the spirit world?

Do you believe the revealed word of God that no one can be saved in His kingdom without receiving the ordinances of salvation which include being baptized?

Do you believe the revealed word of God that declares that little children are saved without baptism through Christ's atonement?

You will find that your investigators' testimonies of the restored gospel will be strengthened as you get them to express their conviction of the principles you introduce. The expression of conviction is a critical step in the development of a person's testimony.

If you are functioning properly the Spirit will guide you in your effort to assess an investigator's understanding and conviction of the message of the restored gospel. If you are skillful in systematically assessing understanding and conviction, you will be effective in your efforts to convert people.

Throughout your mission ask yourself the following questions:

1. Am I doing all I can to present the truths of the gospel in such a way that those I teach can understand them?

2. Do I continually check for understanding as I teach?

3. Do I continually check for conviction of the truths I teach?

4. Am I sensitive to the feelings of investigators?

5. When those I teach answer a question, do I listen to what they say before proceeding with the discussion?

Chapter 35

Handle Questions
and Objections Wisely

When you are presenting a discussion, your investigators will ask questions. You have the responsibility to become skillful in how you handle questions. They fall into two basic categories: (1) sincere questions, and (2) insincere or "baited" questions.

Handling "Baited" Questions

You should *not* attempt to answer a person's question directly unless you are certain he is honestly seeking an answer. If a person's motive in asking you a question is to "bait" you, to hassle or confuse you, you should not attempt to answer the question directly. If you do, you will find yourself on the defensive and your position of strength will be lost. You will automatically be put in the position of trying to prove that your message is true.

With discernment, you, by listening to the tone of a person's voice and recognizing the type of question he asks, will have no difficulty determining if he honestly desires an answer when he asks you a question. If he is hostile or antagonistic towards the Church, it will be evident in his tone of voice. This is also true when someone is not honestly weighing the merits of your message but wants to give you a bad time. When someone asks you a question, ask yourself: "What is his motive for raising the question?"

If you do *not* feel he is honestly seeking an answer, keep the following points in mind.

1. *Do not raise your voice.* People usually speak louder or softer in direct proportion to the loudness or softness of the voice of the person to whom they are speaking. Therefore, you can usually control the other person's tone of voice by your own.

2. *Respond indirectly.* When someone attacks you or the Church in a statement or a question, the natural tendency is to strike back or to react directly. If you succumb to this tendency, you will find yourself arguing with people. On the other hand, if you learn to respond to certain comments and questions indirectly and act intelligently, you can avoid arguments.

The following are ways you can respond indirectly to a person's question:

A. Explain that nothing would be accomplished by answering the question.

Example:

Missionary: Sir, we know nothing would be accomplished by our attempting to answer that question, but before we leave, we want to tell you that we are here because of our conviction of certain truths. (The missionary then bears testimony.)

B. Say that the question asked is not the real issue; the issue is: Was Joseph Smith a prophet? or Is the Book of Mormon true?

Example:

"Your question is not the real issue. The real question is whether or not the Book of Mormon is true. I can promise you that if you will read it and ask God if it is true, with real intent and sincere desire, he will reveal the truth of it to you."

C. Ask a question in return instead of answering the question.

Example:

"Do you believe God answers prayers?" "Do you believe the Bible is the word of God?"

D. Explain that a certain reference contains a written answer better than the one you could give.

Example:

"That very question is answered thoroughly in _____ (refer to pamphlet or book). I can't explain it as well as it is stated there so I'd like you to read the answer." (Or, "This pamphlet answers your questions better than I can.")

E. Challenge the person to read the Book of Mormon and respond to the promise in Moroni.

Example:

"Mr. Tolber, I challenge you to read the Book of Mormon and sincerely study, ponder, and pray about the things you read. I know that as you do, you will gain an understanding of the truthfulness of our message."

Handling Honest Questions

If you feel someone is honestly seeking understanding or clarification when he asks you a question, keep the following points in mind.

1. Will the question be answered in a later discussion? If so, you need to weigh very carefully the pros and cons of answering the question or explaining that it will be answered in a later discussion. If you decide to answer it, you need to decide whether it will be advantageous to answer it in depth or answer it briefly and explain that you will answer it in detail in a later discussion.

2. Make certain that you understand the person's question before you attempt to answer it. If necessary, ask the person questions to clarify it.

3. If the question indicates insight on the part of the person or that he is carefully weighing the message, compliment him, telling him that the question is insightful or that it indicates he is weighing the message very carefully.

4. If the question is answered in the scriptures or in a pamphlet, commit the person to read these sources and ponder what they say as well as your answer to the question.

Handling Honest Objections

When a person voices an objection to a point of doctrine you have introduced, it may be either an honest one based on his present beliefs, or it may be hostile and contentious. If it is an honest objection, you should attempt to deal with it. If the person is hostile and contentious, deal with what he says by using the principles discussed previously. If he is sincere and not contentious in voicing the objection, use one of the following principles when you respond to him.

1. *Express empathy* for the person's point of view. In other words, let him know that if you were in his position in terms of training, experience, and background you would probably feel the same way.

Examples:

Mr. Olmstead: I'm sorry, but I have a difficult time accepting the fact that God has a tangible body like mine.

Missionary: If I were in your situation, I'd probably feel the same way. However, once you understand the purpose of life and our relationship to our Heavenly Father, you will be able to understand more fully the truthfulness of this concept. We don't have time to discuss it in detail right now, but our next presentation will deal with that problem in some depth.

2. Pose "what if" questions. When you pose a "what if" question, you

should help your investigator see the importance of the particular doctrine to them personally "if" what you have told them is true.

Examples:

Mr. Tuft: Well, I feel all churches are good, and that God is understanding and doesn't expect us to be unanimous in petty doctrine. The important thing is that we accept Christ as the Savior.

Missionary: Mr. Tuft, on the basis of your previous religious training, I can understand why you feel the way you do. But what if God really did appear to the Prophet Joseph Smith and restored the gospel in its fullness. Suppose he did declare that we need to embrace that gospel in order to return to him. How important would it be to you to belong to that Church?

Mr. Crane: I can't believe that there is just one church that God accepts. I think we could belong to any church and be all right.

Missionary: Mr. Crane, based on your previous religious training, I can understand why you feel the way you do, but if God did restore his Church to the earth, how important would it be for you and your family to belong to that Church?

Mr. Williams: I believe that all we need is the Bible.

Missionary: Mr. Williams, based on your previous religious training, I can understand why you feel the way you do, but if God did reveal another book of scripture through a modern-day prophet, how important would that book be to you?

3. *Compliment the person* before you attempt to deal with the objection.

Example:

Mr. Page: I read the Bible every day, and I really don't feel I need any other scriptures. I get enough spiritual truth from it.

Missionary: It's commendable that you read the Bible every day. Very few people do. The fact that you study the Bible indicates that you are genuine in desiring to know what the Lord wants you to know.

Note: The missionary should then proceed to explain further the importance of the Book of Mormon as a witness of Christ and how Mr. Page can obtain greater insight regarding the Savior and his message from reading this book.

4. *Let him know that you can appreciate his point of view,* and then *express a fervent testimony* of the truthfulness of the point of doctrine that has been introduced. Your testimony should contain the promise that if he prayerfully weighs the truths you have introduced, he will come to a conviction that they have been revealed by God through modern-day revelation.

Example:

Mr. Ebert: According to the Book of Revelation, we don't need any more scriptures. John said that we shouldn't add to the Bible or take away from it, and that's what you are trying to do.

Missionary: We can appreciate your point of view. However, we want you to know that God has never stated that he would not add to or take away from the Bible. I know that God loves us as much today as he did his children anciently, and because of that love he speaks through a prophet today just as he spoke through Noah, Abraham, or Moses. I know that the Book of Mormon is the word of God, because I've read it, and prayed about it, and received a spiritual witness of its truthfulness. As you read the Book of Mormon and prayerfully consider its truthfulness, you will come to the same conviction that it is the revealed word of God.

5. *Draw a parallel* between the person's objection and a situation in the Bible .

Example:

Mr. Bracy: I really don't think it's necessary to have modern-day prophets. We have enough guidance from the teachings of the Savior.

Missionary: Have you ever stopped to think that as the Savior was teaching the fullness of the gospel, there were those who challenged the need for what he was teaching? Their response to his message was that they had Moses and his teachings, and they didn't need any further revelation. After the Savior was crucified, God continued to reveal his will to mankind through Peter, Paul, and the other apostles. Only the honest in heart accepted the need for modern-day revelation back at the time of Christ. The same is true today.

6. *Address the objection itself.* In many instances, people will disagree with the truths you teach because they have not clearly understood what you have taught them. When this is the case, the objection can be overcome by:

a. Explain the concept or doctrine in your own words and, if necessary, use examples to clarify the subject.

Example:

Mr. Stinson: If baptism is so important, you ought to be baptized as soon as possible. I've always been taught that little children should be baptized.

Missionary: Mr. Stinson, when we understand the true nature of baptism, we can see why the Lord disapproves of the baptism of infants. Baptism is a covenant, a commitment made by a responsible person.

b. Clarify the concept or doctrine through the scriptures. When you refer to scriptures, be sure your intent is to clarify, rather than prove.

Example:

Mr. Sorenson: If baptism is so important, you ought to be baptized as soon as possible. I've always been taught that little children should be baptized.

Missionary: Mr. Sorenson, you're not the only person who has had those kinds of feelings. Because of that, the Lord revealed to the prophet Mormon some important truths concerning baptism. These few verses that you are going to read are part of a letter Mormon wrote to his son Moroni. There were many good honest-in-heart people at that time who felt the same way about baptism. Would you please read verses 5 through 12 of Moroni chapter 8 ?

Do Not Contend

Joseph Smith counseled:

Let the Elders be exceedingly careful about unnecessarily disturbing and harrowing up the feelings of the people. Remember that your business is to preach the Gospel in all humility and meekness, and warn sinners to repent and come to Christ. Avoid contentions and vain disputes with men of corrupt minds who do not desire to know the truth. Remember that "it is a day of warning and not a day of many words." If they receive not your testimony in one place, flee to another, remembering to cast no reflections, nor throw out any bitter sayings. If you do your duty, it will be just as well with you, as though all men embraced the gospel. (Joseph Smith, *History of the Church*, 1:468.)

If a person expresses an objection in a hostile tone of voice, you should not attempt to respond to it directly. The suggestions introduced previously for responding indirectly to insincere questions also apply when a person expresses an objection in a hostile tone of voice.

The following excerpts from a talk given by Elder Marvin J. Ashton, during a recent general conference of the Church, clearly state the position of the Church regarding contention:

A few months ago word reached some of our missionaries in a remote South Pacific island that I would soon be visiting there for two or three days. When I arrived, the missionaries were waiting anxiously to share with me some anti-Mormon literature that was being circulated in their area. They were disturbed by the accusations and were eager to plan retaliation.

The elders sat on the edge of their chairs as I read the slander and false declarations issued by a minister who apparently felt threatened by their presence and successes. As I read the pamphlet containing the malicious and ridiculous statements, I actually smiled, much to the surprise of my young associates. When I finished, they asked, "What do we do now? How can we best counteract such lies?"

I answered, "To the author of these words, we do nothing. We have no time for contention. We only have time to be about our Father's business. Contend with no man. Conduct yourselves as gentlemen with calmness and conviction and I promise you success."

Perhaps a formula for those missionaries and all of us to follow can be found in Helaman, Chapter five, verse thirty, of the Book of Mormon. "And it came to pass when they heard this voice, and beheld that it was not a voice of thunder, neither was it a voice of a great tumultuous noise, but behold, it was a still voice of perfect mildness, as if it had been a whisper, and it did pierce even to the very soul—"

There never has been a time when it is more important for us as members of The Church of Jesus Christ of Latter-day Saints to take a stand, remain firm in our convictions, and conduct ourselves wisely under all circumstances. We must not be manipulated or enraged by those who subtly foster contention over issues of the day.

When issues are in contradiction to the laws of God, the Church must take a stand and state its position. We have done this in the past and will continue to do so in the future when basic moral principles are attacked. There are those in our society who would promote misconduct and immoral programs for financial gain and popularity. When others disagree with our stand we should not argue, retaliate in kind, or contend with them. We can maintain proper relationships and avoid the frustrations of strife if we wisely apply our time and energies.

Ours is to conscientiously avoid being abrasive in our presentations and declarations. We need constantly to remind ourselves that when we are unable to change the conduct of others, we will go about the task of properly governing ourselves.

Certain people and organizations are trying to provoke us into contention with slander, innuendos, and improper classifications. How unwise we are in today's society to allow ourselves to become irritated, dismayed, or offended because others seem to enjoy the role of misstating our position or involvement. Our principles or standards will not be less than they are because of the statements of the contentious. Ours is to explain our position through reason, friendly persuasion, and accurate facts. Ours is to stand firm and unyielding on the moral issues of the day and the eternal principles of the gospel, but to contend with no man or organization. Contention builds walls and puts up barriers. Love opens doors. Ours is to be heard and teach. Ours is not only to avoid contention, but to see that such things are done away.

"For verily, verily I say unto you, he that hath the spirit of contention is not of me, but is of the devil, who is the father of contention, and he stirreth up the hearts of men to contend with anger, one with another.

"Behold, this is not my doctrine, to stir up the hearts of men with anger, one against another; but this is my doctrine, that such things should be done away." (3 Nephi 11:29, 30)

We need to be reminded that contention is a striving against one another, especially in controversy or argument. It is to struggle, fight, battle, quarrel, or dispute. Contention never was and never will be an ally of progress. Our loyalty will never be measured by our participation in controversy. Some misunderstand the realm, scope, and dangers of contention. Too many of us are inclined to declare, "Who, me? I am not contentious, and I'll fight anyone who says I am." There are still those among us who would rather lose a friend than an argument. How important it is to know how to disagree without being disagreeable. It behooves all of us to be in the position to involve ourselves in factual discussions and meaningful study, but never in bitter arguments and contention. ("No Time for Contention," *Ensign*, May 1978, pp. 7, 8.)

Throughout your mission you should ask yourself the following questions:

1. When I respond to objections, do I keep my voice soft?

2. Whenever someone attacks me or the Church, do I react indirectly, using the guidelines contained in this chapter?

3. Before I answer a question, do I make every effort to determine if the person is honestly seeking clarification and understanding?

4. Am I able to avoid being manipulated or enraged by those who subtly foster contention over issues of the day?

5. Do I conscientiously avoid being abrasive in our presentations and declarations?

6. Do I preach the gospel in all humility and meekness?

Chapter 36

Stress Modern-Day Revelation

As you teach your investigators, you have the responsibility to consistently stress modern-day revelation. The Lord has commanded: "These words are not of men nor of man, but of me; wherefore, you shall testify they are of me and not of man." (D&C 18:34.)

When you follow the guidelines specified in this chapter, you will be effective in fulfilling this charge. After you have introduced a particular doctrine(s), follow the guidelines in Chapter 34 to determine whether or not your investigators understand and believe what you have taught them. Once your investigators indicate that they believe what you have taught, stress that your message is from God and was revealed through a modern-day prophet. Explain that, even though these doctrines are alluded to vaguely in the ancient scriptures, if it were not for modern-day revelation, you would not be in a position to share these gospel truths with them.

The following statement by Elder Bruce R. McConkie clearly explains the importance of stressing modern-day revelation:

When you get into the active operation of your proselyting program, this is a concept you absolutely must have. It has been our traditional course in days past, unfortunately all too frequently, to say, "Here is the Bible, and the Bible says this and this, and therefore the gospel has been restored." Well now, there is no person on earth that believes the Bible more than I do. I read it and ponder its words. I know that what is in it is true. But let me tell you, it is not the Bible that brings people into the Church; it is the Book of Mormon and latter-day revelation. We can use the Bible to lay a foundation, and to point

215

people's attention to Joseph Smith and the Book of Mormon, but until we get involved with latter-day revelation, the processes of conversion does not begin to operate in any substantial degree in the heart of an investigator. The Lord said to Joseph Smith: "... this generation shall have my word through you..." (D&C 5:10.) That is his decree. They either get it through Joseph Smith or they do not get it, and our whole perspective is: Joseph Smith and the Book of Mormon, the Book of Mormon and Joseph Smith. (Mission Presidents' Seminar, June 21, 1975.)

If you fail to stress the role of Joseph Smith in receiving modern-day revelation, your investigators may believe the doctrines you teach, but they will not accept Joseph Smith as a prophet, and consequently they will not join the Church.

Example:

Missionary: This evening, Brother Jones, we have discussed several beautiful gospel truths (discussion D). Based upon what we have taught you, is there any doubt in your mind that the gospel of Jesus Christ will be made available to all people, even if they never hear of Christ in this life?

Mr. Jones: No, it is obvious from the scripture you read in 1 Corinthians 15:29 that ordinances for the dead were performed by the disciples of Christ.

Missionary: The thing you must remember, Brother Jones, is that, even though reference is made to the doctrine of salvation for the dead in the Bible, prior to 1820 this doctrine was not taught or understood by any of the ministers of the world. The only reason we understand this doctrine and have been able to share it with you is that the particulars of the doctrine were revealed to the Prophet Joseph Smith. In other words, if it were not for modern-day revelation through a prophet of God, we still would not understand the doctrine of salvation for the dead.

Unless your investigators understand clearly the role of Joseph Smith as the recipient of modern-day revelation in the establishment of the Church of Jesus Christ on the earth in these latter days, they will not be truly converted to the gospel. As this understanding grows in them, they will acquire a new appreciation for him as a man, and more especially for his role as a prophet of God. When they do so, they will be inclined to express gratitude to God for calling a modern-day prophet and will express their conviction that Joseph Smith was truly a prophet of God.

You can facilitate the development of this sense of gratitude in the lives of your investigators if you will consistently point out that the love of God is evidenced in the things that he revealed through the Prophet Joseph Smith.

Example:

"God loves us and it is his desire that we understand his true nature. That is why he appeared to Joseph Smith."

Help your investigators understand that everything God did through Joseph Smith was motivated by his love for his children on earth.

Example:

> Missionary: Joseph Smith's vision is an example of God's love for us. It is God's desire that we understand him so we can worship him properly. If God had not appeared to the Prophet Joseph Smith, we would still not know that our Heavenly Father is a glorified being with a body of flesh and bone. Every time God reveals a truth to the world through a prophet, it is an expression of his love for us.

In stressing modern-day revelation, you should become conversant with specific scriptures which you can use to reinforce the role of revelation in the Kingdom of God. The following are a few examples:

> 1 Corinthians 2:10-4
> John 8:26
> 1 Corinthians 14:6
> Ephesians 3:4-5
> Matthew 16:17
> Matthew 4:4
> Deuteronomy 8:3
> Amos 3:7
> Genesis 18:17-18

Do not make the mistake of assuming that if people accept the doctrines that you introduce, they will automatically accept the Church and desire to be baptized. It has been found that people quite readily accept the doctrines covered in the various discussions, but mere acceptance of these doctrines does not necessarily result in a desire to join the Church. A desire to join the Church is tied very directly to conviction on the part of your investigators that Joseph Smith is a prophet. As a missionary you have the responsibility to help your investigators develop a love and appreciation for the Prophet Joseph. If you fail in this responsibility, you will see many people accept the basic doctrines that you introduce, but they will not be inclined to join the Church.

The best way to insure that your investigators develop a love and appreciation for the Prophet Joseph Smith is to make extensive use of the Book of Mormon in your teaching. This can be accomplished by: (1) referring to scriptures in the Book of Mormon frequently when you are presenting a discussion, (2) committing your investigator(s) to read specific passages in the Book of Mormon at the conclusion of every discussion, (3) selecting passages in the Book of Mormon that will have particular appeal to an investigator and reading the passages out loud with them. For example, if your investigator family has expressed concern about life after death, you could read Alma 40:7-14 with them, (4) consistently citing examples of doctrines that are vague in the Bible that are clarified by the Book of Mormon (i.e., infant baptism), and (5) making your investigator families aware of the promises the Lord made in the Book of Mormon (i.e., 3 Nephi 18:19-20, 3 Nephi 20:22, Moroni 10:32-33).

In addition, you have the responsibility to consistently stress the role of continuing revelation through a living prophet. You can accomplish this by means of your personal testimony, reference to talks given by the prophet of the Church and published in the various Church periodicals, and reference to the general conferences of the Church. By the time a family is baptized, they should have a clear understanding that Jesus Christ is literally the head of the Church and is directing it by means of revelation through a living prophet and apostles. The family should understand the basic organization of the Church consisting of the First Presidency and the Twelve Apostles, and their role in directing its affairs under inspiration from our Father in Heaven. It is absolutely essential that each convert be committed to follow the counsel of local Church leaders and understand the blessings that follow if he is obedient to those who preside over him.

When you discuss modern-day revelation, you should also systematically review the principles and doctrines you have been able to share with the family as a result of it. This review should consist of a brief summary of all the discussions you have covered with the family thus far, and you should stress again that without modern-day revelation these truths would be lost to the world.

Throughout your mission ask yourself the following questions:

1. As I teach, do I consistently stress modern-day revelation?

2. Do those I teach understand the role of Joseph Smith in receiving modern revelation?

3. Do I have an understanding of the role Joseph Smith played in the establishment of the Church?

4. Do I consistently express gratitude to God for calling a modern-day prophet?

5. Do I make extensive use of the Book of Mormon in my teaching?

6. Do I consistently express my conviction that Joseph Smith was truly a prophet of God?

7. Am I helping those I teach develop a love and appreciation for the Prophet Joseph Smith?

Chapter 37

Commit Your Investigators

No matter how skillful you become in other aspects of missionary work, unless you perfect your ability to commit people, you will never be totally effective in bringing families into the waters of baptism. Once you are functioning properly, you should focus on the principles introduced in this chapter until you are consistently committing the people you teach.

Commitments That Result in Conversion

Unfortunately, some missionaries fail to distinguish between the two terms *contact* and *investigator*. In many instances the two terms are used interchangeably, when, in fact, there is a major difference. The dictionary defines a *contact* as someone with whom we merely make contact. In contrast, an *investigator* is someone who studies by close examination and systematic inquiry. Generally a person will not join the Church unless he is willing to investigate the gospel systematically. For this reason, you should be resolved to get people to make commitments that will result in investigation of the gospel. A commitment is a pledge or an agreement to do something. In the case of missionary work, commitments are actions that will result in conversion. The following are examples:

Agreeing to a return appointment.

Agreeing to pray.

Agreeing to read missionary tracts and other literature.

Agreeing to attend church.

Agreeing to repent.

Agreeing to fast.

Agreeing to be baptized.

You should personally resolve to be bold in consistently committing your investigator to do things that lead to conversion. As a general rule, the best time to commit your investigator is when the Spirit has been manifest and felt by him.

You need to cultivate discernment so that you will not attempt to commit an investigator beyond his capacity. Generally, commitments should increase progressively in difficulty. For example, you may feel a need to commit an investigator to attend church meetings before you commit him to stop smoking. The Spirit will help you select appropriate commitments for each investigator.

In many instances, teaching must accompany committing. For example, as you commit someone to fast, it is absolutely essential that you teach him how to fast. Obviously, you cannot commit someone to fast unless he knows how to fast.

Requirements for Success in Getting People to Make Commitments

You will be successful in getting people to make commitments when you:

1. Are totally committed to the work.

2. Truly love the people. Joseph Smith said, "I possess the principle of love." Love is a prerequisite to getting people to make commitments. Pure love dispels people's fear of ulterior motives on your part. Trust is built upon love. Once people are convinced that you are honestly concerned about their welfare, they will be responsive to your efforts to get them to make commitments. Love is something that is felt and discerned, so it cannot be feigned or manufactured. Your effectiveness in getting people to make commitments will be determined to a great extent by the amount of love you have for them. Consequently, unless you truly learn to love the people, you will not be successful in getting them to make commitments. A sense of being loved provides strength and motivation to make and keep commitments.

3. Consistently exercise faith that the people will do what you ask them to do. Your faith is a prime factor in determining how people respond to your requests to pray, read, and observe the Word of Wisdom, etc. Your faith will be enhanced if you will strive to think about the principles, standards, or goals to which you intend to commit your

investigators. Learn to create a mental picture of people praying, being baptized, etc. Repeatedly rehearse in your mind how you will go about committing your investigators. Rehearse specifically what you intend to say. The things you want people to do must be created in your mind and held as a strong vision to ensure their accomplishment. You will be successful in committing people if you train your mind to consistently think about those things you intend to commit your investigators to do and then maintain an attitude of faith after you commit them.

You should make every effort to exercise specific faith in the promise that angels under the direction of the Savior will call people to repentance (see Moroni 7:29-31.) In your prayers request that angels be sent to visit your investigators to assist you in getting them to repent. You should consistently remind yourself that the hosts of heaven beyond the veil will assist you in your efforts to commit people if your faith is sufficient. Remember, your ability to exercise faith is tied to your level of dedication.

Principles for Effectively Committing your Investigators

If you are totally committed to the work, truly love the people, and consistently exercise faith, you will be able to use the following principles very effectively when you are committing each investigator.

1. *Assume that your investigator will make commitments.* Assumption is a valuable tool in getting commitments. You should never suggest with the words you use that you believe there is any possibility the person you are committing won't or can't do what the Lord wants him to do. Words such as *if, maybe, might, perhaps, could,* and *possibly,* cast doubt. When you have a testimony that what you are asking your investigators to do is what the Lord wants them to do, you will find it easy to use such words as *will, when,* or *as.* Assumption is a powerful tool in getting people to make commitments.

Examples:

Less Effective

"Could we possibly come back and talk to your husband?"

"Perhaps you could read the Joseph Smith story."

More Effective

"Would early evening or later be the most convenient time to meet with your husband?"

"I know that as you read the Joseph Smith story and pray sincerely, you will come to know it is true. Will you read it?"

2. *Promise your investigator specific blessings.* As you promise specific blessings, those you teach will not only be motivated to keep the commitment, but their testimonies will be strengthened as they receive

the blessings you have promised them.

Example:

> We promise you that if you prayerfully read those chapters in the Book of Mormon that discuss life after death, the uneasiness that you have about death will be dispelled.

The Lord has stated that all acts of righteousness have specific blessings attached to them. (D&C 130:20-21.) You have the responsibility to find out which blessings follow the commitments you are asking your investigators to keep. The scriptures and the discussions will be a great help in determining those blessings. You should also realize that you have been ordained, set apart, and endowed as an administrator of saving ordinances. You are authorized to speak in the name of Jesus Christ. You are authorized to make promises under the direction of the Spirit in the name of the Lord Jesus Christ as you get people to make commitments.

3. *Let your investigator know that the Lord loves him and that it is His desire that he do what you're asking him to do.* If possible, tie the request you are making to something the Lord has said in the scriptures or through the prophets. It is important that the investigator do things in response to a desire to please the Lord, rather than doing things to please you.

Example:

> Missionary: Brother Stapley, the Lord loves you. Because of his love for you he desires that you pray.

4. *Express your confidence and faith in your investigator's ability to keep commitments.*

Example:

> Missionary: Brother Brown, we are confident you will be able to overcome your coffee habit. We have been impressed with your spirit and desire to keep the Lord's commandments. We want you to know our faith and prayers will be with you for the next few days.

5. *Assure your investigator that the Lord will help him.*

Example:

> Missionary: Brother Brown, we know that as you pray and ask the Lord to help you overcome your cigarette habit, He will help you quit smoking.

6. *Have your investigator respond.* There is a time in the commitment process when you say to your investigator, "Will you _____?"

Examples:

> Missionary: Mr. Salisbury, will you read the Book of Mormon?
>
> Missionary: Mr. Marsh, will you live the Word of Wisdom?
>
> Missionary: Mr. Rushton, will you attend church next Sunday?

Once you have asked your investigator to make a commitment, wait for him to respond. As you commit him, you need to realize that you are asking him to change his current lifestyle (e.g., give up smoking, attend church). It is natural for an investigator to hesitate in responding to requests like these. Some missionaries have a tendency to assume that the investigator is going to say no if he hesitates in his response. As a result, they often interrupt the thoughts of the investigator and attempt to commit him through further discussion. In reality, all that is happening is that the investigator is contemplating the implications of the commitment process. For this reason, you should always wait for the investigator to respond after you ask him specifically to commit to do something. Only when your investigator says, "Yes, I will..." have you succeed in getting a commitment.

If someone resists making a commitment, find out why by asking questions. In your effort to commit people, you need to be discerning. Sometimes the excuses expressed are not really the problem. For example, a man could resist a baptismal commitment and say that he is not sure the gospel is true, when in fact, he knows the gospel is true but is fearful of praying in public.

The Importance of Following Up on Commitments

Always follow up on commitments during subsequent visits with your investigator. Ask specifically about the commitment and discuss how he has done. You should always assume that your investigator has been successful as you follow up on previous commitments.

Example:

Missionary: Mr. and Mrs. Jones, how do you feel now that you've lived the Word of Wisdom for a week?

Mr. Jones: We really feel good, but it's sure been tough.

When a person follows up on a commitment to pray, read, etc., tell him the Lord is pleased.

Example:

Missionary: I know that our Heavenly Father is pleased that you are living this commandment. We have a great love for you and appreciate teaching people who are honest in heart.

If your investigator fails to keep a commitment, find out why by asking questions, and then recommit him.

Accepting Responsibility for Commitments

As you become skillful in getting people to agree to do things that lead to conversion, you will consistently baptize families. Unless your investigators are willing to make commitments, you should make it clear to them that it would serve no purpose to continue meeting with them. Above all else, each investigator should understand that he has the responsibility to do specific things to determine the truthfulness of your message.

If your investigator is not willing to assume this responsibility, you will waste your time in trying to teach him the gospel of Jesus Christ.

If you are not effective in your efforts to commit your investigators, ask yourself the following questions:

1. Do I truly love the people I am teaching?

2. Do those I am teaching know of and feel my love for them?

3. Am I consistently striving to exercise faith that the people will do what I ask them to do?

4. Am I bold in consistently committing people to do the things that will result in their conversion?

5. Am I consistently perfecting my ability to commit people?

6. Does my dedication as a missionary qualify me to ask for and receive guidance and the influence of the Spirit of the Lord as I am committing those I am teaching?

Chapter 38

Teach the Member's Role in the Church

Each time you meet with a person after he has accepted the baptismal challenge, it is absolutely essential that you talk about his membership in the Church. These discussions should focus on both blessings and responsibilities. By the time a person is baptized, he should have a clear understanding of the following: (1) specific blessings and opportunities come from membership in the Church, (2) the Church has a lay (unpaid) ministry and all members are expected to participate and hold various positions in the branch or ward; and (3) the father is the patriarch of his family.

Exactly how you discuss these topics with families will vary according to their particular disposition. For example, if family members are educated and socially outgoing, they most likely will not be fearful of participating and assuming various positions in the branch or ward. However, for many families the idea of speaking and praying in meetings is frightening. You have the responsibility to build their confidence and give them the assurance that once they are baptized and receive the gift of the Holy Ghost, the Lord will sustain them in whatever they are asked to do.

The following are topics suggested for discussion in your effort to get people to realize there are many blessings and opportunities that will result from being a member of The Church of Jesus Christ of Latter-day Saints:

1. The Gift of the Holy Ghost.

2. The priesthood.

3. The blessings associated with partaking of the sacrament.

4. Temple marriage.

5. Fellowship with other members.

6. Home teachers.

7. Leaders honestly concerned about their welfare.

8. Guidance of a living prophet.

9. Modern day scripture.

10. Patriarchal blessings.

11. Special blessings through the priesthood.

12. Help through participating in Relief Society and Primary.

In your discussions with people regarding the expectation that they participate and hold various positions in the branch or ward, discuss their potential role in terms of their unique strengths or abilities. For example, if the woman is skilled in handicrafts, you could talk about her potential role in Relief Society. Put their minds at ease by explaining that the leaders will always consult with them before they ask them to speak, pray, or participate in any way. You will find it helpful to discuss the reaction of other people, who have joined the Church, to membership in a church that has a lay ministry. Let them know all members (including yourself) are a little fearful the first few times they speak in Church meetings. Help them to see how this causes us to learn to rely more on our Father in Heaven. Promise the people the Lord will bless them in their efforts to be equal to anything they are asked to do. Stress that Church callings come from the Lord. Help them understand the role of inspiration in Church callings. Create opportunities for your investigators to talk to other converts about their feelings and experiences as new members of the Church.

If the family has children, make it a point to talk frequently about the children going on missions when they are old enough. You should create a desire in the heart of every young man to fill a mission. Help the family realize what steps they need to take to insure that their sons fill missions.

You have the responsibility to help your investigators realize that the discussions are not intended to teach them all they need to know about the gospel. They should be committed to study the scriptures and other Church publications on a regular basis. In addition, every new member should be committed to read *The Articles of Faith* by James E. Talmage.

If you are not successful in helping your investigators feel basically comfortable about being members of a church in which the members are expected to assume an active role, many good people will not become Church members because of their apprehensions about being called on to speak or pray.

In discussing the role of the father as the patriarch of his family, the following responsibilities and privileges should be covered:

1. Taking charge of family prayer.
2. Blessing the food at meal time.
3. Baptizing his children after he receives the priesthood.
4. Blessing his future children.
5. Confirming his children.
6. Giving his children a father's blessing.
7. Administering to his children.
8. Interviewing his children on a regular basis.
9. Conducting family home evenings.
10. Conducting family councils.

If you are conscientious in your efforts to discuss the family's role in the Church, you will find that your investigators will remain active after they are baptized. This whole process can be further strengthened by suggesting that home teachers systematically cover some of the topics identified in this chapter. This will help insure that your investigators will be able to handle the complex role of being members of the Church.

Throughout your mission ask yourself the following questions:

1. Do I adequately help people prior to their baptism to understand the many blessings and opportunities that will come to them through membership in the Church?
2. Do I help those who have accepted the challenge of baptism understand their role in the Kingdom in terms of participating and holding various positions in the Church?
3. Do I help fathers understand their role as patriarch in their home?
4. Do I help investigators realize that the discussions are not intended to teach them all they need to know about the gospel?
5. Do I commit those I teach to study the scriptures and other Church publications on a regular basis?
6. Do those I teach understand the role of inspiration in Church callings?

7. Am I doing all I can to help those I teach become adequately prepared to accept the responsibilities associated with membership in the Kingdom of God?

Chapter 39

Bless Your Investigators

A s an emissary of the Lord Jesus Christ you have the responsibility
to bless your investigators. The Lord has declared: "Yea, let all
those take their journey, as I have commanded them, going from
house to house, and from village to village, and from city to city."

"And in whatsoever house ye enter, and they receive you, *leave your
blessing upon that house*." (D&C 75:18-19; italics added.)

The Lord expects you to leave your peace and blessing in the homes of
the people you teach. When and how you do this will vary according to the
particular situation. In some instances your first act in the home may be
pronouncing a blessing on the household. At other times, it may prove
more appropriate to bless the family at the conclusion of a discussion.
Usually, the most opportune time to bless the family is immediately after
the father has offered a prayer at the conclusion of your first meeting.
When you pray, you have the responsibility to literally bless the family, not
merely to offer a prayer. The following guidelines will assist you in
formulating the blessing that you will offer in homes of the people you
teach.

1. Obtain permission from the father to bless the family.

   Example:

   Missionary: Mr. Sandgren, before we leave, we would like the privilege
   of leaving a blessing on you and your family. May we do that?

2. Open the prayer by saying, "In the name of Jesus Christ and by the power of the Holy Priesthood which I bear" (do not use the name *Melchizedek*). Sisters would say, "By virtue of our authority as ministers of the Lord Jesus Christ."

3. The primary focus of your blessing should be on the father and his role in leading his family in righteousness.

4. Bless the other members of the family collectively, that they will have health and strength, that the mother will be inspired in her role in directing the affairs of her children, that the children will honor their parents, etc.

5. Bless the family that they will be receptive to truth, that they will be inclined to receive truths that will bless their lives.

6. Express your personal appreciation and your other feelings for the family. Once you have met with the family more than two or three times, it is appropriate to express love and appreciation for them in the blessing.

7. Conclude your blessing by asking the Lord to seal all of these blessings upon this family.

As you learn to bless the families as the Spirit directs, through the power of the Holy Priesthood that you bear, or your authority as a minister of the Lord Jesus Christ, your blessings will have a profound influence on people's conversion. If you are functioning properly, when you bless the family, the Holy Spirit will be manifest. The response of the people to the Spirit is a prime indicator of how receptive they will be to the message of the restored gospel. In carrying out your charge to bless the families you teach, do not be timid in pronouncing specific blessings on individual members of the family or on the family collectively.

You have the responsibility to exercise faith in the authority you have and in your calling as a minister of the Lord Jesus Christ. The Lord has commanded you to bless the family that you teach. If you fail in your responsibility to develop charity which will give you a true love of the people, you will find it difficult to pronounce the type of blessing that the Lord would have you pronounce on the families you teach. You will be prone to be uneasy at discharging this responsibility. You'll be very timid in your expression of specific blessings in behalf of the family. The Savior provided an excellent example during his ministry among the Nephites. He blessed the people on several occasions.

> And it came to pass that when they had all been brought, and Jesus stood in the midst, he commanded the multitude that they should kneel down upon the ground.
>
> And it came to pass that when they had knelt upon the ground, Jesus

groaned within himself, and said: Father, I am troubled because of the wickedness of the people of the house of Israel.

And when he had said these words, he himself also knelt upon the earth; and behold he prayed unto the Father, and the things which he prayed cannot be written, and the multitude did bear record who heard him.

And after this manner do they bear record: The eye hath never seen, neither hath the ear heard, before, so great and marvelous things as we saw and heard Jesus speak unto the Father;

And no tongue can speak, neither can there be written by any man, neither can the hearts of men conceive so great and marvelous things as we both saw and heard Jesus speak; and no one can conceive of the joy which filled our souls at the time we *heard him pray for us unto the Father.* (3 Nephi 17:13-17; italics added.)

In the process of blessing a family, you have the opportunity to teach. In many ways people are more receptive to the truth when it is expressed in a prayer instead of in direct conversation: "... their hearts were open and they did understand in their hearts the words which he prayed." (3 Ne. 19:33.)

The response of people to a blessing will provide you an indication of their receptiveness to the message of the restored gospel. Some will be so strongly touched by your blessing that there will be tears in their eyes at the conclusion of the blessing. (See 3 Ne. 17:17, 18.) Others will not take you seriously and will not sense the significance of the blessing you have offered. There will be all kinds of reactions. If people are grateful for the blessing or are touched by it, they will probably be receptive to the gospel. The Spirit will prompt you, and you will know whether or not you should proceed to meet with the family again.

As a general rule you should bless the family every time you meet with them. You should always decide in advance which missionary will bless the family. The missionary who is going to pronounce the blessing should reflect on it and formulate ahead of time what he intends to say. However, this mental preparation should not dictate exactly what is said in the blessing. As you are blessing the family, the Spirit may prompt you to say things you had not previously considered.

Throughout your mission ask yourself the following questions:

1. Am I developing the spirit of charity which will give me a true love for the people I teach?

2. Do my companion and I determine in advance who will offer the blessing?

3. Am I bold in my expression of specific blessings on the family?

4. Before I pronounce a blessing, do I reflect on it and formulate ahead of time what I intend to say?

5. Am I open to the promptings of the Spirit whenever I leave a blessing?

Chapter 40

Express Love and Appreciation

In your association with your investigators, it is absolutely essential that you express your love and appreciation for them on a regular basis. The most opportune times to tell the family how you feel about them are (1) when you are preparing them to receive a discussion and (2) when you are concluding a meeting (immediately after one of you has blessed the family).

Your expressions of love to your investigators will greatly facilitate their conversion. As you express your love and appreciation for your investigators, focus on the character traits that are Christlike—the family's humility, the family's goodness, the family's solidarity. Help them to see that they do stand apart from the world and are exemplary of the things the Savior desires of us. Discuss the growth you have noticed in their ability to pray, to express their love to each other, to understand the scriptures, to repent, etc.

Let them know you are confident that they can live up to the Lord's expectations. Express your anticipation of the contribution they will make as members of the Church. Talk about the time when the sons of the family will fulfill missions, etc.

In your daily prayers you should consistently seek the gift of charity because the gift of charity will cause you to truly love the people you are teaching. It will give you the warmth and sensitivity so critical to your success when you are teaching people the gospel. The gospel of Jesus

Christ is a gospel of love, and it has to be taught in the spirit of love.

Once you are able to openly and sincerely express your love for your investigators, you will catch the spirit of your labors. You will begin to experience the sweet joy associated with this labor of love. You will find yourself making statements like the following to your parents:

"Words cannot express the joy I have experienced this past week."

"I never dreamed that I could grow so close to people so quickly."

"I find myself loving these people like my own family."

"Mom and Dad, I wish you could meet these choice people. They are the greatest."

Once your investigators sense your great love for them, they will be responsive to your requests that they repent, attend Church, etc. Once your investigators experience the tremendous bond of love that will develop between you and them, you should help them to realize that this same bond of love exists among the members of the Church generally. You should make it a point to express your love and respect for the various members of the ward or branch and especially the presiding authorities: the stake president, the bishop, etc. Help them to see that this is a characteristic of the true Church of Jesus Christ and that in a very literal sense people are "no more strangers and foreigners, but fellow citizens with the saints, and of the household of God." (Ephesians 2:19.) You will find that all your investigators will strongly identify with your love and concern for them and that the power and influence of your love will cause them to then identify with the doctrines and teachings of the Church.

Throughout your mission ask yourself the following questions:

1. Do I express my love and appreciation for our investigators on a regular basis?

2. When I express my love and appreciation for our investigators, do I focus on those character traits that are Christlike (e.g., their humility, their solidarity, their concern for each other)?

3. Do I discuss with the family the growth that we have noticed in them?

4. Am I expressing my confidence in the family's ability to live up to the Lord's expectations?

5. Am I consistently praying to receive the gift of charity?

6. Do I make it a point to express my love and respect for the members of the ward or branch and especially for the presiding authorities?

Chapter 41

Summary of Section 4

The chapters in this section make it clear that teaching the gospel involves much more that merely reciting memorized dialogues. As a missionary you have the responsibility to become skillful in making yourself believed.

You should be resolved to follow President Joseph F. Smith's counsel:

> ... they [missionaries] should teach as nearly as they can after the manner of the Master. (*Gospel Doctrine*, p. 364.)

As you do, you will be endowed with the Spirit, and you will teach with power and authority. You have the assurance that if you use the principles and procedures introduced in this section, people will believe your message and will become members of the Church. In contrast, if you do not strive to consistently improve you ability to get people to believe your message, the Spirit will not continue to sustain you in your labors.

You should reread the chapters in this section every month and evaluate your own performance in terms of the principles and procedures introduced. Once you become skillful in the use of these principles and procedures, you have the responsibility to do everything in your power to assist other missionaries in their effort to improve their ability to make themselves believed.

Chapter 42

Introduction to Section 5

The greatest deterrent to effective missionary work is the tendency of most missionaries to become lax once they can handle the routine of missionary work. In any effort associated with the Kingdom of God, if you fail to consistently improve your performance you will regress (lose ground). As the prophets have explained the law of eternal progression, they have made it clear that in spiritual matters we must either improve or we will decrease. It is impossible to stand still. Consequently, if you fail to consistently improve your ability to discharge your duties as a missionary, your effectiveness will decrease. President Kimball has said that our present level of performance is not acceptable either to ourselves or the Lord. He has consistently encouraged us to make up our minds, collectively and individually, to improve the effectiveness of our missionary effort.

We are remembering that the Lord of heaven and earth, whose program it is and who has created and peopled this earth—He is anxious. He commanded that we continue and increase our efforts to reach the people. We continue to read his earnest statements that the gospel must go to all the world, to every creature, every clime, every people, every soul. It calls for an "all-out" effort. This appeal is not for the rich or the poor, the successful or the intelligentsia, but to every heart and mind in the world—to every corner of the earth. *We are still far from our goal. Though we have made some excellent advances, we are still far from the mark. We still look at the teeming millions in the many lands with which we have to do. We still see numerous nations*

236

without a knowledge of their Savior, their Redeemer, without the gospel and its saving and exalting principles. (Spencer W. Kimball, Regional Representatives Seminar, Oct. 2, 1975.)

Sensing keenly the adverse effect of mediocrity in missionary work, President Kimball has requested that missionaries consistently *increase the perfection of their performance.* The chapters in this section will assist you in your efforts to consistently perfect your performance throughout your mission.

Chapter 43

Consistently Strive to Improve

When the Lord requires something of us, he has made it clear that if we do our part, he will compensate for our limited abilities. The thing you need to remember is that this promise does not apply if you fail to do your part. Your part in any endeavor is determined by your ability and the opportunity you have had to perfect your performance. For example, if a missionary has a difficult time memorizing the discussions and has been in the field only three weeks, the Lord would be tolerant of the fact that he is not able to give a very smooth discussion. The Holy Spirit will compensate for weaknesses in the presentation. The graph below depicts the role of the Spirit in compensating for your limitations if you consistently strive to perfect your performance.

The performance level required to qualify for the Spirit will increase each month. If you fail to consistently perfect your ability to handle various aspects of missionary work, there will be a gap between your actual level of performance and the level of performance you could have achieved if you were consistently applying yourself. When this happens, you will not experience a full endowment of the Spirit.

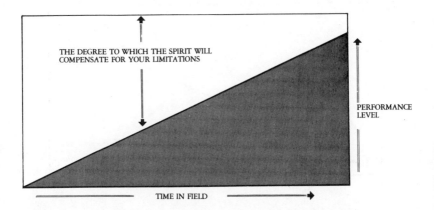

In the illustration below you will note that once the missionary is no longer striving to perfect his performance, his performance level decreases. Consequently, a gap develops between the level of performance required to qualify for the Spirit and the missionary's actual performance level.

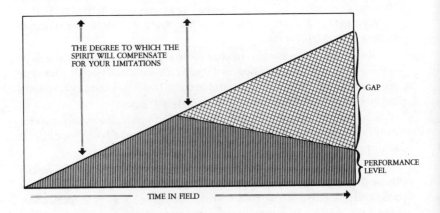

As you approach your mission, you should find consolation in the fact that the Lord will compensate for your weaknesses or limitations if you are consistently striving to *perfect your performance.* More than anything else, you should resolve to be steady in your growth.

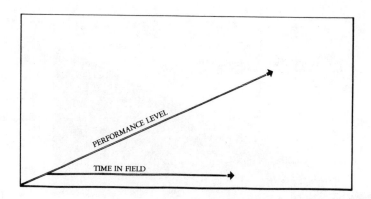

"We must be constant, we must not weary in well-doing." (President Spencer W. Kimball, Regional Representatives Seminar, Sept. 29, 1978.)

If your growth pattern is steady and constant, your effectiveness as a missionary will increase by a greater factor each subsequent month you are in the field.

In the diagram below, you will note that the increase in the missionary's level of effectiveness is greater each subsequent month he is striving to *improve his performance.* The results or benefits from effort on your part will *increase* each month if you are consistently trying to *perfect your performance.*

If you are not consistent in your efforts, your growth pattern will be erratic. When this happens you will spend a substantial part of your time regaining lost ground each time you become lax. If this happens, you will never realize your full potential as a missionary.

To a great extent you have to start all over in your efforts to qualify for the full endowment of the Spirit each time you become lax in your efforts to improve.

You have the assurance that as you apply yourself consistently throughout your mission, you will become very effective in your missionary labors. In the Lord's work, persistence results in perfection. (See D&C 67:13.) In a very literal sense your abilities will increase line upon line if you consistently strive to *perfect your performance.* As you do, the Lord has promised that you will accomplish great things. (See D&C 64:33.)

In contrast, if you are ever content with a minimal effort, you will be limited in your effectiveness. The Lord is not pleased with medocrity.

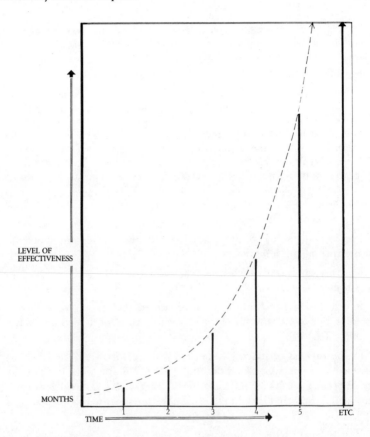

LEVEL OF
EFFECTIVENESS

MONTHS

TIME ⟹   1   2   3   4   5   ETC.

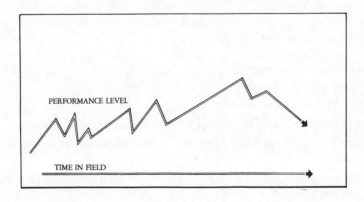

PERFORMANCE LEVEL

TIME IN FIELD

I know thy works, that thou art neither cold nor hot: I would thou wert cold or hot. So then because thou art lukewarm, and neither cold nor hot, I will spue thee out of my mouth. (Revelation 3:15-16.)

President Kimball has expressed the same sentiment:

Are you satisfied with either the stake mission or the full-time mission? Are we getting as many conversions as we should? I don't know if there is any blame. I don't know where it is. We wouldn't want to blame anybody, but is it the missionaries? Is it our program? Is it our leaders? Is it the way we handle the matter? What is the reason that we are receiving less than 100,000 people a year with a third that many missionaries, ever growing? That's something for us to be thinking about. (Regional Representatives Seminar, Oct. 2, 1975.)

I certainly would not like to appear critical of our missionaries generally, but I wonder if our stride is long enough. (Regional Representatives Seminar, Apr. 5, 1976.)

President Joseph F. Smith made the following statement about the performance of missionaries:

There are many excellent men but very few really good missionaries. (*Gospel Doctrine*, p. 356.)

In order to be persistent in your missionary endeavors, you will need to resolve not to let your mind turn back to your old interests and ways. (See D&C 67:14.)

In the process of striving to perfect your performance, the Lord has counseled that you should not become weary in doing what is right day after day (see D&C 64:33 and Galations 6:9). You will not realize the full benefits of doing what is right if you have the tendency to become weary of doing what is right.

You should make a personal resolve to be a good missionary throughout your entire mission, remembering that a level of performance that is considered good early in your mission will not be acceptable a month or so later. The Lord expects you to consistently improve your ability to do missionary work.

You should make it a practice to consistently evaluate your performance throughout your mission. In your effort to evaluate yourself, there are some basic indicators you should always consider:

1. Do you find the work enjoyable?

2. Are more and more people agreeing to receive the discussions?

3. Are you becoming more effective in your efforts to get people to repent?

4. Are you inclined to go the extra mile in your efforts to bring people into the Church?

More than any other scripture, the 58th section of the Doctrine and Covenants provides a basis for evaluating your performance.

> For behold, it is not meet that I should command in all things; for he that is compelled in all things, the same is a slothful and not a wise servant; wherefore he receiveth no reward. Verily I say, men should be anxiously engaged in a good cause, and do many things of their own free will, and bring to pass much righteousness; for the power is in them, wherein they are agents unto themselves. And inasmuch as men do good they shall in nowise lose their reward. (D&C 58:26-29.)

You should make it a policy to review personally the self-evaluation questions found at the end of each chapter and also review them with your companion at least once a month throughout your mission. The purpose of these questions is to provide you some way to assess your compliance with certain principles (such as obedience, motives, dedication, etc.) and your ability to use various proselyting principles. As you evaluate your performance in this way, you will be able to set appropriate and challenging goals according to your individual and companion needs. Elder Thomas S. Monson has said:

> When performance is measured, performance improves. When performance is measured and reported, the rate of improvement accelerates.

In order to meet the Lord's expectations, you will need to consistently strive to perfect your performance. This will be accomplished in part by consistently reviewing the chapters in this book. You should establish a review schedule with your companion. Your schedule should reflect your personal and companion needs. If your needs dictate, you may want to review some topics more frequently than others. You should plan your schedule, however, so that you will review each chapter at least once every three months.

If you have the responsibility to train a new missionary or other missionaries you preside over as a district or zone leader, you should obtain the *Trainer's Manual* for this book, which has been written to assist you in your responsibility to train other missionaries. It contains study-guide questions for each chapter, additional scriptural references that deal with the topics discussed in the book, and an extensive collection of role-play situations that can be used to practice the various principles introduced in the book.

Throughout your mission ask yourself the following questions:

1. Am I consistently striving to perfect my performance on a daily basis?

2. Am I using my time wisely?

3. Am I steady in my growth pattern?

Chapter 44

Many Are Called,
but Few Are Chosen

In reference to those called to receive the Melchizedek Priesthood, the Lord has said, "Many are called, but few are chosen."(D&C 121:34; 95:5.) Even though thousands are called to fill missions, some missionaries fail to qualify themselves and consequently are not "chosen". To be chosen means that a person qualifies for the special endowments from heaven which enable the Lord to utilize the person to do his work. When a missionary proves himself, he is chosen. When a missionary is chosen and qualifies for the special endowments of the Spirit, the fruits of his labors stand as evidence that he is approved of the Lord. The Lord has said, " ... he that is overcome and bringeth not forth fruits ... is not of me." (D&C 52:18.)

Once you are in the field and get into the routine of missionary work, you should begin to look for the fruits, the evidence that your efforts are acceptable in the eyes of the Lord. This chapter discusses the specific fruits that result when missionaries are chosen by the Lord as a result of their efforts to perfect their performance.

As a missionary you will not be chosen if you are slothful or if your heart is set upon the things of this world and you aspire to the honors of men. If you aspire to the honors of men, you will not learn that the rights of the priesthood are inseparably connected with the powers of heaven, and that the powers of heaven cannot be controlled or handled only upon the principles of righteousness.

Following are some of the fruits of dedicated service.

The Spirit Will Sustain You

When the Spirit sustains you in your labors, you will be invigorated and will approach your appointments with people with anticipation. You will enjoy fasting and find it an uplifting experience. Your reaction to fasting will be positive, not just physical hunger and thirst. Once you are in this frame of mind, time will pass very quickly. You will find the months will appear as weeks and weeks will appear as days. Your hard bed will seem softer, the cold nights will seem warmer, the bland food will be tastier. Things that were previously perceived as inconvenient will no longer occupy your thoughts or distract you from your work. You will have an overwhelming desire to share what you are experiencing with your loved ones. You will find your ability to express your feelings and experiences inadequate. You will look with aniticipation towards the opportunity to express your testimony in zone and district meetings. You will find yourself deriving much more meaning and satisfaction from your personal prayers. You will delight in reading the scriptures and will do so with a lot more insight. In this frame of mind you will find you will not be inclined to become despondent or discouraged. You will find difficult situations challenging instead of discouraging. You will no longer be dependent on letters from home to buoy your spirits. Opportunities to teach will be your first priority instead of activities that are entertaining or a good meal prepared by one of the sisters in the ward. At the conclusion of the day, despite a physical fatigue, you will feel buoyed up, lifted, and you will approach the ensuing day with anticipation and excitement.

You Will Experience Joy

Once you are successful in cultivating the Spirit, you will find missionary work very rewarding. You will not have any difficulty doing these things required of missionaries (getting up at 6:30, proselyting a certain number of hours per day). You will delight in the work, just as did Ammon and the sons of Mosiah who experienced "incomprehensible joy." (Alma 28:8, 26:15.)

The Lord has promised that you will have joy in the fruit of your labor. (D&C 6:31, 75:21.) One of the sweetest forms of joy we experience in this life comes when we are instruments in the hands of the Lord in seeing someone else come into the Church. The Lord has said:

> And if it so be that you should labor all your days in crying repentance unto this people and bring, save it be one soul unto me, how great shall be your joy with him in the kingdom of my Father!
>
> And now, if your joy will be great with one soul that you have brought

unto me into the kingdom of my Father, how great will be your joy if you
should bring many souls unto me! (D&C 18:15,16.)

Joy is a gift of the spirit. A person is not capable of experiencing joy unless
he gains a remission of his sins. (Mosiah 4:3, 20; Alma 22:15.) So when you
begin to experience joy in your labors, you have the assurance you have been
forgiven of your sins.

You Will Feel Compelled to Overcome Difficulties

There will be many occasions throughout your mission when you will
be faced with situations that are challenging and difficult. These
challenges will come from particular areas of labor, companions, the
climate, the food, the people, or from unexpected circumstances. If you
have the Spirit, you will not become discouraged by difficulties; you will
feel compelled to overcome them. With the Lord's help you will resolve
them. In contrast, if you do not have the Spirit, you will become
despondent and discouraged when you encounter difficulties.

You Will Be Confident

As you qualify yourself and experience the sustaining influence of the
Spirit in your labors, you will not fear any aspect of missionary work. You
will feel at ease teaching people sophisticated in the ways of the world in
terms of education, wealth, or position. As the Lord fulfills his promise
that you will not be fearful in your labors if you are prepared (see D&C
38:30), you will have poise and maturity way beyond your years of
experience.

You Will Have a Charitable Disposition

Once you are successful in cultivating the gift of charity, you will
evidence the following characteristics. You will be long-suffering, you will
be kind, you will not envy, you will not be puffed up, you will be inclined to
serve the interests of others, you will not be easily provoked, you will not
think about evil things, you will rejoice in the truth, you will bear the
infirmities and afflictions you experience in the course of your mission
with patience, and you will be inclined to believe all truth associated with
the gospel of Jesus Christ. You will evidence a prevailing hope in the
promise made in the holy scriptures that you will be able to endure all
things required of you without wavering in your commitment to the
gospel of Jesus Christ.

Once you are in this frame of mind, your mission president will trust
you to be a companion to anyone. The Lord will virtually trust your
capacity to relate with all people. He will trust you with the responsibility
of teaching people the gospel of Jesus Christ. You will be endowed with
the ability to lift the spirits of all with whom you associate. You will have
the ability to inspire your companions to do better and to inspire your

investigators to remove themselves from the ways of the world. With this frame of mind you will be totally unselfish, and you will be stripped of vanity. Virtue will garnish your thoughts unceasingly. You will be endowed with the full confidence that the Lord will sustain you in your labors according to your righteous endeavors. You will be totally unselfish in your desire to bless the lives of other people. You will not be bothered by inconveniences. You will delight in the sacrifices required of you as a missionary. You will be inclined to put the interest and the welfare of others before your own. Families you teach will praise your name, and your companions will hold your name in great esteem and look back with fond memories on their association with you, having a keen awareness of the profound influence you had on their lives.

The Spirit Will Be Manifest in Your Labors

As you are magnified in your calling, the Spirit will be manifest in your labors in a variety of ways. Inspiration will become commonplace in the course of your daily routine. The various gifts of the Spirit (e.g., discernment, the power to heal the sick, facility with language) will accompany your labors. When you teach a family or when you are called upon to speak to a congregation, you will speak with power and authority and will have the ability to motivate people to action. You will receive specific inspiration regarding the families you are teaching and your companions. If you are called to preside over other missionaries, you will receive specific inspiration regarding their welfare.

Your ability to express yourself in writing will be enhanced, and more importantly your ability to express will be magnified, your ability to understand will be facilitated. As these things occur in your life, you will truly know what it means to be endowed with the powers of the Spirit. You will understand the workings of the Spirit, and you will be able to teach others regarding its workings that they in turn may enjoy its fruits as you have.

You Will Not Be Content with Mediocrity

When you receive a full endowment of the Spirit, you will be impelled to perfect your performance, and you will no longer be content with mediocrity in any aspect of your life. Through the power of discernment you will be sensitive to conversations that are inappropriate and conduct that is inappropriate. Consequently, your overall performance in every aspect of missionary work will improve. Even things that previously were difficult for you will come with ease. You will be much more insightful regarding your weaknesses and will be able to see clearly the steps that you need to take in order to overcome them. You will be endowed with the ability to see clearly how to deal with problems that arise in your relationship with other missionaries or in your proselyting activities with your investigators.

Your mission president will have total confidence that under any set of circumstances you will resolve to do the right thing. He will trust you to assume any leadership responsibility. You will be endowed with the ability to prompt and inspire others to do better. You will find yourself taking much more pride in your standard of excellence in all that is required of you. Most importantly, you will be inclined to do the right things for the right reason. Your overall motivation to excel will be an outgrowth of your love for the Lord Jesus Christ and your effort to respond to his charge to have an eye single to his glory. Consequently, you will find it easy to let others assume the role of baptizing investigators or confirming investigators whom you have taught, whether they be companions or members of the ward or branch. You will not be concerned with personal recognition. You will not be preoccupied with position or status.

You Will Be Physically Renewed

As you draw close to the Spirit, you will experience an increase in vitality and physical endurance. As you engage in missionary work and come to realize how physically demanding it is, your sense of gratitude for the physical renewal that comes from the Spirit will increase.

The following quote from Parley P. Pratt describes the total effect the Spirit has on people:

> The gift of the Holy Ghost adapts itself to all these organs or attributes. It quickens all the intellectual faculties; increases, enlarges, expands and purifies all the natural passions and affections and adapts them, by the gift of wisdom, to their lawful use. It inspires, develops, cultivates and matures all the fine-toned sympathies, joys, kindred feelings and affections of our nature. It inspires virtue, kindness, goodness, tenderness, gentleness, and charity. It develops beauty of person, form, and features.
>
> *It tends to health, vigor, animation, social feeling. It invigorates all the faculties of the physical and intellectual man.* It strengthens and gives tone to the nerves. In short, it is, as it were, marrow to the bones, joy to the heart, light to the eyes, music to the ears, and life to the whole being. (Parley P. Pratt, *The Key to Theology*, pp. 99-100.)

You Will Be Committed to Missionary Work

As you approach the end of your mission, you will catch the vision that your responsibility to missionary work will never end. You will find the following statement by Brigham Young totally consistent with your own thinking:

> We wish the brethren to understand the facts just as they are. That is, there is neither man nor woman in this Church who is not on a mission. That

mission will last as long as they live.…I wish to make this request that all of the Elders who return from missions consider themselves just as much on a mission here (in Utah) as in England or in any other part of the world.…When he has been home a week, month, year or ten years the spirit of preaching and the spirit of the gospel ought to be within him like a river flowing forth to the people in good words teaching precepts and examples. If this is not the case, he does not fill his mission. (*Discourses of Brigham Young*, p. 322.)

You will sense very keenly that your responsibility to persuade men to repent will never end in this life.

As you return from your mission, you will be just as inclined to set baptismal goals as you were in the mission field. Then you will proceed to exercise faith, and you will see people join the Church each year. You will experience the joy of seeing someone join the Church every year following your mission. In some instances you might be one of several who influence someone to join the Church, but you will have the satisfaction of playing a role in the conversion process.

Over the years the Lord will consistently call upon you to perform specific tasks that will afford you the opportunity to draw on the powers of heaven. You will know that you are playing a part in preparing the earth for Christ's second coming.

You will be instrumental in motivating many young people to resolve to go on missions. Even more importantly, you will help them catch a vision of their potential if they truly dedicate themselves in the mission field.

In the course of your life, as a result of your various labors associated with missionary work, you will directly and indirectly be responsible for the conversion of thousands of people.

Throughout your life the Lord will sustain you in all your endeavors (e.g., schooling, your profession, your Church work). You will be recognized as a person of honor and integrity, and you will enjoy stature in your profession and in the community where you reside.

At the last day you will have the assurance that you are not among those who say, "Lord, Lord, have we not prophesied in thy name? and in thy name have cast out devils? and in thy name done many wonderful works?" And the Lord will say, "I never knew you! depart from me ye that work iniquity." (Matthew 7:21-23.) In the *Doctrinal New Testament Commentary*, Elder Bruce R. McConkie explains that this scripture in Matthew refers to those who received the Melchizedek Priesthood and during some period of their life were able to call down the powers of heaven to heal the sick and perform other miracles, and yet did not continue to magnify their callings in the priesthood and consequently failed to live up to the oath and covenants associated with the Melchizedek Priesthood.

If you prove yourself and are chosen by the Lord to do his work (e.g., baptize people and train other missionaries), your mission experience will bring you close to your Heavenly Father, and your mission will provide you a spiritual foundation that will serve you throughout your life.

As you approach the end of your mission, ask yourself the following questions:

1. Am I experiencing joy in doing missionary work?

2. Am I experiencing the sustaining influence of the Spirit?

3. Am I confident?

4. Do I have a charitable disposition?

5. Am I able to recognize when the Spirit is manifest in my labors?

6. Am I perfecting my performance?

7. Am I determined to continue living the high standards of performance I have lived throughout my mission?

8. Am I proceeding to exercise faith that I will see people join the Church each year following my mission?

9. Am I resolved to do all I can to motivate young people to go on a mission?

10. Am I going to continue to magnify my callings in the Priesthood?

Chapter 45

Summary of Section 5

The 39th section of the Doctrine and Covenants is a revelation given through Joseph Smith, the prophet, to James Covill. In requesting this particular revelation, James Covill had made a covenant with the Lord that he would obey any commandments that the Lord would give him through Joseph Smith. In the revelation James Covill is promised several special blessings conditioned on his obedience to the Lord's commandments.

... you shall receive my Spirit, and a blessing so great as you never have known.

And if thou do this, I have prepared thee for a greater work. Thou shalt preach the fulness of my gospel, which I have sent forth in these last days, the covenant which I have sent forth to recover my people, which are of the house of Israel.

And it shall come to pass that power shall rest upon thee; thou shalt have great faith, and I will be with thee and go before thy face.

Thou art called to labor in my vineyard, and to build up my church, and to bring forth Zion, that it may rejoice upon the hills and flourish. (D&C 39:10-13.)

Section 40 of the Doctrine and Covenants is a revelation received by Joseph Smith regarding the same James Covill.

Behold, verily I say unto you, that the heart of my servant James Covill was right before me, for he covenanted with me that he would obey my word.

251

And he received the word with gladness, but straightway Satan tempted him; and the fear of persecution and the cares of the world caused him to reject the word.

Wherefore he broke my covenant, and it remaineth with me to do with him as seemeth me good. Amen. (D&C 40:1-3.)

As you were set apart for your mission you likewise received a personal revelation from your Father in Heaven in which specific blessings were enumerated. In many instances, for those of you who have received patriarchal blessings, reference is made to your mission and your potential success as a missionary. You must keep foremost in your mind the fact that these blessings are contingent on your faithfulness and obedience. Through disobedience and slothfulness, you jeopardize all these blessings and promises. As was the case with James Covill, if you are diligent in your labors the Lord will keep his word in helping you realize various promises and blessings. If you are slothful in your labors, he will do with you as he sees fit.

At any point in your mission if you are not being effective in your teaching, you should carefully review every chapter in this book to help determine why. You have the complete assurance that if you are complying with the principles and using the proselyting procedures taught in this book, you will be successful in coverting people. You should maintain an abiding confidence in the Lord's promise that as modern-day missionaries function properly they will be successful in their efforts to convert people.

Index

About the Author

Grant Von Harrison is a native of Cedar City, Utah. He received his B.A. degree from Brigham Young University in 1962; his M.A. from Adams State College in 1965; and his doctorate in Instructional Science from UCLA in 1969.

Dr. Harrison taught for the Church educational system for seven years. He worked as a project associate and consultant for the institute for Educational Development, and was a human factors analyst with System Development Corporation.

Since joining the Brigham Young University faculty in 1969, he has developed numerous instructional programs. He is the author of the books *Understanding Your Divine Nature, Tools for Missionaries,* and *Seeing With an Eye of Faith.* He is the author and developer of the structured tutoring model which has provided the basis for literacy programs the Church is using in South America; he has also developed and authored various instructional materials designed to be used by nonprofessionals to teach reading, mathematics, and foreign languages.